Introduction to Computing and Problem Solving with PYTHON

REVISED EDITION

Jeeva Jose
Associate Professor, Department of Computer Applications
Baselios Poulose II Catholicos College[BPC]
Piravom - 686 664, Ernakulam District, Kerala, India

P. Sojan Lal
Professor, Department of Computer Science and Engineering
Mar Baselios Institute of Technology and Science[MBITS]
Kothamangalam - 686 693, Ernakulam District, Kerala, India

KHANNA BOOK PUBLISHING CO. (P) LTD.
Publisher of Engineering and Computer Books
4C/4344, Ansari Road, Darya Ganj, New Delhi-110002
Phone : 011-23244447-48 **Mobile:** +91-9910909320
E-mail : contact@khannabooks.com
Website : www.khannabooks.com

Dear Readers,

To prevent the piracy, this book is secured with HIGH SECURITY HOLOGRAM on the front title cover. In case you don't find the hologram on the front cover title, please write us to at contact@khannabooks.com or whatsapp us at +91-99109 09320 and avail special gift voucher for yourself.

Specimen of Hologram on front Cover title:

Moreover, there is a SPECIAL DISCOUNT COUPON for you with EVERY HOLOGRAM.

How to avail this SPECIAL DISCOUNT:

Step 1: Scratch the hologram
Step 2: Under the scratch area, your "coupon code" is available
Step 3: Logon to www.khannabooks.com
Step 4: Use your "coupon code" in the shopping cart and get your copy at a special discount
Step 5: Enjoy your reading!

Price: ₹ 355.00

ISBN: 978-93-82609-81-0

Introduction to Computing & Problem Solving with PYTHON
by Jeeva Jose, P. Sojan Lal

First Edition: 2015
Revised Edition: 2018
Reprint: 2025

To view complete list of books, Please scan the QR Code:
KPH

Published by:
Khanna Book Publishing Co. (P) Ltd.
CIN: U22110DL1998PTC095547

Visit us at: **www.khannabooks.com**
Write us at: **contact@khannabooks.com**

Printed in India.

Acknowledgement

Thanks to God for leading us and guide us the days ahead.

Blessings from God, teachers and parents are the key success factors for its accomplishment and our "Pranams".

We would like to express our sincere thanks to all people who have motivated and supported us in bringing out this book. We express our heartfelt thanks to Python Software Foundation for providing the Python logo for using in this book.

Mr. Vijo Mathew who mentored and supported us from its concept to reality deserves special thanks. We are also thankful to Late P. M. Poulose, Mrs Chinnamma Poulose and Prof. Shiny S. Lal, who had been consistently inspired and supported unconditionally for the success of these projects.

We acknowledge our special gratefulness to Dr. K. Poulose Jacob and Dr. A. Unnikrishnan for their proficient guidance and sincere encouragements.

We owe our gratitude to the Management of BASELIOS POULOSE II CATHOLICOS COLLEGE, Piravom, Kerala and MAR BASELIOS INSTITUTE OF TECHNOLOGY AND SCIENCE [MBITS], Kothamangalam, Kerala, India for the ways and means they provided in writing this book.

The role played by our colleague Mr. Shajan P.X in the installation of Python is invaluable. We also express our sincere thanks to all our colleagues for their motivation and encouragement.

We would like to express our gratitude to Dr. V.M. Domkundwar for his encouragement and guidance in bringing out this book as well as earlier book, "A course in computer programming with Numerical Techniques".

We are thankful to our family members for their moral support and appreciation in writing this book. We also express sincere thanks to our students, friends and well-wishers for their critical comments and valuable suggestions.

We would like to express our gratitude to Mr. Mukul Seth, Director, Khanna Book Publishing, New Delhi for the keen interest shown in publishing this book. Finally, thanks to all Editorial team members of Khanna Book Publishing, New Delhi for their patience, reviews and suggestions.

Authors

Foreword

Introduction to Computing and Problem Solving with PYTHON is a title which would attract many, interested in mastering the art of Programming in a language that is fast gaining importance. Python is powerful, fast; is friendly and easy to learn. Python is developed under an OSI-approved open source license, making it freely usable and distributable, even for commercial use.

Going through the book chapters along with their solved lab exercises, one can expect to gain capability to design algorithmic solution to problems and to convert algorithms to Python Programs, leading towards becoming a Python professional.

The book follows a style of presentation which suits any class of learners, though focused on approved syllabi of several universities.

Dr. K. Poulose Jacob
PhD [Computer Engg.]

PRO VICE CHANCELLOR
Cochin University of Science and Technology,
Kochi, Kerala, India

About the Authors

Jeeva Jose completed PhD in Computer Science from Mahatma Gandhi University, Kerala, India and is a faculty member at BPC College, Kerala. Her passion is teaching and areas of interests include World Wide Web, Data Mining and Cyber laws. She has been in higher education for the last 15 years and has completed three research projects funded by UGC and KSCSTE. She has published more than twenty research papers in various refereed journals and conference proceedings. She has edited three books and has given many invited talks in various conferences. She is a recipient of ACM-W Scholarship provided by Association for Computing Machinery, New York.

P. Sojan Lal was awarded PhD from Cochin University of Science and Technology, Kerala, India. He is Professor, Department of Computer Science and Engineering, MBITS, Kerala, India and Research Supervisor for PhD programs of University of Petroleum & Energy Studies, Dehra Dun, India as well as School of Computer Sciences, Mahatma Gandhi University, Kerala, India. He has 29 years of academic and industrial experience with 60 publications inclusive of two technical books. His joint publications are recorded with World Records India (2014) for most number of papers in several international technical journals within short duration. He has also obtained MBA from Strathclyde Business School, Scotland, UK and is a Fellow of The Institution of Engineers (FIE-India). He was the District Operating Board Member for ASME, Middle East and Africa region. He is a member of ISTE, ASME, IEEE, CSI and Engineering Council (UK). He is listed in Marquis who's Who in the World since 2009 as the biographical reference representing the world's most accomplished individuals.

Preface

Python is a widely used general-purpose, high-level programming language. This is an Open Source Software and its source code is available with a license in which the Copyright holder provides the rights to study, change, and distribute the software to anyone and for any purpose. This can run on any hardware platform (PC, Mac, Sun Sparc, etc.) or software platform (Linux, MacOS, Unix, Windows, etc.). Its design philosophy emphasizes code readability, and its syntax allows programmers to express concepts in least lines of code than in languages like C++ or Java. Python supports multiple programming paradigms, including object-oriented, imperative and functional programming or procedural styles. It features a dynamic type system and automatic memory management and has a large and comprehensive standard library.

Python was conceived in the late 1980s and its implementation was started in December 1989 by Guido van Rossum at Centrum Wiskunde & Informatica which is a research center in Netherlands .The non-profit organization Python Software Foundation fosters development of the Python community and is responsible for various processes within the Python community, including developing the core Python distribution, managing intellectual rights, developer conferences including PyCon, and raising funds. The softwares like YouTube, DropBox, Instagram, etc. are to name a few which is written in Python.

Python is used in many application domains. The Python Package Index lists thousands of third party modules for Python. Python's standard library and the community-contributed modules allow for endless possibilities. In Web and Internet development, Python offers many choices of Web development like Django and Pyramid for Frame work, Flask and Bottle for Micro-frameworks and advanced content management systems such as Plone & Django CMS. In addition to this, Python's standard library supports many Internet Protocols such as HTML, XML, JSON, E-mail processing, FTP, IMAP etc. Python is in education presently from post secondary and Government is utilizing this for Administration, Homeland Security, Public Safety, Traffic Control, Urban Infrastructure etc. In Business Python is using in domains such as Consumer Goods Industry, Aviation, Medical, Industrial, Financial services, GIS & Mapping, Marine and Lighting. Python is used in areas of Customer Relationship Management (CRM), Content & Document Management, Energy Conservation, E-Commerce, Enterprise Resource Planning (ERP), Knowledge Management, Manufacturing, Product Development, Project Management, Quality Control, Six Sigma, Lean, Relational Online Analytical Processing (ROLAP), Risk Management, Simulation etc. In Network Programming, Python is used to control Firmware updates, bringing desktop applications to the Internet etc. In Software, Python plays a right role in Accessibility, Code Generation, Computer Graphics, Cross-platform Development, Data Mining, Documentation Development, E-mail, Embedded Systems, Functional Testing, Groupware, Legacy System Integration, Rapid Application Development, RSS aggregator, User Interface, Visual Effects etc.

Python is widely used in areas such as Biology, Geography, Language Processing, Astrology etc. Based on the application, many packages and libraries are developed in Python. SciPy is a collection of packages for Mathematics, Science, and Engineering. Pandas is a data analysis and modeling library. IPython is a powerful interactive shell that features easy editing and recording of a work session, and supports visualizations and parallel computing.

This book will help every student, teacher and researcher to understand the computing basics and advanced Python Programming language. The simple style of presentation makes this a friend for self learners.

The first two Chapters introduce the reader on digital computers and programming. The third Chapter gives an introduction to Python which includes reserved keywords, identifiers, variables and operators. The fourth Chapter gives detailed explanation about data types and their operations. Chapter 5 illustrates flow control techniques which include decision making and looping. Functions are covered in Chapter 6. Chapter 7 explains built-in modules, user defined modules, packages, time, calendar and datetime modules. File handling is covered in Chapter 8. The entire concept of Object Oriented Programming is explained in Chapter 9. Various Exception Handling techniques are explained in Chapter 10. The Chapters 11 & 12 cover advanced topics like Python Regular Expressions and Database Programming in detail.

All Chapters have worked out programs, illustrations, review and frequently asked interview questions. More than 300 solved lab exercises available in this book is tested in Python 3.4.3 version for Windows. Please note that the syntax in early versions of Python and UNIX version of Python is slightly different from Python 3.4.3 for Windows.

Contents

01 Introduction to Computers

CONTENTS

1.1 Introduction

The present computer technology is highly advanced and captures each and every aspect of human life. The computers are used in houses, banks, railways, air traffic controls, police departments, hospitals, oil and gas fields, chemical plants, meteorology department, telecom and so on. The application of these computers varies from video games, handling banking transactions, office and plant automations, research and developments, displaying of signals, controlling process equipment, design of machinery and fabrics, communication, war field applications, under water study, image processing, medicine, resource planning, language translation, electronic mail (e-mail), e-commerce, e-post, e-learning, blended learning, e-banking, internet applications, weather forecast, mobile applications, simulation and training of a number of scenarios like pilot training and a lot more.

A small computer attached on a human body can easily monitor status of blood pressure, insulin and can also take corrective measures by injecting the appropriate medicines with the required dosage, without human intervention. Even the low level of medicine in the human body or variation in the threshold value of some key parameters of human body shall be alerted by giving appropriate alarms. Nanotechnology is the latest trend in this direction. Bioinformatics, a hybrid combination of Information Technology, Biotechnology and Life Science, are also in the way forward. Thus computers are becoming inevitable part of human life.

The term computer can logically be applied to any calculating device. The computers can broadly be classified as **analog**, **digital** and **hybrid** computers. The analog computer is like thermometer, pressure gauge, voltmeter, ammeter and speedometer, which measures continuous types of data and gives an analogue signal on a **calibrated** dial gauge. Slide rule is also an example of an analog computer.

All digital computers are general-purpose machines, which are capable of handling and processing large amount of data and discrete quantities. It gives some information or result. Hybrid computers are the combination of analog and digital computers that are normally used for controlling equipment on chemical plants, oil and gas fields and War field weapons. In a chemical plant or in a continuous process industry, the field instruments measure the field parameters (analog) such as pressure, temperature, volume and transmits the converted digital signal (values in discrete quantity) to a digital computer. The digital computer periodically checks and interprets the field parameters and transmits back an appropriate action, if required. Some of the actions are opening or closing of a valve through an actuator, reducing the temperature inside a vessel, giving a (pressure/ temperature/ volume high or low) warning to an operator or even shutting down the unit or the complete plant when the parameter reaches to a threshold (preset) value. ABB, ROSEMOUNT, FOXBORO and HONEYWELL are few vendors who are supplying such online monitoring system called DCS (Digital Control System). We come across many digital and analog computers in most of our day-to-day life. Personal Computers (PC), like desktop, laptop and tablets are digital computers.

1.2 Components of Digital Computer

All the required instruction and data are given to the Central Processing Unit (CPU) of the computer through the input unit. Keyboard, mouse, digitizer, floppy drive, hard disk (also called Winchester), tape drive, CD/DVD drive, OD drive (Optical Disk), scanner, USB flash drive (also known as data stick, pen drive, keychain drive, thumb drive and jump drive), external hard disk drive etc. are some examples of input unit. The CPU consists of a Control unit, an Arithmetic and Logic Unit (ALU) and a Primary memory popularly known as RAM (Random Access Memory). All the arithmetic and logic operations are performed in ALU. The intermediate results and some operational data, as per the requirement and capacity of the computer, are kept in RAM. The control unit controls all the operations of a computer. All the results of computations are sent out to the user through the Output unit. The combination of ALU and Control unit is known as CPU, Central Processing Unit. Fig. 1.1 shows the block diagram of a digital computer.

Video Display Unit (VDU), plotter, floppy drive, Winchester disk drive, CD/DVD drive (Reader or with writer, CD RW/DVD RW), magnetic tape, printer, USB flash drive and external hard disk drive are some of the output devices. Some DVD RW drive is available with light scribe for printing CD/DVD title and pictures over the CD/DVD. Any storage media like floppy, magnetic tape and hard disk,USB flash drive and external hard disk are called secondary memory, which stores the information permanently. The primary memory (RAM) is volatile as the data in RAM will be automatically erased, when the system is powered off. Large amount of data and Program codes can be stored in these secondary memories. Both primary and secondary memory are divided into small locations to store the data and Programs. This is similar to a Library with lots of rooms and stacks for storing books. Each location of memory has an address similar to location identifier in Library for each book. Every storage media, like RAM, flash memory, tape, internal and external hard disk etc, has different access time. Hence the time required to retrieve the data from each storage-devices are different. RAM retrieves the data very fast compared with all other secondary memory devices. Usually, Personal Computers (PC) with RAM's of sizes 512 MB (Mega Byte) to 8GB (Giga Byte) are popular. Personal Computers are having a capability to extend this RAM capacity to a certain limit (could be in multiples of 128MB/ 256MB/ 512MB/ 1GB/ 2GB/ 4GB/ 8GB). The extension of RAM depends upon the maximum addressable memory limit available in each CPU. Most of the PC motherboards are having additional memory slots for upgrading its RAM. The performance of a computer is generally measured with the speed of CPU. Popular desktop and laptop PCs are with 2.0 GHz of CPU speed and above. Functionality of all other auxiliary devices and the communication bus also plays a vital role in determining the efficiency of a computer. As an example, the physical condition of road is a major factor for comfort driving.

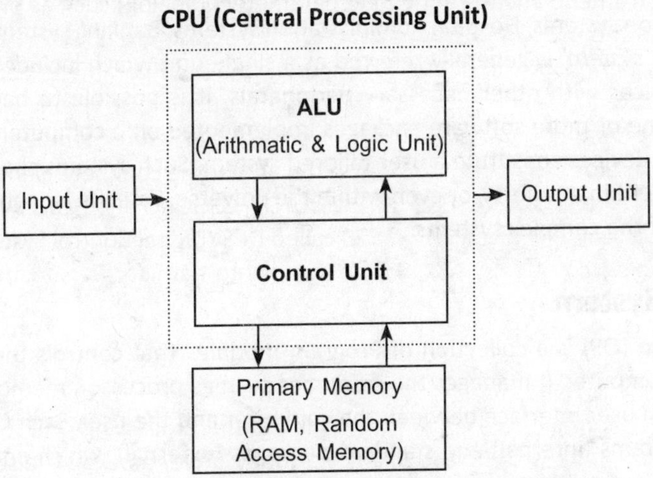

Fig. 1.1: Block Diagram of a Digital Computer

All digital computers are running under an operating system like DOS, Windows 2000, Windows NT, Windows ME, Windows XP (Professional or Home edition), Windows 7, Windows 8, Windows 10, Linux, VAX-VMS, Unix and CP/M. More details of operating system are given in the Section 1.4. All these operating systems are software for managing the functionalities of a computer, and it interacts with the user.

1.3 Hardware and Software

Hardware is the physical component of a computer where as the software is a set of Programs used to run the computer. Motherboard (Main Printed Circuit Board -PCB- of a computer where CPU is mounted), CPU, floppy drive, keyboard, mouse, cam (used for video conferencing/ internet chatting), CD drive, USB flash drive, monitor and power supply units are examples of the hardware components of computer. Scanner, printer, plotter, microphone and camera are examples of hardware peripheral devices connected to a digital computer.

Few examples of Application **software** are MS (Microsoft) Office packages (Word, Excel, Power Point), MS Access, MS Project and Primavera (both are used for project Planning), AutoCAD, Freelance,

Visio (these three are used for design /& drafting), MATHLAB (graphics application), Maximo (from IBM) for Computerized Materials and Maintenance Management for major industries and federal government which is having more than 10,000 Corporate customers. Compilers for different computer languages (Section 1.7) and all Operating Systems (OS) are software (Section 1.4). OS is an interface between the user and the hardware of a computer.

MSN Messenger, GoogleTalk, Skype, ICQ, Yahoo messenger and WhatsApp messenger are used for online chatting with or without video conferencing. Yahoo, Gmail, Hotmail, AOL, ureach and Rediffmail are some popular e-mail service providers. *Gmail* has become so popular e-mail service provider within a short span of time because of its unique features in handling messages and large free space availability (more than 15 GB inbox space and increasing) to preserve messages from deletion. A number of video game softwares are also available with internet.

Some software used by certain large industries are tailored to end-user requirement like Railway and Airline reservation systems, Hospital Administration systems, Banking systems and communication systems. The word '*system*' is generally referred as a single unit which includes hardware, software, communication devices with other necessary peripherals. It is possible to have many sub-systems within a 'system'. One or more software packages implemented on a computer hardware along with required peripheral devices constitute a user tailored system. Such systems shall be in a single room, the entire building, within a country, or even within the universe. Satellite launching systems and radar systems are some of the complex systems.

1.4 Operating System

An Operating System (OS) is a collection of Program modules that controls the functions (routines) performed by the computer. It manages the resources such as processor, memory, input-output (I/O) devices and acts as a user interface between the computer and the user. Each OS includes a series of special control Programs (internal) and standard packages (external), which enable the computer to operate efficiently. Control Program is always in execution and standard packages are invoked (called) as and when it is required. These are called internal and external commands respectively in DOS (Disc Operating System). External commands are commonly referred as utilities in many operating systems.

OS provides a lot of services to the users. It sometimes behaves like a watchman and safeguards the computer. It also acts like a labor and executes all the commands provided by the user with one hundred-percentage loyalty to his master. OS is like a traffic police who controls the heavy traffic (of data and results) in a very efficient manner. Certain jobs are done routinely and others are done after receiving a command from the user. System time and date updates are done regularly by the system where as installation and un-installation of a Program is done only after proper instructions from the user. Data and Programs are kept in files. OS does storing and retrieval of such files from the storage media. These files are kept in different groups of locations, which are called directories (folders). These directories can have subdirectories (subfolders). The maximum numbers of subdirectories are defined by each operating system and its version. This is similar to books in any traditional Library, classified with its subject and type. We shall find all journals such as IEEE /ACM/ IASTED/ EURASIP/ ASME etc. in one room with separate classification based on title. Different areas like Engineering, Medical, Commerce, Science, Arts and Literature are some major grouping of books in a Library. Further, engineering wing could be divided into Civil, Mechanical, Electrical, Electronics, Computer,

Instrumentation and Biomedical. These locations can be further sub-divided. The following Fig. 1.2 illustrates how the directories and subdirectories are maintained in Windows.

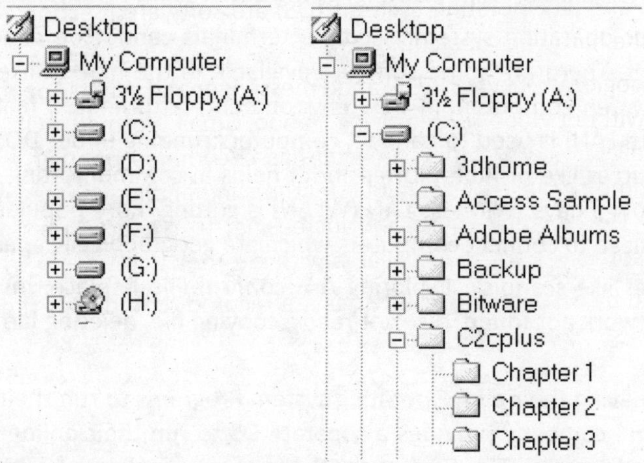

Fig. 1.2: Display of Directories in Windows Operating system

The + symbol in Fig 1.2 indicates the existence of a sub-directory. The letter (C:) indicates the directories in hard disk where as the letter (A:) indicates the contents of floppy disk directories and files of a computer. Other drives (D:) & (E:) are commonly used as logical drives in hard disk itself. In Fig. 1.2, (F:) and (G:) are also logical drives in the hard disk. A hard disk can be partitioned (broken down) into many logical drives. This will ease the house keeping of directories and filing system in a better way. The partitioning (logical separation) of a hard disk is done by the operating system utilities (software). The operating system safeguards the boundary of each logical drives. The drive (H:) in the Fig. 1.2 is referring to a CD drive. A typical directory is analogous to a super market or a department store. The storage capacity depends upon the size of the room or building and the policy of stacking the material. The store may have storage place at a very far-off place and materials are taken in and out in bulk quantities through some transport service as and when required. LAN, WAN, intranet or internet assist in carrying out these jobs for various computer applications. The connection between the systems could be with wire or wireless. Now a days wireless network connections are getting more popular.

A series of 3-tier railway compartment is typical in arranging more occupants compared to a conventional hotel room. Here we noticed that each application has different policy and supported by various services like transportation for the smooth running of the business. The above referenced directories shall be in computer hard disk floppy, flash memory, DVD or in a CD. Double layer DVDs are becoming more popular due to the huge data storage capacity (4TB) and portability. Light scribe CDs are accepted by its unique feature of labeling the CD by the CD writer itself.

Some Operating System (OS) like Windows even protects the system from loosing the data from power failure. A recovery procedure for the lost data is done automatically by the operating system whenever the computer is abnormally restarted. Some OS like WindowsNT and Unix takes care of communication between computers. They are called multiuser operating system. Linux is considered to be a stable OS, with various flavours available. For example Ubuntu, Fedora, Mint, Puppy, TinyCore, Zorin etc.

Apple computers are running under an OS called Macintosh. Their systems are much more reliable, but expensive and hence limited use. Recent Apple systems in the market comes with an option to choose MS Windows or Macintosh while booting, giving better choice for its customers.

DOS is a single user operating system. Multiple terminals cannot be connected to computers under such environment. There are some software available in the market like LL5, which are used for communicating between computers in DOS environment, with limited features. But Local Area Network (Novel Netware LAN) is used to connect computers running under DOS operating system to pool the common resources like printer, plotter and it helps in communicating and transferring data between computers. Now a days, Wireless LAN (WLAN) is getting more popular. Wide Area Network (wired WAN) has been used to connect computers which are geographically apart.

Automatic messages like scandisk, Exploring A:\, confirm File Replace, insufficient memory, no paper in the printer, network not found, disc not ready, copying file, deleting file etc. are generated by the OS.

Many vendors are having their own Operating system Programs to run their special Programs. As an example *"Rosemount"* company provides a separate OS to run their online monitoring Programs called DCS (Digital Control System). This OS along with the special packages (called application software or customized software) controls a complete chemical plant, oil and gas field, or a steel plant.

Android is a mobile operating system written on the Linux kernel. It is developed by Google. More than a million devices across the globe including smartphones and tablets are using the Android operating system. The first beta version was released in November 2007 and the first commercial version Android 1.0 was released in September 2008. Several versions of Android have been released since 2008. All versions of Android except Android 1.0 and Android 1.1 are given names based on confectionery theme. Cupcake (version 1.5), Donut (version 1.6), Eclair (version 2.0–2.1), Froyo (version 2.2–2.2.3), Gingerbread (version 2.3–2.3.7), Honeycomb (version 3.0–3.2.6), Ice Cream Sandwich (version 4.0–4.0.4), Jelly Bean (version 4.1–4.3.1), KitKat version(4.4–4.4.4), and Lollipop (5.0–5.1.1) are the versions of Android available and many more are expected to follow.

1.5 Drivers

A *'driver'* is software, which has a close link with the hardware and operating system. We can call the *driver* as bridging low-level software between hardware and operating system. All hardware manufactures has to develop this *bridge*, so that all installed hardware like printers, plotters, scanners and add on PCB cards will have compatibility with each other. Windows95, Windows98, Windows2000, Windows ME, Windows XP, Windows 7, Windows 8 and Windows 10 operating systems have plug and play feature. This means that whenever a new hardware designed for plug and play feature is connected to a computer, it automatically detects and installs the required drivers either from the hard disk or from the CD provided by the hardware manufacturer. In Linux and DOS user has to manually install new drivers for new hardware components. Drivers can also be downloaded from internet. Fig 1.3 shows the relationship between user, operating system, driver and hardware.

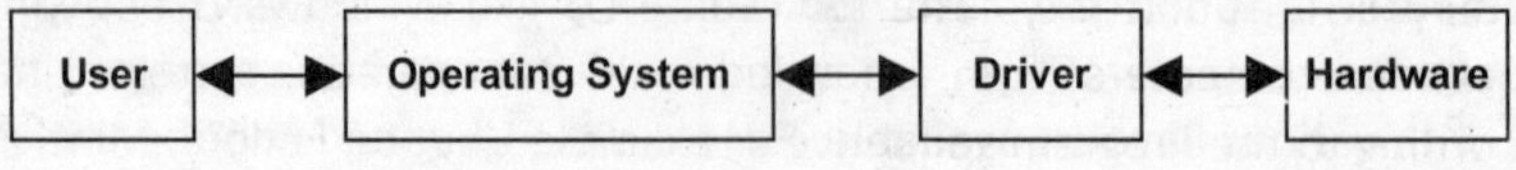

Fig 1.3: Relationship between user, operating system, driver and hardware

The use of a proper 'driver' gives us the complete feature of a hardware component. So a driver created/ developed by the hardware manufacturer and certified by the OS Developer are highly recommended.

1.6 Languages of Computer

We, human being, are using different languages for communicating each other. Although English is the most popular language for communication, thousands of other languages also exists. Generally mother tongue is the easiest language for us. However, we may have to use many other languages like Hindi, Arabic, German, French, Spanish and Chinese depending up on the circumstances. Similarly, we must learn at least one language, which is acceptable for computer for effective communication.

The computers understand low-level language called **machine language**. It is very hard for us to study this language. Hence, **high-level languages** like FORTRAN, BASIC, COBOL, C, C++, Java, SQL, LISP, PYTHON, ALGOL, HTML and Pascal were developed over the past decades. Each one of them is having their own advantages. Python is a widely used general-purpose, high-level programming language. Its design philosophy emphasizes code readability, and its syntax allows programmers to express concepts in least lines of code than in languages like C++ or Java. Python supports multiple programming paradigms, including object-oriented, imperative and functional programming or procedural styles. It features a dynamic type system and automatic memory management. It also has a large and comprehensive standard library. YouTube, DropBox, Instagram, etc. are few softwares are which is developed in Python. In Web and Internet development, Python offers many choices of Web development like Django and Pyramid for Frame work, Flask and Bottle for Micro-frameworks and advanced content management systems such as Plone & Django CMS. In addition to this, Python's standard library supports many Internet Protocols such as HTML, XML, JSON, E-mail processing, FTP, IMAP etc.

Assembly Languages are bridged between high-level languages and machine languages. It has lower level primitives and operations. Some system Programmers write the Program directly in assembly language. It has limited primitives, but more powerful and efficient.

1.7 Translators (Compiler, Interpreter and Assembler)

Translator can be classified in to three categories- compiler, interpreter and assembler.

The computer understands only machine languages as mentioned in the previous section. Here comes the necessity of a decoder to translate from high-level to low-level and vice versa. This is done by a sequence of Programs (*A* Program *is a set of instruction to a computer to perform a certain task*) called language processors or Translators. It could be a **compiler, interpreter or an assembler**.

The high-level languages are converted to its corresponding machine language by a set of Programs called compiler or interpreter. The **compiler** compiles (translates) the entire Program in high-level language *(source code)* into its machine language *(object code)* before execution starts. Therefore, the object code will be completely ready, normally as an EXE file in the system prior to execution and these EXE file does not require the compiler to run at any time. We can say that EXE files are easily portable.

An **interpreter** reads the first line of the source code and then translates into its machine language and then executes. The process of translation and execution will be repeated for each line of the source code according to the Program sequence. Here the source code will be translated many times, whenever a Program segment repeats. Hence more time is required for translation by an interpreter.

Also the portability of the Programs is restricted, as the Program requires the support of the interpreter to run all the time. It is similar to a person visiting China without any knowledge of Chinese language. He always requires an interpreter to speak to any person who knows only Chinese. Python is an interpreted language.

Some software may have both interpreter and compiler modes. This will help the Programmer to verify certain modules of Program by the interpreter. The process of compilation and execution may be time consuming for minor changes and testing. The final code after testing and validation will be distributed with its compiled version. Also in compiler mode the Programmer can preserve the source code with them. Many source codes are preserved due to its high value. It must have taken a lot of resources to develop and may use some efficient Programming techniques to write the source code and so on.

An **assembler** translates the assembly level language to machine language. The speed, compactness and close association with hardware are the advantages of assembly language over high level languages. Application Programs are seldom written in assembly language. Instead, only time-critical parts are written in assembly (for example an interface subroutine for direct hardware access). Device driver Programs (Section 1.5) and Embedded System Programs are stored in PROM (Programmable Read Only Memory)/(EPROM) Erasable Programmable Read Only Memory Chips, micro controllers (for chemical plant and automobile) and telecom devices use assembly language. Fig. 1.4 shows sequence of language coding.

High level language

↓↓ (Compiler/ interpreter)

Assembly Language

↓↓ (Assembler)

Machine Level Language

Fig 1.4: Sequence of language coding

1.8 Personal Computer

The evolution of Personal Computer (PC) has begin with the invention of 8085 Intel processor. The series of processors 8086, 80286, 80386, 80486 and Pentium Processors have come into the market in Intel family of processors. The families of Pentium processors are of different types like Pentium MMX, PII, PIII and PIV. The speed of each processor and its processing capability normally varies depending upon the type of processor. Desktop computers and Laptop computers comes under the category of PC. The present PCs are of higher processing and storage capability than the earlier Super computers! The following Fig. 1.5 shows the speed of Pentium processors.

PI, PMMX	60 - 233 MHz
PII	233- 450 MHz
PIII	450 – 1200 MHz (i.e. 1.2 GHz)
PIV	1.4 GHz to 2.4GHz and above

Fig. 1.5: Speed of Pentium Processors

Apart from Intel, processors from other manufacturers like AMD and Cyrix are common in the PC market. Processors like Intel Celeron, Intel Centrino are some of the releases from Intel. AMD K6, AMD Athlon, AMD Duron, AMD sempron, Cyrix MII, and Cyrix MIII are processors from AMD and Cyrix respectively. Intel core processors replaced mid to high end processors of Pentium and Celeron Series of processors. The Intel core processors includes Intel Core i7, Intel Core i5, Intel Core i3, and Core M. Fig 1.6 shows the speed of Intel Core processors.

Core i7	3.4-4GHz
Core i5	3-3.5GHz
Core i3	3.4-3.8GHz
Core M	900 MHz -1.2 GHz

Fig. 1.6: Speed of Intel Core Processors

1.9 Internet and E-commerce

The internet is getting more popular in our daily life and also in various business sectors. Huge pool of data is available through internet. The usage of internet has increased considerably with the advancement in communication and hardware/software technology.

E-commerce has led to the development of areas of conventional trading. Customers can trade through the internet using a PC/ laptop. Banking transactions between accounts, payment of bills, purchasing of air and railway tickets are performed through internet. The spaces for warehouses for physical storage of items inside towns/ cities are getting diminished as the customer can place orders through the internet. This helps to reduce the selling prize of each item, by having a warehouse in the suburbs of the city. The dealers can also do their business even without having a warehouse. www.thejari.com is one of the major and popular e-commerce website in UAE. www.amazon.com is popular site for purchasing of books, and makemytrip.com is used for online airticket/hotel reservation, with extended personal service. Flipkart allows you for on-line purchase of various electronics goods, items for men, women, kids, home, furniture, books, automobile and sports goods.

1.10 Search Engines

Some of the popular *search engines* are listed below. Electronic searches for a particular topic, documents and images are done in internet using *search engines*. Google, one among the search engines, has received wider acceptance within a short span of time. The search is performed based on the keyword supplied by the user. It is very important to use the appropriate 'key word' to have the best results. Right *key words* shall be chosen based on the vital content of search. However, we will not take guarantee for the content of any website.

1. www.yahoo.com
2. www.google.com
3. www.msn.com

1.11 Conclusion

This Chapter gives an overview about the components of a digital computer, primary memory and various secondary storage devices. A detailed description of various software including application software and different types of operating systems are discussed. A comparison of languages like machine language, assembly language and high level languages is done. The functions of compilers, assemblers and interpreters are discussed. Advanced technologies like internet, electronic commerce and search engines are explained.

1.12 Review Questions

1. What are the uses of Digital computers?
2. Distinguish between Analog and Digital computers.
3. Explain the components of a Digital computer with the help of a block diagram.
4. Illustrate hardware and software with examples.
5. Explain Operating System and its uses.
6. What is a 'driver' and what are their functions?
7. Why do we need different levels of languages like high level and low level?
8. Give some examples for high level languages.
9. Why do you need an assembler?
10. Explain compiler and interpreter.
11. What are the uses of search engines in internet? Name any two search engines.
12. Have you ever used search engines? Was it beneficial? If so how?
13. What are the keywords used by you in search engine? Did you get the correct result?
14. Briefly explain the evolution of Personal Computers. You may use any search engine to find the answer from the internet.

02 Program Logic and Flowcharts

CONTENTS

2.1 Introduction to Program Logic

An ordinary calculator performs all arithmetic operations like multiplication, division, addition and subtraction where as all digital computers have decision-making capacity in addition to the arithmetic operations. This decision-making capability is called logical operations and it is utilized to implement all the applications like industrial automation, simulation and commercial use as explained in detail in the first chapter. The capability of a computer to perform comparisons on two values (data) like greater than, less than, equal to, not equal to, greater than or equal to, and less than or equal to (6 logical operations) helps in decision making. All digital computers are designed to accept commands from the user. They process the data and gives out some information or result.

Any given problem is identified with its business requirement along with the feasibility to implement it along with available hardware, and other resources. Further, a methodical approach is required to solve the problems. The formulated sequence of steps to solve a given problem is called **Algorithm** for that problem. An algorithm describes the step-by-step procedure to solve a problem. The following example illustrates a simple algorithm to make a coffee.

Algorithm 2.1

1. Wash the kettle.
2. Connect the kettle to power supply.

3. Wash the mugs and spoons.
4. Fill the kettle with water.
5. Switch on the kettle.
6. Mix milk powder, sugar and coffee powder with cold water.
7. Wait until the water boils. (Assuming that the kettle automatically switch off when the water boils)
8. Pour the hot water into the mug and stir it.
9. Serve the coffee.

We repeat the steps from 6 through 9 to serve/prepare more coffee for the amount of water contained in the kettle. When the water is not sufficient enough, we repeat from step 4 through 9. Here, we apply our logical thinking capability (power of brain) to judge the quantity of water and temperature of boiled water. We are sure that you can think of a different approach for making coffee.

Similarly, we generate lots of logical decisions in our life like planning for future, shopping, arranging marriage or functions, sending kids to school, constructing a house, drawing money from a bank and even catching a train. Traveling abroad may require more vigilant steps like checking the validity of the passport, arranging visa, arranging cash/ travelers cheque/ credit card, details about the place and weather, making schedule of the intended travel, booking of airline ticket and so on. Also, some alternatives have to be planned, for successfully achieving the planned objectives.

Certain tasks are systematically formulated and we do certain tasks routinely without much logical thinking. It is a must to have properly documented algorithm to give instructions to a computer. This helps to co-ordinate various experts working in a project and to complete the project in time.

2.2 Methodology of Problem Solving

System Analysis: It is the phase where the "System Analyst" interacts with the client and analyses their requirement. He/She review the requirement, analyses the feasibility of the project, formulate alternative/ better optimum solution/s, summarizes the steps of the proposal/s. Followed by this, the analyst understands availability and nature of data (/its source), reviews various user needs, formulates the practical feasibility in implementation of the model in their premises and estimates the system resources (both hardware and system model). Based on this analysis and estimation of resources, the system analyst develops an algorithm. Further a Data Flow Diagram (DFD) is drawn in which more details of input (data) and output (result/ information/ action) are given. The data paths, storage medium etc will also be marked in the data flow diagram. Programming is the next phase, in which flowchart is coded into a high level language. These codes could be in a suitable highlevel language like Python. The process of debugging removes all syntax errors in the Program. The logical errors could be traced during validation. There shall be variation in the practice for each industry.

- Programmers, system analyst, experts from vendor and client will be validating the Program (software package). The testing is performed by the testing department of the software company and later with quality assurance team of the client, generally called as User Acceptance Test.
- The compiler prompts all syntax errors during compilation. The Programmer has to correct each one of them and after that only the compiler generates an EXE file. An EXE file is ready for execution, independent of the compiler. A number of test values are given including boundary values during

validation. Necessary modifications may be done in the algorithm or source code as required. The tested model is implemented and monitored for certain period of time and then handed over to the client. In certain cases a proto type shall be made and tested.

- During the transition period, a team of vendor representatives shall normally be available on work site to ensure the proper administration and initial training of the system to the end-users. This system requires further on site reviews and validation to satisfy the end-users.
- Upgradation of the system software will be required due to dynamic change in customer demand, introduction of newer version of other linked software or upgradation of the operating system itself. High-end hardware availability, improved communication network and business requirement due to market competency have forced a customer to go for hardware and software upgradation. Some times vendors may support earlier release only for a certain period of time, after releasing a newer version. Many of the earlier client-server based packages have been written as web based software packages with the advancement of internet technology.

We have described the role of a system analyst above. Now he has to implement the system satisfying the user requirements with a feasible algorithm followed by designing a flowchart. We shall explain more details of flowchart in the next Section to follow.

2.3 Flowcharts

Some form of planning is necessary before solving any common day-to-day problems. For shopping, one prepares the list of material, sequence of the shops for purchasing the materials, estimates the cost of material and so on. This planning is often done automatically without much formal thinking. But when a problem is to be solved using a computer, it becomes essential to represent all the decisions to be taken by the machine, actions to be performed and the sequence in which these are to be preformed. The diagrammatic representation of the actions and their sequences are known as **flowchart**.

The flowchart is represented using various symbols as shown in Fig. 2.1. The decision is represented by a diagonal box, actions or process by a rectangular box and input/output by a parallelogram shaped box. The boxes are connected by directed lines which shows the sequence of execution.

Sometimes, it can happen that the person who formulates the problem is unaware of the Programming details and the Programmer may not be in a position to formulate the problem. Under such a circumstance, the flowchart acts as a link between the two. Another advantage of the flowchart is that it easily helps to understand the logic of a Program written by different Programmers. In addition to this, the flowchart helps the Programmer to modify the existing Program, if required. Flowchart is used not only as a problem planning aid but also as documentation of the procedure for problem solving.

The flowchart is the natural way of expressing the relationship between different parts of a Program that would otherwise require many pages of extensive language to describe. Here we remember the phrase, *"one picture is worth more than thousand words"*. The overall logical thinking can be improved with the help of a flowchart . The flowchart can also be used to establish the relation between many Program modules or even between different application Programs. This is required when the main Program assign certain tasks to other Programs, called sub Programs. This applies when a project is divided into many modules and submodules, based on its function. Communication alignment and data handling between each module are vital.

In a hospital management system there could be modules like inpatient, outpatient, registration, pharmacy, laboratory, payments and so on. Some modules in hotel management system are front office, reservation, payments, inventory, restaurant, health clubs and maintenance. For a chain of hotel groups, the application extends between many countries using available or dedicated communication network.

Here, we concentrate only on simple flowcharts. Complex flowchart construction is outside the extent of this book. **Visio** is one of the popular software used for drawing flowcharts and other drawings.

Q 2.1: What are the uses of flowchart?

2.4 Flowcharts Symbols

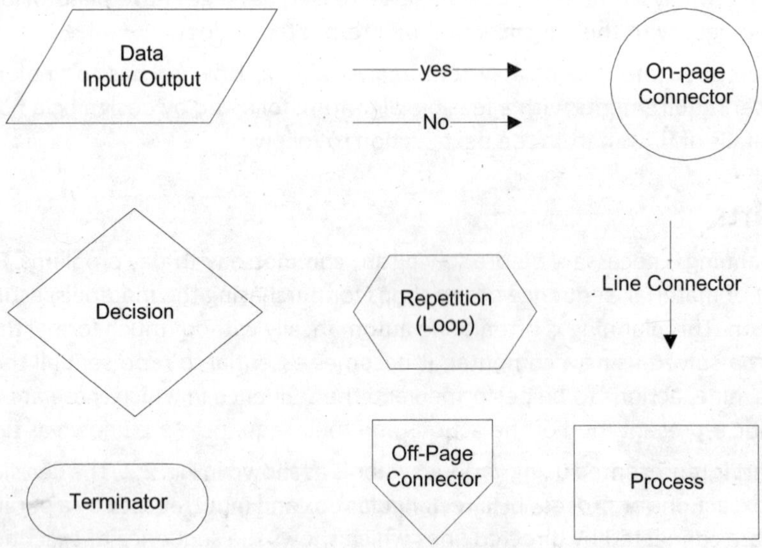

Fig 2.1: Flowchart Symbols

We shall demonstrate these symbols with some example.

Q 2.2. Develop an algorithm and draw a flowchart to find the sum of two numbers

A flowchart is given in Fig. 2.2 for the algorithm 2.2. One to one correspondence between the algorithm and flowchart can be noticed. Execution of the Program starts in step 1. The value of variable 'a' and 'b' are given through some input device, say keyboard. In step 3, the value of 'a' and 'b' are added and it is stored in a variable called 'sum'. The computer, in step 4, gives out the results along with the given value of variables. The Program terminates in the last step which is step 5.

Algorithm 2.2

1. Start execution.
2. Input the two values to the computer, say a, b.

3. Add the two values and store it in 'sum'.
4. Output the two values supplied and the result.
5. Stop execution.

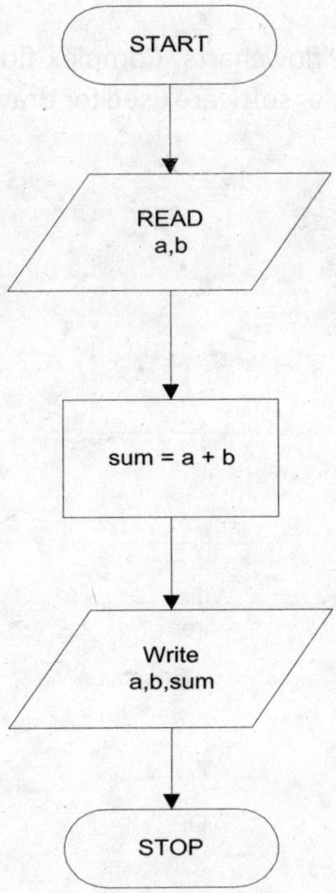

Fig. 2.2: Flowchart to find the sum of two numbers

2.5 Exercise

Q 2.3 Develop an algorithm to find the area of circle. Draw a flowchart for the algorithm.

Given: Area = πr^2

Algorithm 2.3

1. Start execution.
2. Input the value of 'r' to the computer.
3. Calculate *Area* = πr^2.
4. Output the input and result (r and area).
5. Stop execution

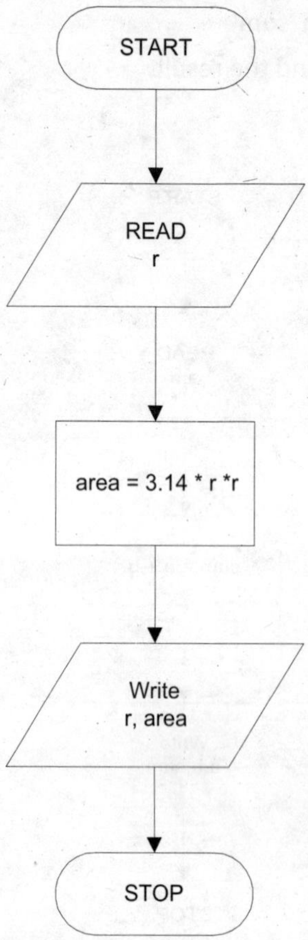

Fig. 2.3: Flowchart to find the area of circle

Q 2.4 Develop an algorithm and draw flowchart to find the simple interest of a deposit.

Given: I = PNR (I: the interest, P: the principal amount, N: No of years, R: Rate of interest)

Algorithm 2.4

1. Start execution.
2. Input the value of p, n, r to the computer.
3. Calculate *i= p * n * r*
4. Output the input and result (p, n, r, i and area).
5. Stop execution

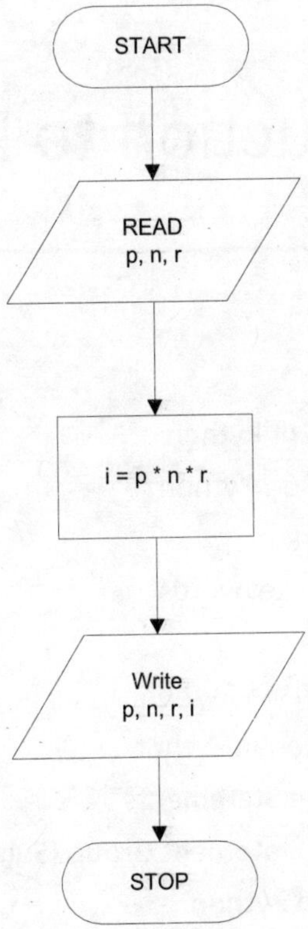

Fig. 2.4: Flowchart to find interest rate

2.6 Conclusion

We have briefly introduced the Programming logic and flowchart in this Chapter. Various flowchart symbols and example flowchart are illustrated.

2.7 Review Questions

1. Describe various modules of a railway reservation system.
2. Describe a simple banking system with various modules.
3. Explain the various symbols used for drawing a flowchart.
4. Develop an algorithm and draw a flowchart to find the area of a rectangle.
5. Develop an algorithm and draw a flowchart, to find the area of a triangle. Use any formula.
6. Develop an algorithm and draw a flowchart for temperature conversion from Fahrenheit (f) to degree Celsius (c). Hint: c = 5 * (f-32) / 9
7. Develop an algorithm and draw a flowchart to travel abroad (US or Europe) as far as you can, keeping one alternate option.

03 Introduction to Python

CONTENTS

Python was developed by Guido van Rossum at the National Research Institute for Mathematics and Computer Science in Netherlands during 1985-1990. Python is derived from many other languages, including ABC, Modula-3, C, C++, Algol-68, SmallTalk, Unix shell and other scripting languages. Rossum was inspired by Monty Python's Flying Circus, a BBC comedy series and he wanted the name of his new language to be short, unique and mysterious. Hence he named it Python. It is a general-purpose interpreted, interactive, object-oriented and high-level Programming language. Python source code is available under the GNU General Public License (GPL) and it is now maintained by a core development team at the National Research Institute.

3.1 Features of Python

a) **Simple and easy-to-learn** – Python is a simple language with few keywords, simple structure and its syntax is also clearly defined. This makes Python a beginner's language.

b) **Interpreted and Interactive** - Python is processed at runtime by the interpreter. We need not compile the program before executing it. The Python prompt interact with the interpreter to interpret the programs that you have written. Python has an option namely interactive mode which allows interactive testing and debugging of code.

c) **Object-Oriented** – Python supports Object Oriented Programming (OOP) concepts that encapsulate code within objects. All concepts in OOPs like data hiding, operator overloading, inheritance etc. can be well written in Python. It supports functional as well as structured programming.

d) **Portable** - Python can run on a wide variety of hardware and software platforms and has the same interface on all platforms. All variants of Windows, Unix, Linux and Macintosh are to name a few.

e) **Scalable** - Python provides a better structure and support for large programs than shell scripting. It can be used as a scripting language or can be compiled to bytecode (intermediate code that is platform independent) for building large applications.

f) **Extendable** - You can add low-level modules to the Python interpreter. These modules enable programmers to add to or customize their tools to be more efficient. It can be easily integrated with C, C++, COM, ActiveX, CORBA, and Java.

g) **Dynamic** - Python provides very high-level dynamic data types and supports dynamic type checking. It also supports automatic garbage collection.

h) **GUI Programming and Databases** - Python supports GUI applications that can be created and ported to many libraries and windows systems, such as Windows Microsoft Foundation Classes (MFC), Macintosh and the X Window system of Unix. Python also provides interfaces to all major commercial databases.

i) **Broad Standard Library** - Python's library is portable and cross platform compatible on UNIX, Linux, Windows and Macintosh. This helps in the support and development of a wide range of applications from simple text processing to browsers and complex games.

3.2 How to Run Python

There are three different ways to start Python.

a) Using Interactive Interpreter

You can start Python from Unix, DOS, or any other system that provides you a command-line interpreter or shell window. Get into the command line of Python. For Unix/Linux, you can get into interactive mode by typing `$python or python%`. For Windows/Dos it is `C:>python`.

Invoking the interpreter without passing a script file as a parameter brings up the following prompt–

```
$ python
Python 2.7.10 (default, Sep 27 2015, 18:11:38)
[GCC 5.1.1 20150422 (Red Hat 5.1.1-1)] on linux2
Type "help", "copyright", "credits" or "license" for more
information.
>>>
```

Type the following text at the Python prompt and press the Enter:

```
>>> print("Programming in Python!")
```

The result will be as given below.

```
Programming in Python!
>>>
```

b) Script from the Command Line

This method invokes the interpreter with a script parameter which begins the execution of the script and continues until the script is finished. When the script is finished, the interpreter is no longer active. A Python script can be executed at command line by invoking the interpreter on your application, as follows.

For Unix/Linux it is `$python script.py` or `python% script.py`. For Windows/Dos it is `C:>python script.py`

Let us write a simple Python program in a script. Python files have extension .py. Type the following source code in a `first.py` file.

```
print("Programming in Python!")
```

Now, try to run this program as follows.

```
$ python first.py
```

This produces the following result:

```
Programming in Python!
```

c) Integrated Development Environment

You can run Python from a Graphical User Interface (GUI) environment as well, if you have a GUI application on your system that supports Python. IDLE is the Integrated Development Environment (IDE) for UNIX and PythonWin is the first Windows interface for Python. All the programs in this book are tested in Python 3.4.3 for Windows.

3.3 Identifiers

A Python identifier is a name used to identify a variable, function, class, module or any other object. Python is case sensitive and hence uppercase and lowercase letters are considered distinct. The following are the rules for naming an identifier in Python.

a) Identifiers can be a combination of letters in lowercase (a to z) or uppercase (A to Z) or digits (0 to 9) or an underscore (_). For example Total and total is different.

b) Reserved keywords (explained in section 3.4) cannot be used as an identifier.

c) Identifiers cannot begin with a digit. For example 2more, 3times etc. are invalid identifiers.

d) Special symbols like @, !, #, $, % etc. cannot be used in an identifier. For example sum@, #total are invalid identifiers.

e) Identifier can be of any length.

Some examples of valid identifiers are total, max_mark, count2, Student etc. Here are some naming conventions for Python identifiers.

- Class names start with an uppercase letter. All other identifiers start with a lowercase letter. Eg: Person
- Starting an identifier with a single leading underscore indicates that the identifier is private. Eg: _sum
- Starting an identifier with two leading underscores indicates a strongly private identifier. Eg: __sum
- If the identifier also ends with two trailing underscores, the identifier is a language-defined special name. foo__

3.4 Reserved Keywords

These are keywords reserved by the programming language and prevent the user or the programmer from using it as an identifier in a program. There are 33 keywords in Python 3.3. This number may vary with different versions. To retrieve the keywords in Python the following code can be given at the prompt. All keywords except True, False and None are in lowercase. The following list in Table 3.1 shows the Python keywords.

```
>>> import keyword
>>> print(keyword.kwlist)
['False', 'None', 'True', 'and', 'as', 'assert', 'break',
'class', 'continue', 'def', 'del', 'elif', 'else', 'except',
'finally', 'for', 'from', 'global', 'if', 'import', 'in', 'is',
'lambda', 'nonlocal', 'not', 'or', 'pass', 'raise', 'return',
'try', 'while', 'with', 'yield']
```

Table 3.1: Python Keywords

False	class	finally	is	return
None	continue	for	lambda	try
True	def	from	nonlocal	while
and	del	global	not	with
as	elif	if	or	yield
assert	else	import	pass	
break	except	in	raise	

3.5 Variables

Variables are reserved memory locations to store values. Based on the data type of a variable, the interpreter allocates memory and decides what can be stored in the reserved memory. Therefore, by assigning different data types to variables, you can store integers, decimals or characters in these variables.

Python variables do not need explicit declaration to reserve memory space. The declaration happens automatically when you assign a value to a variable. The equal sign (=) is used to assign values to variables. The operand to the left of the = operator is the name of the variable and the operand to the right of the = operator is the value stored in the variable.

Example Program

```
a = 100              # An integer assignment
b = 1000.0           # A floating point
name = "John"        # A string

print(a)
print(b)
print(name)
```

Here, 100, 1000.0 and "John" are the values assigned to a, b, and *name* variables, respectively. This produces the following result.

```
100
1000.0
John
```

Python allows you to assign a single value to several variables simultaneously. For example –

```
a = b = c = 1
```

Here, an integer object is created with the value 1, and all three variables are assigned to the same memory location. You can also assign multiple objects to multiple variables. For example

```
a, b, c = 1, 2, "Tom"
```

Here, two integer objects with values 1 and 2 are assigned to variables a and b respectively, and one string object with the value "Tom" is assigned to the variable c.

3.6 Comments in Python

Comments are very important while writing a program. It describes what the source code has done. Comments are for programmers for better understanding of a program. In Python, we use the hash (#) symbol to start writing a comment. A hash sign (#) that is not inside a string literal begins a comment. All characters after the # and up to the end of the physical line are part of the comment. It extends up to the newline character. Python interpreter ignores comment.

Example Program

```
>>>#This is demo of comment
>>>#Display Hello
>>>print("Hello")
```

This produces the following result: `Hello`

For multiline comments one way is to use (#) symbol at the beginning of each line. The following example shows a multiline comment. Another way of doing this is to use triple quotes, either ''' or """.

Example 1

```
>>>#This is a very long sentence
>>>#and it ends after
>>>#Three lines
```

Example 2

```
>>>"""This is a very long sentence
>>>and it ends after
>>>Three lines"""
```

Both Example 1 and Example 2 given above produces the same result.

3.7 Indentation in Python

Most of the programming languages like C, C++ and Java use braces { } to define a block of code. Python uses indentation. A code block (body of a function, loop etc.) starts with indentation and ends with the first unindented line. The amount of indentation can be decided by the programmer, but it must be consistent throughout the block. Generally four whitespaces are used for indentation and is preferred over tabspace. For example

```
if True:
    print("Correct")
else:
  print("Wrong")
```

But the following block generates error as indentation is not properly followed.

```
if True:
    print("Answer")
    print("Correct")
else:
    print("Answer")
  print("Wrong")
```

3.8 Multi-Line Statements

Instructions that a Python interpreter can execute are called statements. For example, a=1 is an assignment statement. if statement, for statement, while statement etc. are other kinds of statements which will be discussed in coming Chapters. In Python, end of a statement is marked by a newline character. But we can make a statement extend over multiple lines with the line continuation character(\). For example:

```
grand_total = first_item + \
              second_item + \
              third_item
```

Statements contained within the [], {}, or () brackets do not need to use the line continuation character. For example

```
months = ['January', 'February', 'March', 'April',
          'May', 'June', 'July', 'August', 'September',
          'October', 'November', 'December']
```

We could also put multiple statements in a single line using semicolons, as follows.

```
a = 1; b = 2; c = 3
```

3.9 Multiple Statement Group (Suite)

A group of individual statements, which make a single code block is called a **suite** in Python. Compound or complex statements, such as if, while, def, and class require a header line and a suite. Header lines begin the statement (with the keyword) and terminate with a colon (:) and are followed by one or more lines which make up the suite. For example

```
if expression :
    suite
elif expression :
    suite
else :
    suite
```

3.10 Quotes in Python

Python accepts single ('), double (") and triple (''' or """) quotes to denote string literals. The same type of quote should be used to start and end the string. The triple quotes are used to span the string across multiple lines. For example, all the following are legal.

```
word = 'single word'
sentence = "This is a short sentence."
paragraph = """This is a long paragraph. It consists of
            several lines and sentences."""
```

3.11 Input, Output and Import Functions

3.11.1 Displaying the Output

The function used to print output on a screen is the print statement where you can pass zero or more expressions separated by commas. The print function converts the expressions you pass into a string and writes the result to standard output.

Example 1

```
>>>print("Learning Python is fun and enjoy it.")
```

This will produce the following output on the screen.

```
Learning Python is fun and enjoy it.
```

Example 2

```
>>>a=2
>>>print("The value of a is",a)
```

This will produce the following output on the screen.

```
The value of a is 2
```

By default a space is added after the text and before the value of variable a. The syntax of *print* function is given below.

```
print(*objects, sep=' ', end='\n', file=sys.stdout, flush=False)
```

Here, `objects` are the values to be printed. `Sep` is the separator used between the values. Space character is the default separator. `End` is printed after printing all the values. The default value for end is the new line. `File` is the object where the values are printed and its default value is `sys.stdout` (screen). Flush determines whether the output stream needs to be flushed for any waiting output. A True value forcibly flushes the stream. The following shows an example for the above syntax.

Example

```
>>>print(1,2,3,4)
>>>print(1,2,3,4,sep='+')
>>> print(1,2,3,4,sep='+',end='%')
```

The output will be as follows.

```
1 2 3 4
1+2+3+4
1+2+3+4%
```

The output can also be formatted to make it attractive according to the wish of a user. This will be discussed in the subsequent Chapters.

3.11.2 Reading the Input

Python provides two built-in functions to read a line of text from standard input, which by default comes from the keyboard. These functions are **raw_input** and **input.**

`raw_input function`

The raw_input([prompt]) function reads one line from standard input and returns it as a string (removing the trailing newline). This prompts you to enter any string and it would display same string on the screen. raw_input function is not supported by Python 3.4.3 for Windows.

Example

```
str = raw_input("Enter your name: ");
print("Your name is : ", str)
```

Output

```
Enter your name: Collin Mark
Your name is : Collin Mark
```

input function

The input([prompt]) function is equivalent to raw_input, except that it assumes the input is a valid Python expression and returns the evaluated result to you.

Example 1

```
n = input("Enter a number ");
print("The number is : ", n)
```

Output

```
Enter a number: 5
The number is : 5
```

Example 2

```
n = input("Enter an expression ");
print("The result is : ", n)
```

Output

```
Enter an expression: 5*2
The result is : 10
```

3.11.3 Import function

When the program grows bigger or when there are segments of code that is frequently used, it can be stored in different modules. A module is a file containing Python definitions and statements. Python modules have a filename and end with the extension `.py`. Definitions inside a module can be imported to another module or the interactive interpreter in Python. We use the `import` keyword to do this. For example, we can import the `math` module by typing in `import math`.

```
>>> import math
>>> math.pi
3.141592653589793
```

3.12 Operators

Operators are the constructs which can manipulate the value of operands. Consider the expression a = b + c. Here a, b and c are called the operands and +, = are called the operators. There are different types of operators. The following are the types of operators supported by Python.

- Arithmetic Operators
- Comparison (Relational) Operators
- Assignment Operators
- Logical Operators

- Bitwise Operators
- Membership Operators
- Identity Operators

Let us have a look on all operators one by one.

3.12.1 Arithmetic Operators

Arithmetic operators are used for performing basic arithmetic operations. The following are the arithmetic operators supported by Python. Table 3.2 shows the arithmetic operators in Python.

Table 3.2: Arithmetic Operators in Python

Operator	Operation	Description
+	Addition	Adds values on either side of the operator.
-	Subtraction	Subtracts right hand operand from left hand operand.
*	Multiplication	Multiplies values on either side of the operator.
/	Division	Divides left hand operand by right hand operand.
%	Modulus	Divides left hand operand by right hand operand and returns remainder.
**	Exponent	Performs exponential (power) calculation on operators.
//	Floor Division	The division of operands where the result is the quotient in which the digits after the decimal point are removed.

Example Program

```
a, b, c = 10, 5, 2
print("Sum=", (a+b))
print("Difference=", (a-b))
print("Product=", (a*b))
print("Quotient=", (a/b))
print("Remainder=", (b%c))
print("Exponent=", (b**2))
print("Floor Division=", (b//c))
```

Output

```
Sum= 15
Difference= 5
Product= 50
Quotient= 2
Remainder= 1
Exponent= 25
Floor Division= 2
```

3.12.2 Comparison Operators

These operators compare the values on either sides of them and decide the relation among them. They are also called relational operators. Python supports the following relational operators. Table 3.3 shows the comparison or relational operators in Python.

Table 3.3: Comparison (Relational Operators) in Python

Operator	Description
==	If the values of two operands are equal, then the condition becomes true.
!=	If values of two operands are not equal, then condition becomes true.
>	If the value of left operand is greater than the value of right operand, then condition becomes true.
<	If the value of left operand is less than the value of right operand, then condition becomes true.
>=	If the value of left operand is greater than or equal to the value of right operand, then condition becomes true.
<=	If the value of left operand is less than or equal to the value of right operand, then condition becomes true.

Example Program

```
a,b=10,5
print("a==b is", (a==b))
print("a!=b is", (a!=b))
print("a>b is", (a>b))
print("a<b is", (a<b))
print("a>=b is", (a>=b))
print("a<=b is", (a<=b))
```

Output

```
a==b is False
a!=b is True
a>b is True
a<b is False
a>=b is True
a<=b is False
```

3.12.3 Assignment Operators

Python provides various assignment operators. Various shorthand operators for addition, subtraction, multiplication, division, modulus, exponent and floor division are also supported by Python. Table 3.4 provides the various assignment operators.

Table 3.4: Assignment Operators

Operator	Description
=	Assigns values from right side operands to left side operand.
+=	It adds right operand to the left operand and assign the result to left operand.
-=	It subtracts right operand from the left operand and assign the result to left operand.
*=	It multiplies right operand with the left operand and assign the result to left operand.
/=	It divides left operand with the right operand and assign the result to left operand.
%=	It takes modulus using two operands and assign the result to left operand.
**=	Performs exponential (power) calculation on operators and assign value to the left operand.
//=	It performs floor division on operators and assign value to the left operand.

The assignment operator = is used to assign values or values of expressions to a variable. Example: a = b+ c. For example c+=a is equivalent to c=c+a. Similarly c-=a is equivalent to c=c-a, c*=a is equivalent to c=c*a, c/=a is equivalent to c=c/a, c%=a is equivalent to c=c%a, c**=a is equivalent to c=c**a and c//=a is equivalent to c=c//a.

Example Program

```
a,b=10,5
a+=b
print(a)
a,b=10,5
a-=b
print(a)
a,b=10,5
a*=b
print(a)
a,b=10,5
a/=b
print(a)
b,c=5,2
b%=c
print(b)
b,c=5,2
b**=c
print(b)
b,c=5,2
b//=c
print(b)
```

Output

```
15
5
50
2
1
25
2
```

3.12.4 Bitwise Operators

Bitwise operator works on bits and performs bit by bit operation. The following are the bitwise operators supported by Python. Table 3.5 gives a description of bitwise operators in Python.

Table 3.5: Bitwise Operators

Operator	Operation	Description
&	Binary AND	Operator copies a bit to the result if it exists in both operands.
|	Binary OR	It copies a bit if it exists in either operand.
^	Binary XOR	It copies the bit if it is set in one operand but not both.
~	Binary Ones Complement	It is unary and has the effect of 'flipping' bits.
<<	Binary Left Shift	The left operands value is moved left by the number of bits specified by the right operand.
>>	Binary Right Shift	The left operands value is moved right by the number of bits specified by the right operand.

Let *a* = 60 (`0011 1100` in binary) and *b* = 2 (`0000 0010` in binary)

Example Program

```
a,b=60,2
print(a&b)
print(a|b)
print(a^b)
print(~a)
print(a>>b)
print(a<<b)
```

Output

```
0
62
62
```

```
-61
15
240
```

Consider the first print statement `a&b.` Here a = 0011 1100

b = 0000 0010

When a bitwise and is performed, the result is 0000 0000 . This is 0 in decimal. Similar is the case for all the print statements given above.

3.12.5 Logical Operators

Table 3.6 shows the various logical operators supported by Python language.

Table 3.6: Logical Operators

Operator	Operation	Description
and	Logical AND	If both the operands are true then condition becomes true.
or	Logical OR	If any of the operands are true then condition becomes true.
not	Logical NOT	Used to reverse the logical state of its operand.

Example Program

```
a,b,c,d=10,5,2,1
print((a>b)and(c>d))
print((a>b)or(d>c))
print(not(a>b))
```

Output

```
True
True
False
```

3.12.6 Membership Operators

Python's membership operators test for membership in a sequence, such as strings, lists, or tuples. There are two membership operators as explained below in Table 3.7. Strings, lists and tuples will be covered in the forthcoming Chapter.

Table 3.7: Membership Operators

Operator	Description
in	Evaluates to true if the variables on either side of the operator point to the same object and false otherwise.
not in	Evaluates to true if it does not finds a variable in the specified sequence and false otherwise.

Example Program

```
s='abcde'
print('a' in s)
print('f' in s)
print('f'not in s)
```

Output

```
True
False
True
```

3.12.7 Identity Operators

Identity operators compare the memory locations of two objects. There are two Identity operators as shown in below Table 3.8.

Table 3.8: Identity Operators

Operator	Description
is	Evaluates to true if the variables on either side of the operator point to the same object and false otherwise.
is not	Evaluates to false if the variables on either side of the operator point to the same object and true otherwise.

Example Program

```
a,b,c=10,10,5
print(a is b)
print(a is c)
print(a is not b)
```

Output

```
True
False
False
```

3.12.8 Operator Precedence

The following Table 3.9 lists all operators from highest precedence to lowest. Operator associativity determines the order of evaluation when they are of the some precedence and are not grouped by parenthesis. An operator may be left-associative or right-associative. In left-associative, the operator falling on the left side will be evaluated first, while in right-associative, operator falling on the right will be evaluated first. In Python '=' and '**' are right-associative while all other operators are left-associative.

Table 3.9: Operator Precedence

Operator	Description
**	Exponentiation (raise to the power)
~,+, -	Complement, unary plus and minus
*, /, %, //	Multiply, divide, modulo and floor division

Operator	Description
+, -	Addition and subtraction
>>, <<	Right and left bitwise shift
&	Bitwise 'AND'
^ ,|	Bitwise exclusive `OR' and regular `OR'
<=, < >,>=	Comparison operators
<>, ==, !=	Equality operators
= ,%= ,/=, //= ,-= ,+=, *= ,**=	Assignment operators
is, is not	Identity operators
in, not in	Membership operators
not, or, and	Logical operators

3.13 Conclusion

This Chapter gives an introduction to Python, its features, programming constructs like identifiers, reserved keywords, variables and various operators with illustrated examples. This Chapter also covers the purpose of indentation, the usage of comments, multi-line statements, multiple statements and quotes in Python, each one with illustrated examples. The basic Input/Output and import functions covered in this Chapter helps to handle the input, output and import operations in Python. Moreover how to execute Python is explained in this Chapter.

3.14 Review Questions

1. List some of the features of Python.
2. Is Python a case sensitive language?
3. How can you run Python?
4. Give the rules for naming an identifier in Python.
5. How can you give comments in Python?
6. What are multi-line statements?
7. What do you mean by suite in Python?
8. Briefly explain the Input and Output functions used in Python.
9. What is the purpose of import function?
10. What is the purpose of // operator?
11. What is the purpose of ** operator?
12. What is the purpose of is operator?
13. What is the purpose of not in operator?
14. Briefly explain the various types of operators in Python.
15. List out the operator precedence in Python.

04 Data Types and Operations

CONTENTS

The data stored in memory can be of many types. For example, a person's name is stored as alphabets, age is stored as a numeric value and his or her address is stored as alphanumeric characters. Python has the following standard data types.

- Numbers
- String
- List
- Tuple
- Set
- Dictionary

4.1 Numbers

Number data types store numeric values. Number objects are created when you assign a value to them. For example `a = 1, b = 20.` You can also delete the reference to a number object by using the del statement. The syntax of the del statement is as follows.

```
del variable1[,variable2[,variable3[....,variableN]]]]
```

You can delete a single object or multiple objects by using the del statement. For example

```
del a
del a,b
```

Python supports four different numerical types.

- int (signed integers)
- long (long integers, they can also be represented in octal and hexadecimal)
- float (floating point real values)
- complex (complex numbers)

Integers can be of any length, it is only limited by the memory available. A floating point number is accurate up to 15 decimal places. Integer and floating points are separated by decimal points. 1 is integer, 1.0 is floating point number. Complex numbers are written in the form, x + yj, where x is the real part and y is the imaginary part.

Example Program

```
a,b,c,d=1,1.5,231456987,2+9j
print("a=",a)
print("b=",b)
print("c=",c)
print("d=",d)
```

Output

```
a= 1
b= 1.5
c= 231456987
d= (2+9j)
```

4.1.1 Mathematical Functions

Python provides various built-in mathematical functions to perform mathematical calculations. The following Table 4.1 provides various mathematical functions and its purpose. For using the below functions, all functions except abs(x), max(x1,x2,...xn), min(x1,x2,...xn), round(x[,n]) and pow(x,y) need to import the math module because these functions reside in the math module. The math module also defines two mathematical constants `pi` and `e`. Modules will be discussed in Chapter 7.

Table 4.1: Mathematical Functions

Function	Description
abs(x)	Returns the absolute value of x.
sqrt(x)	Finds the square root of x.
ceil(x)	Finds the smallest integer not less than x.
floor(x)	Finds the largest integer not greater than x.

Function	Description
pow(x,y)	Finds x raised to y.
exp(x)	Returns e^x ie exponential of x.
fabs(x)	Returns the absolute value of x.
log(x)	Finds the natural logarithm of x for x>0.
log10(x)	Finds the logarithm to the base 10 for x>0.
max(x1,x2,...xn)	Returns the largest of its arguments.
min(x1,x2,....xn)	Returns the smallest of its arguments.
round(x,[n])	In case of decimal numbers, x will be rounded to n digits.
modf(x)	Returns the integer and decimal part as a tuple. The integer part is returned as a decimal.

Example Program

```
import math
print("Absolute value of -120:",abs(-120))
print("Square root of 25:",math.sqrt(25))
print("Ceiling of 12.2:", math.ceil(12.2))
print("Floor of 12.2:", math.floor(12.2))
print("2 raised to 3:", pow(2,3))
print("Exponential of 3:",math.exp(3))
print("Absolute value of -123:", math.fabs(-123))
print("Natural Logarithm of 2:", math.log(2))
print("Logarithm to the Base 10 of 2:",math.log10(2))
print("Largest among 10, 4, 2:",max(10,4,2))
print("Smallest among 10,4, 2:",min(10,4,2))
print("12.6789 rounded to 2 decimal places:",round(12.6789,2))
print("Decimal part and integer part of 12.090876:", math.
modf(12.090876))
```

Output

```
Absolute value of -120: 120
Square root of 25: 5.0
Ceiling of 12.2: 13
Floor of 12.2: 12
2 raised to 3: 8
Exponential of 3: 20.085536923187668
Absolute value of -123: 123.0
Natural Logarithm of 2: 0.6931471805599453
```

```
Logarithm to the Base 10 of 2: 0.3010299956639812
Largest among 10, 4, 2: 10
Smallest among 10,4, 2: 2
12.6789 rounded to 2 decimal places: 12.68
Decimal part and integer part of 12.090876:
(0.09087599999999973, 12.0)
```

4.1.2 Trigonometric Functions

There are several built-in trigonometric functions in Python. The function names and its purpose are listed in Table 4.2.

Table 4.2: Trigonometric Functions

Function	Description
sin(x)	Returns the sine of x in radians.
cos(x)	Returns the cosine of x in radians.
tan(x)	Returns the tangent of x in radians.
asin(x)	Returns the arc sine of x, in radians.
acos(x)	Returns the arc cosine of x, in radians.
atan(x)	Returns the arc tangent of x, in radians.
atan2(y,x)	Returns atan(y / x), in radians.
hypot(x,y)	Returns the Euclidean form, sqrt(x*x + y*y).
degrees(x)	Converts angle x from radians to degrees.
radians(x)	Converts angle x from degrees to radians.

Example

```
import math
print("Sin(90):",math.sin(90))
print("Cos(90):",math.cos(90))
print("Tan(90):",math.tan(90))
print("asin(1):",math.asin(1))
print("acos(1):",math.acos(1))
print("atan(1):",math.atan(1))
print("atan2(3,2):",math.atan2(3,2))
print("Hypotenuse of 3 and 4:",math.hypot(3,4))
print("Degrees of 90:",math.degrees(90))
print("Radians of 90:",math.radians(90))
```

Output

```
Sin(90): 0.893996663601
```

```
Cos(90): -0.448073616129
Tan(90): -1.99520041221
asin(1): 1.57079632679
acos(1): 0.0
atan(1): 0.785398163397
atan2(3,2): 0.982793723247
Hypotenuse of 3 and 4: 5.0
Degrees of 90: 5156.62015618
Radians of 90: 1.57079632679
```

4.1.3 Random Number Functions

There are several random number functions supported by Python. Random numbers have applications in research, games, cryptography, simulation and other applications. Table 4.3 shows the commonly used random number functions in Python. For using the random number functions, we need to import the module `random` because all these functions reside in the `random` module.

Table 4.3: Random Number Functions

Function	Description
choice(sequence)	Returns a random value from a sequence like list, tuple, string etc.
shuffle(list)	Shuffles the items randomly in a list. Returns none.
random()	Returns a random floating-point number which lies between 0 and 1.
randrange([start,] stop [,step])	Returns a randomly selected number from a range where start shows the starting of the range, stop shows the end of the range and step decides the number to be added to decide a random number.
seed([x])	Gives the starting value for generating a random number. Returns none. This function is called before calling any other random module function.
uniform(x,y)	Generates a random floating-point number n such that n>x and n<y.

Example

```
import random
s='abcde'
print("choice(abcde):", random.choice(s))
list = [10,2,3,1,8,19]
print("shuffle(list):", random.shuffle(list))
print("random.seed(20):", random.seed(20))
print("random():",random.random())
print("uniform(2,3):", random.uniform(2,3))
print("randrange(2,10,1):",random.randrange(2,10,1))
```

Output

```
choice(abcde): b
shuffle(list): None
random.seed(20): None
random(): 0.905639676175
uniform(2,3): 2.68625415703
randrange(2,10,1): 8
```

4.2 Strings

Strings in Python are identified as a contiguous set of characters represented in the quotation marks. Python allows for either pairs of single or double quotes. Subsets of strings can be taken using the slice operator ([ ] and [:]) with indexes starting at 0 in the beginning of the string and ending at -1.The plus (+) sign is the string concatenation operator and the asterisk (*) is the repetition operator. The % operator is used for string formatting which will be discussed in Section 4.2.2.

Example Program

```
str = 'Welcome to Python Programming '
print(str) # Prints complete string
print(str[0]) # Prints first character of the string
print(str[11:17]) # Prints characters starting from 11th to 17th
print(str[11:]) # Prints string starting from 11th character
print(str * 2) # Prints string two times
print(str + "Session") # Prints concatenated string
```

Output

```
Welcome to Python Programming
W
Python
Python Programming
Welcome to Python Programming Welcome to Python Programming
Welcome to Python Programming Session
```

4.2.1 Escape Characters

An escape character is a character that gets interpreted when placed in single or double quotes. They are represented using backslash notation. These characters are non printable. The following Table 4.4 shows the most commonly used escape characters and their description.

Table 4.4: Escape Characters

Escape Characters	Description
\a	Bell or alert
\b	Backspace
\f	Formfeed
\n	Newline
\r	Carriage Return
\s	Space
\t	Tab
\v	Vertical Tab

4.2.2 String Formatting Operator

This operator is unique to strings and is similar to the formatting operations of the printf() function of the C Programming language. The following Table 4.5 shows various format symbols and their conversion.

Table 4.5: Format Symbols and their Conversion

Format Symbols	Conversion
%c	Character
%s	String
%i	Signed Decimal Integer
%d	Signed Decimal Integer
%u	Unsigned Decimal Integer
%o	Octal Integer
%x	Hexadecimal Integer (lowercase letters)
%X	Hexadecimal Integer(uppercase letters)
%e	Exponential notation with lowercase letter 'e'
%E	Exponential notation with uppercase letter 'E'
%f	Floating-point real number

The following example shows the usage of various string formatting functions.

Example Program

```
#Demo of String Formatting Operators
print("The first letter of %s is %c " %('apple', 'a')) #usage of
%s and %c
print("The sum=%d" %(-12)) #usage of %d
print("The sum=%i" %(-12)) #usage of %i
print("The sum=%u" %(12)) #usage of %u
```

```
print("%o is the octal octal equivalent of %d" %(8,8)) #usage of %o
print("%x is the hexadecimal equivalent of %d" %(10,10))#usage
of %x
print("%X is the hexadecimal equivalent of %d" %(10,10))#usage
of %X
print("%e is the exponential equivalent of %f"
%(10.98765432,10.98765432)) #usage of %e and %f
print("%E is the exponential equivalent of %f"
%(10.98765432,10.98765432)) #usage of %E and %f
print( "%.2f" %(32.1274)) #usage of %f for printing upto two
decimal places
```

Output

```
The first letter of apple is a
The sum=-12
The sum=-12
The sum=12
10 is the octal octal equivalent of 8
a is the hexadecimal equivalent of 10
A is the hexadecimal equivalent of 10
1.098765e+01 is the exponential equivalent of 10.987654
1.098765E+01 is the exponential equivalent of 10.987654
32.13
```

4.2.3 String Formatting Functions

Python includes a large number of built-in functions to manipulate strings.

1. **len(string)**- Returns the length of the string

   Example Program

```
#Demo of len(string)
s='Learning Python is fun!'
print("Length of", s, "is", len(s))
```

   Output

```
Length of Learning Python is fun! is 23
```

2. **lower()** – Returns a copy of the string in which all uppercase alphabets in a string are converted to lowercase alphabets.

   Example Program

```
#Demo of lower()
s='Learning Python is fun!'
print(s.lower())
```

Output

```
learning python is fun!
```

3. **upper()** – Returns a copy of the string in which all lowercase alphabets in a string are converted to uppercase alphabets.

Example Program

```
#Demo of upper()
s='Learning Python is fun!'
print(s.upper())
```

Output

```
LEARNING PYTHON IS FUN!
```

4. **swapcase()** – Returns a copy of the string in which the case of all the alphabets are swapped. ie. all the lowercase alphabets are converted to uppercase and vice versa.

Example Program

```
#Demo of swapcase()
s='LEARNing PYTHON is fun!'
print(s.swapcase())
```

Output

```
learnING python IS FUN!
```

5. **capitalize()** – Returns a copy of the string with only its first character capitalized.

Example Program

```
#Demo of capitalize()
s='learning Python is fun!'
print(s.capitalize())
```

Output

```
Learning python is fun!
```

6. **title()** - Returns a copy of the string in which first character of all the words are capitalized.

Example Program

```
#Demo of title()
s='learning Python is fun!'
print(s.title())
```

Output

```
Learning Python Is Fun!
```

7. **lstrip()** – Returns a copy of the string in which all the characters have been stripped(removed) from the beginning. The default character is whitespaces.

Example Program

```
#Demo of lstrip()
s='     learning Python is fun!'
print(s.lstrip())
s='*******learning Python is fun!'
print(s.lstrip('*'))
```

Output

```
learning Python is fun!
learning Python is fun!
```

8. **rstrip()** - Returns a copy of the string in which all the characters have been stripped(removed) from the beginning. The default character is whitespaces.

Example Program

```
#Demo of rstrip()
s='learning Python is fun!     '
print(s.rstrip())
s='learning Python is fun!******'
print(s.rstrip('*'))
```

Output

```
learning Python is fun!
learning Python is fun!
```

9. **strip()** - Returns a copy of the string in which all the characters have been stripped(removed) from the beginning and end . It performs both `lstrip()` and `rstrip()`. The default character is whitespaces.

Example Program

```
#Demo of strip()
s='    learning Python is fun!     '
print(s.strip())
s='******learning Python is fun!******'
print(s.strip('*'))
```

Output

```
learning Python is fun!
learning Python is fun!
```

10. **max(str)** – Returns the maximum alphabetical character from string `str`.

Example Program

```
#Demo of max(str)
```

```
s='learning Python is fun'
print('Maximum character is :', max(s))
```

Output

```
Maximum character is : y
```

11. **min(str)** - Returns the minimum alphabetical character from string `str`.

Example Program

```
#Demo of min(str)
s='learning-Python-is-fun'
print('Minimum character is :', min(s))
```

Output

```
Minimum character is : -
```

12. **replace(old, new [,max])** – Returns a copy of the string with all the occurrences of substring `old` is replaced by `new`. The `max` is optional and if it is specified, the first occurrences specified in `max` are replaced.

Example Program

```
# Demo of replace(old, new[,max])
s="This is very new.This is good"
print(s.replace('is', 'was'))
print(s.replace('is', 'was', 2))
```

Output

```
Thwas was very new.Thwas was good
Thwas was very new.This is good
```

13. **center(width, fillchar)** – Returns a string centered in a length specified in the `width` variable. Padding is done using the character specified in the `fillchar`. Default padding is space.

Example Program

```
# Demo of center(width, fillchar)
s="This is Python Programming"
print(s.center(30, '*'))
print(s.center(30))
```

Output

```
**This is Python Programming**
  This is Python Programming
```

14. **ljust(width[,fillchar])** – Returns a string left-justified in a length specified in the `width` variable. Padding is done using the character specified in the `fillchar`. Default padding is space.

Example Program

```
# Demo of ljust(width[,fillchar])
s="This is Python Programming"
print(s.ljust(30, '*'))
print(s.ljust(30))
```

Output

```
This is Python Programming****
This is Python Programming
```

15. **rjust(width[,fillchar])** – Returns a string right-justified in a length specified in the `width` variable. Padding is done using the character specified in the `fillchar`. Default padding is space.

Example Program

```
# Demo of rjust(width[,fillchar])
s="This is Python Programming"
print(s.rjust(30, '*'))
print(s.rjust(30))
```

Output

```
****This is Python Programming
    This is Python Programming
```

16. **zfill(width)** - The method `zfill()` pads string on the left with zeros to fill `width`.

Example Program

```
# Demo of zfill(width)
s="This is Python Programming"
print(s.zfill(30))
```

Output

```
0000This is Python Programming
```

17. **count(str,beg=0,end=len(string))** – Returns the number of occurrences of `str` in the range `beg` and `end`.

Example Program

```
# Demo of count(str,beg=0,end=len(string))
s="This is Python Programming"
print(s.count('i',0,10))
print(s.count('i',0,25))
```

Output

```
2
3
```

18. find(str,beg=0,end=len(string)) – Returns the index of `str` if `str` occurs in the range `beg` and `end` and returns -1 if it is not found.

Example Program

```
# Demo of find(str,beg=0,end=len(string))
s="This is Python Programming"
print(s.find('thon',0,25))
print(s.find('thy'))
```

Output

```
10
-1
```

19. rfind(str,beg=0,end=len(string)) – Same as **`find`**, but searches backward in a string.

Example Program

```
# Demo of rfind(str,beg=0,end=len(string))
s="This is Python Programming"
print(s.rfind('thon',0,25))
print(s.rfind('thy'))
```

Output

```
10
-1
```

20. index(str,beg=0,end=len(string)) – Same as that of find but raises an exception if the item is not found.

Example Program

```
# Demo of index(str,beg=0,end=len(string))
s="This is Python Programming"
print(s.index('thon',0,25))
print(s.index('thy'))
```

Output

```
10
Traceback (most recent call last):
File "main.py", line 4, in <module>
  print s.index('thy')
ValueError: substring not found
```

21. rindex(str,beg=0,end=len(string)) – Same as index but searches backward in a string.

Example Program

```
# Demo of rindex(str,beg=0,end=len(string))
```

```
s="This is Python Programming"
print(s.rindex('thon',0,25))
print(s.rindex('thy'))
```

Output

```
10
Traceback (most recent call last):
File "main.py", line 4, in <module>
  print s.index('thy')
ValueError: substring not found
```

22. **startswith(suffix, beg=0,end=len(string))**- It returns `True` if the string begins with the specified suffix, otherwise return `False`.

Example Program

```
# Demo of startswith(suffix,beg=0,end=len(string))
s="Python Programming is fun"
print(s.startswith('is',10,21))
s="Python Programming is fun"
print(s.startswith('is',19,25))
```

Output

```
False
True
```

23. **endswith(suffix, beg=0,end=len(string))**- It returns `True` if the string ends with the specified suffix, otherwise return `False`.

Example Program

```
# Demo of endswith(suffix,beg=0,end=len(string))
s="Python Programming is fun"
print(s.endswith('is',10,21))
s="Python Programming is fun"
print(s.endswith('is',0,25))
```

Output

```
True
False
```

24. **isdecimal()** - Returns `True` if a unicode string contains only decimal characters and `False` otherwise. To define a string as unicode string, prefix 'u' to the front of the quotation marks.

Example Program

```
# Demo of isdecimal()
s=u"This is Python 1234"
```

```
print(s.isdecimal())
s=u"123456"
print(s.isdecimal())
```

Output

```
False
True
```

25. isalpha() – Returns `True` if string has at least 1 character and all characters are alphabetic and `False` otherwise.

Example Program

```
# Demo of isalpha()
s="This is Python1234"
print(s.isalpha())
s="Python"
print(s.isalpha())
```

Output

```
False
True
```

26. isalnum()- Returns `True` if string has at least 1 character and all characters are alphanumeric and `False` otherwise.

Example Program

```
# Demo of isalnum()
s="***Python1234"
print(s.isalnum())
s="Python1234"
print(s.isalnum())
```

Output

```
False
True
```

27. isdigit() – Returns `True` if string contains only digits and `False` otherwise.

Example Program

```
# Demo of isdigit()
s="***Python1234"
print(s.isdigit())
s="123456"
print(s.isdigit())
```

Output

```
False
True
```

28. islower() – Returns `True` if string has at least 1 cased character and all cased characters are in lowercase and `False` otherwise.

Example Program

```
# Demo of islower()
s="Python Programming"
print(s.islower())
s="python Programming"
print(s.islower())
```

Output

```
False
True
```

29. isupper() – Returns `True` if string has at least one cased character and all cased characters are in uppercase and `False` otherwise.

Example Program

```
# Demo of isupper()
s="Python Programming"
print(s.isupper())
s="PYTHON ProgramMING"
print(s.isupper())
```

Output

```
False
True
```

30. isnumeric() – Returns `True` if a unicode string contains only numeric characters and `False` otherwise.

Example Program

```
# Demo of isnumeric()
s=u"Python Programming1234"
print(s.isnumeric())
s=u"12345"
print(s.isnumeric())
```

Output

```
False
True
```

31. isspace() – Returns `True` if string contains only whitespace characters and `False` otherwise.

Example Program

```
# Demo of isspace()
s="Python Programming"
print(s.isspace())
s="    "
print(s.isspace())
```

Output

```
False
True
```

32. istitle() - Returns `True` if string is properly "titlecased" and `False` otherwise. Title case means each word in a sentence begins with uppercase letter.

Example Program

```
#Demo of istitle()
s="Python Programming is fun"
print(s.istitle())
s="Python Programming Is Fun"
print(s.istitle())
```

Output

```
False
True
```

33. expandtabs(tabsize=8) - It returns a copy of the string in which tab characters ie. '\t' are expanded using spaces using the given tabsize. The default tabsize is 8.

Example Program

```
#Demo of expandtabs(tabsize)
s="Python\tProgramming\tis\tfun"
print( s.expandtabs())
s="Python\tProgramming\tis\tfun"
print(s.expandtabs(10))
```

Output

```
Python  Programming     is      fun
Python    Programming         is        fun
```

34. join(seq) - Returns a string in which the string elements of sequence have been joined by a separator.

Example Program

```
# Demo of join(seq)
s="-"
seq=("Python", "Programming")
print(s.join(seq))
s="*"
seq=("Python", "Programming")
print(s.join(seq))
```

Output

```
Python-Programming
Python*Programming
```

35. split(str="", num=string.count(str)) - Returns a list of all the words in the string, using `str` as the separator (splits on all whitespace if left unspecified), optionally limiting the number of splits to num.

Example Program

```
#Demo of split(str="",num=string.count(str))
s="Python Programming is fun"
print(s.split(' '))
s="Python*Programming*is*fun"
print(s.split('*'))
s="Python*Programming*is*fun"
print(s.split('*',2))
```

Output

```
['Python', 'Programming', 'is', 'fun']
['Python', 'Programming', 'is', 'fun']
['Python', 'Programming', 'is*fun']
```

36. splitlines(num=string.count('\n') - Splits string at all (or num) NEWLINEs and returns a list of each line with NEWLINEs removed. If num is specified, it is assumed that line breaks need to be included in the lines.

Example Program

```
#Demo of splitlines(num=string.count('\n'))
s="Python\nProgramming\nis\nfun"
print(s.splitlines( ))
print(s.splitlines(0))
print(s.splitlines(1))
```

Output

```
['Python', 'Programming', 'is', 'fun']
['Python', 'Programming', 'is', 'fun']
['Python\n', 'Programming\n', 'is\n', 'fun']
```

4.3 List

List is an ordered sequence of items. It is one of the most used data type in Python and is very flexible. All the items in a list do not need to be of the same type. Items separated by commas are enclosed within brackets [ ]. To some extent, lists are similar to arrays in C. One difference between them is that all the items belonging to a list can be of different data type. The values stored in a list can be accessed using the slice operator ([ ] and [:]) with indices starting at 0 in the beginning of the list and ending with -1. The plus (+) sign is the list concatenation operator and the asterisk (*) is the repetition operator.

Example Program

```
first_list = ['abcd', 147, 2.43, 'Tom', 74.9]
small_list = [111, 'Tom']
print(first_list)# Prints complete list
print(first_list[0])# Prints first element of the list
print(first_list[1:3])# Prints elements starting from 2nd till 3rd
print(first_list[2:])# Prints elements starting from 3rd element
print(small_list * 2)# Prints list two times
print(first_list + small_list) # Prints concatenated lists
```

Output

```
['abcd', 147, 2.43, 'Tom', 74.9]
abcd
[147, 2.43]
[2.43, 'Tom', 74.9]
[111, 'Tom', 111, 'Tom']
[['abcd', 147, 2.43, 'Tom', 74.9, 111, 'Tom']
```

We can update lists by using the slice on the left hand side of the assignment operator. Updates can be done on single or multiple elements in a list.

Example Program

```
#Demo of List Update
list = ['abcd', 147, 2.43, 'Tom', 74.9]
print("Item at position 2=", list[2])
list[2]=500
print("Item at position 2=", list[2])
print("Item at Position 0 and 1 is", list[0],list[1])
list[0]=20; list[1]='apple'
print("Item at Position 0 and 1 is", list[0],list[1])
```

Output

```
Item at position 2= 2.43
Item at position 2= 500
Item at Position 0 and 1 is abcd 147
Item at Position 0 and 1 is 20 apple
```

To remove an item from a list, there are two methods. We can use `del` statement or `remove()` method which will be discussed in the subsequent session.

Example Program

```
#Demo of List Deletion
list = ['abcd', 147, 2.43, 'Tom', 74.9]
print(list)
del list[2]
print("List after deletion: ", list)
```

Output

```
['abcd', 147, 2.43, 'Tom', 74.9]
List after deletion:  ['abcd', 147, 'Tom', 74.9]
```

4.3.1 Built-in List Functions

1. **len(list)** – Gives the total length of the list.

Example Program

```
#Demo of len(list)
list1 = ['abcd', 147, 2.43, 'Tom']
print(len(list1))
```

Output

```
4
```

2. **max(list)** – Returns item from the list with maximum value.

Example Program

```
#Demo of max(list)
list1 = [1200, 147, 2.43, 1.12]
list2 = [213, 100, 289]
print("Maximum value in: ", list1, "is",  max(list1))
print("Maximum value in: ", list2, "is",  max(list2))
```

Output

```
Maximum value in:  [1200, 147, 2.43, 1.12] is 1200
Maximum value in:  [213, 100, 289] is 289
```

3. **min(list)** – Returns item from the list with minimum value.

   Example Program

```
#Demo of min(list)
list1 = [1200, 147, 2.43, 1.12]
list2 = [213, 100, 289]
print("Minimum value in: ", list1, "is", min(list1))
print("Minimum value in: ", list2, "is", min(list2))
```

   Output

```
Minimum value in:  [1200, 147, 2.43, 1.12] is 1.12
Minimum value in:  [213, 100, 289] is 100
```

4. **list(seq)** – Returns a tuple into a list.

   Example Program

```
#Demo of list(seq)
tuple = ('abcd', 147, 2.43, 'Tom')
print("List:", list(tuple))
```

   Output

```
List: ['abcd', 147, 2.43, 'Tom']
```

5. **map(aFunction,aSequence)** - One of the common things we do with list and other sequences is applying an operation to each item and collect the result. The **map(aFunction, aSequence)** function applies a passed-in function to each item in an iterable object and returns a list containing all the function call results.

   Example Program

```
str=input("Enter a list(space separated):")
lis=list(map(int,str.split()))
print(lis)
```

   Output

```
Enter a list(space separated):1 2 3 4
[1, 2, 3, 4]
```

In the above example, a string is read from the keyboard and each item is converted into int using map(aFunction,aSequence) function.

4.3.2 Built-in List Methods

1. **list.append(obj)** – This method appends an object obj passed to the existing list.

   Example Program

```
#Demo of list.append(obj)
list = ['abcd', 147, 2.43, 'Tom']
```

```
print("Old List before Append:", list)
list.append(100)
print("New List after Append:", list)
```

Output

```
Old List before Append: ['abcd', 147, 2.43, 'Tom']
New List after Append: ['abcd', 147, 2.43, 'Tom', 100]
```

2. **list.count(obj)** – Returns how many times the object obj appears in a list.

Example Program

```
#Demo of list.count(obj)
list = ['abcd', 147, 2.43, 'Tom',147,200,147]
print("The number of times", 147, "appears in", list, "=",list.
count(147))
```

Output

```
The number of times 147 appears in['abcd', 147, 2.43, 'Tom',
147, 200, 147]= 3
```

3. **list.remove(obj)** – Removes object obj from the list.

Example Program

```
#Demo of list.remove(obj)
list1 = ['abcd', 147, 2.43, 'Tom']
list1.remove('Tom')
print(list1)
```

Output

```
['abcd', 147, 2.43]
```

4. **list.index(obj)** - Returns index of the object obj if found, otherwise raise an exception indicating that value does not exist.

Example Program

```
#Demo of list.index(obj)
list1 = ['abcd', 147, 2.43, 'Tom']
print(list1.index(2.43))
```

Output

```
2
```

5. **list.extend(seq)** – Appends the contents in a sequence seq passed to a list.

Example Program

```
#Demo of list.extend(seq)
```

```
list1 = ['abcd', 147, 2.43, 'Tom']
list2 = ['def', 100]
list1.extend(list2)
print(list1)
```

Output

```
['abcd', 147, 2.43, 'Tom', 'def', 100]
```

6. **list.reverse()** – Reverses objects in a list.

   Example Program

```
#Demo of list.reverse()
list1 = ['abcd', 147, 2.43, 'Tom']
list1.reverse()
print(list1)
```

Output

```
['Tom', 2.43, 147, 'abcd']
```

7. **list.insert(index,obj)** – Returns a list with object obj inserted at the given index.

   Example Program

```
#Demo of list.insert(index,obj)
list1 = ['abcd', 147, 2.43, 'Tom']
print("List before insertion:",list1)
list1.insert(2,222)
print("List after insertion:",list1)
```

Output

```
List before insertion: ['abcd', 147, 2.43, 'Tom']
List after insertion: ['abcd', 147, 222, 2.43, 'Tom']
```

8. **list.sort([func])** – Sorts the items in a list and returns the list. If a function is provided, it will compare using the function provided.

   Example Program

```
#Demo of list.sort([func])
list1 = [890, 147, 2.43, 100]
print("List before sorting:",list1)
list1.sort()
print("List after sorting:",list1)
```

Output

```
List before sorting: [890, 147, 2.43, 100]
List after sorting: [2.43, 100, 147, 890]
```

9. **list.pop(obj=list[-1])** – Removes or returns the last object obj from a list.

Example Program

```
#Demo of list.pop(obj=list[-1])
list1 = ['abcd', 147, 2.43, 'Tom']
print("List before poping",list1)
list1.pop(-1)
print("List after poping:",list1)
```

Output

```
List before poping ['abcd', 147, 2.43, 'Tom']
List after poping: ['abcd', 147, 2.43]
```

4.4 Tuple

A tuple is another sequence data type that is similar to the list. A tuple consists of a number of values separated by commas. The main differences between lists and tuples are lists are enclosed in square brackets ([ ]) and their elements and size can be changed, while tuples are enclosed in parentheses (( )) and cannot be updated. Tuples can be considered as read-only lists.

Example Program

```
first_tuple = ('abcd', 147, 2.43, 'Tom', 74.9)
small_tuple = (111, 'Tom')

print(first_tuple)# Prints complete tuple
print(first_tuple[0])# Prints first element of the tuple
print(first_tuple[1:3])# Prints elements starting from 2nd till 3rd
print(first_tuple[2:])# Prints elements starting from 3rd element
print(small_tuple * 2)# Prints tuple two times
print(first_tuple + small_tuple) # Prints concatenated tuples
```

Output

```
('abcd', 147, 2.43, 'Tom', 74.9)
abcd
(147, 2.43)
(2.43, 'Tom', 74.9)
(111, 'Tom', 111, 'Tom')
('abcd', 147, 2.43, 'Tom', 74.9, 111, 'Tom')
```

The following code is invalid with tuple whereas this is possible with lists.

```
first_list = [ 'abcd', 147 , 2.43, 'Tom', 74.9 ]
first_tuple = ('abcd', 147, 2.43, 'Tom', 74.9)
tuple[2] = 100    # Invalid syntax with tuple
list[2] = 100     # Valid syntax with list
```

To delete an entire tuple we can use the `del` statement. It is not possible to remove individual items from a tuple. Eg. del tuple

4.4.1 Built-in Tuple Functions

1. **len(tuple)** – Gives the total length of the tuple.

   Example Program

```
#Demo of len(tuple)
tuple1 = ('abcd', 147, 2.43, 'Tom')
print(len(tuple1))
```

   Output

```
4
```

2. **max(tuple)** – Returns item from the tuple with maximum value.

   Example Program

```
#Demo of max(tuple)
tuple1 = (1200, 147, 2.43, 1.12)
tuple2 = (213, 100, 289)
print("Maximum value in: ", tuple1, "is",  max(tuple1))
print("Maximum value in: ", tuple2, "is",  max(tuple2))
```

   Output

```
Maximum value in:  (1200, 147, 2.43, 1.12) is 1200
Maximum value in:  (213, 100, 289) is 289
```

3. **min(tuple)** – Returns item from the tuple with minimum value.

   Example Program

```
#Demo of min(tuple)
tuple1 = (1200, 147, 2.43, 1.12)
tuple2 = (213, 100, 289)
print("Minimum value in: ", tuple1, "is",  min(tuple1))
print("Minimum value in: ", tuple2, "is",  min(tuple2))
```

   Output

```
Minimum value in:  (1200, 147, 2.43, 1.12) is 1.12
Minimum value in:  (213, 100, 289) is 100
```

4. **tuple(seq)** – Returns a list into a tuple.

   Example Program

```
#Demo of tuple(seq)
list = ['abcd', 147, 2.43, 'Tom']
print("Tuple:", tuple(list))
```

Output

```
Tuple: ('abcd', 147, 2.43, 'Tom')
```

4.5 Set

Set is an unordered collection of unique items. Set is defined by values separated by comma inside braces { }. It can have any number of items and they may be of different types (integer, float, tuple, string etc.). Items in a set are not ordered. Since they are unordered we cannot access or change an element of set using indexing or slicing. We can perform set operations like union, intersection, difference on two sets. Set have unique values. They eliminate duplicates. The slicing operator [] does not work with sets.

Example Program

```
# Demo of Set Creation
s1={1,2,3} #set of integer numbers
print(s1)
s2={1,2,3,2,1,2}#output contains only unique values
print(s2)
s3={1, 2.4, 'apple', 'Tom', 3}#set of mixed data types
print(s3)
#s4={1,2,[3,4]}#sets cannot have mutable items
#print s4 # Hence not permitted
s5=set([1,2,3,4])#using set function to create set from a list
print(s5)
```

Output

```
set([1, 2, 3])
set([1, 2, 3])
set([1, 3, 2.4, 'apple', 'Tom'])
set([1, 2, 3, 4])
```

4.5.1 Built-in Set Functions

1. **len(set)** – Returns the length or total number of items in a set.

Example Program

```
#Demo of len(set)
set1 = {'abcd', 147, 2.43, 'Tom'}
print(len(set1))
```

Output

```
4
```

2. **max(set)** – Returns item from the set with maximum value.

Example Program

```
#Demo of max(set)
set1 = {1200, 147, 2.43, 1.12}
set2 = {213, 100, 289}
print("Maximum value in: ", set1, "is",  max(set1))
print("Maximum value in: ", set2, "is",  max(set2))
```

Output

```
Maximum value in:  {1200, 1.12, 2.43, 147} is 1200
Maximum value in:  {289, 100, 213} is 289
```

3. **min(set)** – Returns item from the set with minimum value.

Example Program

```
#Demo of min(set)
set1 = {1200, 147, 2.43,1.12}
set2 = {213, 100, 289}
print("Minimum value in: ", set1, "is",  min(set1))
print("Minimum value in: ", set2, "is",  min(set2))
```

Output

```
Minimum value in:  {1200, 1.12, 2.43, 147} is 1.12
Minimum value in:  {289, 100, 213} is 100
```

4. **sum(set)** – Returns the sum of all items in the set.

Example Program

```
#Demo of sum(set)
set1 = {147, 2.43}
set2 = {213, 100, 289}
print("Sum of elements in", set1, "is",  sum(set1))
print("Sum of elements in", set2, "is",  sum(set2))
```

Output

```
Sum of elements in {147, 2.43} is 149.43
Sum of elements in {289, 100, 213} is 602
```

5. **sorted(set)**- Returns a new sorted set. The set does not sort itself.

Example Program

```
#Demo of sorted(set)
set1 = {213, 100, 289, 40, 23, 1, 1000}
```

```
set2 = sorted(set1)
print("Sum of elements before sorting", set1)
print("Sum of elements after sorting", set2)
```

Output

```
Sum of elements before sorting {1, 100, 289, 1000, 40, 213, 23}
Sum of elements after sorting {1, 23, 40, 100, 213, 289, 1000}
```

6. **enumerate(set)** – Returns an enumerate object. It contains the index and value of all the items of set as a pair.

Example Program

```
#Demo of enumerate(set)
set1 = {213, 100, 289, 40, 23, 1, 1000}
print("enumerate(set):", enumerate(set1))
```

Output

```
enumerate(set): <enumerate object at 0x7f0a73573690>
```

7. **any(set)** – Returns True, if the set contains at least one item, False otherwise.

Example Program

```
#Demo of any(set)
set1 = set()
set2={1,2,3,4}
print("any(set):", any(set1))
print("any(set):", any(set2))
```

Output

```
any(set): False
any(set): True
```

8. **a11(set)** – Returns True, if all the elements are true or the set is empty.

Example Program

```
#Demo of all(set)
set1 = set()
set2={1,2,3,4}
print("all(set):", all(set1))
print("all(set):", all(set1))
```

Output

```
all(set): True
all(set): True
```

4.5.2 Built-in Set Methods

1. **set.add(obj)** – Adds an element obj to a set.

   Example Program

```
#Demo of set.add(obj)
set1={3,8,2,6}
print("Set before addition:",set1)
set1.add(9)
print("Set after addition:", set1)
```

   Output

```
Set before addition: {8, 2, 3, 6}
Set after addition: {8, 9, 2, 3, 6}
```

2. **set.remove(obj)** – Removes an element obj from the set. Raises KeyError if the set is empty.

   Example Program

```
#Demo of set.remove(obj)
set1={3,8,2,6}
print("Set before deletion:",set1)
set1.remove(8)
print("Set after deletion:", set1)
```

   Output

```
Set before deletion: {8, 2, 3, 6}
Set after deletion: {2, 3, 6}
```

3. **set.discard(obj)** - Removes an element obj from the set. Nothing happens if the element to be deleted is not in the set.

   Example Program

```
#Demo of set.discard(obj)
set1={3,8,2,6}
print("Set before discard:",set1)
set1.discard(8)
print("Set after discard:", set1)# Element is present
set1.discard(9)
print("Set after discard:",set1)#Element is not present
```

   Output

```
Set before discard: {8, 2, 3, 6}
Set after discard: {2, 3, 6}
Set after discard: {2, 3, 6}
```

4. **set.pop()** – Removes and returns an arbitrary set element. Raises KeyError if the set is empty.

   Example Program

```
#Demo of set.pop()
set1={3,8,2,6}
print("Set before pop:",set1)
set1.pop()
print("Set after poping:", set1)
```

   Output

```
Set before pop: {8, 2, 3, 6}
Set after poping: {2, 3, 6}
```

5. **set1.union(set2)** – Returns the union of two sets as a new set.

   Example Program

```
#Demo of set1.union(set2)
set1={3,8,2,6}
print("Set1:",set1)
set2={4,2,1,9}
print("Set2:",set2)
set3=set1.union(set2)#Unique values will be taken
print("Union:", set3)
```

   Output

```
Set1: {8, 2, 3, 6}
Set2: {9, 2, 4, 1}
Union: {1, 2, 3, 4, 6, 8, 9}
```

6. **set1.update(set2)** – Update a set with the union of itself and others. The result will be stored in set1.

   Example Program

```
#Demo of set1.update(set2)
set1={3,8,2,6}
print("Set1:",set1)
set2={4,2,1,9}
print("Set2:",set2)
set1.update(set2)#Unique values will be taken
print("Update Method:", set1)
```

   Output

```
Set1: {8, 2, 3, 6}
```

```
Set2: {9, 2, 4, 1}
Update Method: {1, 2, 3, 4, 6, 8, 9}
```

7. **set1.intersection(set2)** – Returns the intersection of two sets as a new set.

   Example Program

```
#Demo of set1.intersection(set2)
set1={3,8,2,6}
print("Set1:",set1)
set2={4,2,1,9}
print("Set2:",set2)
set3 = set1.intersection(set2)
print("Intersection:", set3)
```

   Output

```
Set1: {8, 2, 3, 6}
Set2: {9, 2, 4, 1}
Intersection: {2}
```

8. **set1.intersection_update()** – Update the set with the intersection of itself and another. The result will be stored in set1.

   Example Program

```
#Demo of set1.intersection_update(set2)
set1={3,8,2,6}
print("Set1:",set1)
set2={4,2,1,9}
print("Set2:",set2)
set1.intersection_update(set2)
print("Intersection:", set1)
```

   Output

```
Set1: {8, 2, 3, 6}
Set2: {9, 2, 4, 1}
Intersection_update: {8, 2, 3, 6}
```

9. **set1.difference(set2)** – Returns the difference of two or more sets into a new set.

   Example Program

```
#Demo of set1.difference(set2)
set1={3,8,2,6}
print("Set1:",set1)
set2={4,2,1,9}
print("Set2:",set2)
```

```
set3= set1.difference(set2)
print("Difference:", set3)
```

Output

```
Set1: {8, 2, 3, 6}
Set2: {9, 2, 4, 1}
Difference: {8, 3, 6}
```

10. **set1.difference_update(set2)** – Remove all elements of another set set2 from set1 and the result is stored in set1.

    Example Program

```
#Demo of set1.difference_update(set2)
set1={3,8,2,6}
print("Set1:",set1)
set2={4,2,1,9}
print("Set2:",set2)
set1.difference_update(set2)
print("Difference Update:", set1)
```

Output

```
Set1: {8, 2, 3, 6}
Set2: {9, 2, 4, 1}
Difference Update: {8, 3, 6}
```

11. **set1.symmetric_difference(set2)**- Return the symmetric difference of two sets as a new set.

    Example Program

```
#Demo of set1.Symmetric_difference(set2)
set1={3,8,2,6}
print("Set1:",set1)
set2={4,2,1,9}
print("Set2:",set2)
set3=set1.symmetric_difference(set2)
print("Symmetric Difference :", set3)
```

Output

```
Set1: {8, 2, 3, 6}
Set2: {9, 2, 4, 1}
Symmetric Difference: {1, 3, 4, 6, 8, 9}
```

12. **set1.difference_update(set2)** – Update a set with the symmetric difference of itself and another.

    Example Program

```
#Demo of set1.symmetric_difference_update(set2)
```

```
set1={3,8,2,6}
print("Set1:",set1)
set2={4,2,1,9}
print("Set2:",set2)
set1.symmetric_difference_update(set2)
print("Symmetric Difference Update:", set1)
```

Output

```
Set1: {8, 2, 3, 6}
Set2: {9, 2, 4, 1}
Symmetric Difference Update: {1, 3, 4, 6, 8, 9}
```

13. **set1.isdisjoint(set2)** – Returns True if two sets have a null intersection.

Example Program

```
#Demo of set1.isdisjoint(set2)
set1={3,8,2,6}
print("Set1:",set1)
set2={4,7,1,9}
print("Set2:",set2)
print("Result of set1.isdisjoint(set2):", set1.isdisjoint(set2))
```

Output

```
Set1: {8, 2, 3, 6}
Set2: {9, 7, 4, 1}
Result of set1.isdisjoint(set2): True
```

14. **set1.issubset(set2)** - Returns True if set1 is a subset of set2.

Example Program

```
#Demo of set1.issubset(set2)
set1={3,8}
print("Set1:",set1)
set2={3,8,4,7,1,9}
print("Set2:",set2)
print("Result of set1.issubset(set2):", set1.issubset(set2))
```

Output

```
Set1: {8, 3}
Set2: {1, 3, 4, 7, 8, 9}
Result of set1.issubset(set2): True
```

15. set1.issuperset(set2) – Returns True, if set1 is a super set of set2.

Example Program

```
#Demo of set1.issuperset(set2)
set1={3,8,4,6}
print("Set1:",set1)
set2={3,8,}
print("Set2:",set2)
print("Result of set1.issuperset(set2):", set1.issuperset(set2))
```

Output

```
Set1: {8, 3, 4, 6}
Set2: {8, 3}
Result of set1.issuperset(set2): True
```

4.5.3 Frozenset

Frozenset is a new class that has the characteristics of a set, but its elements cannot be changed once assigned. While tuples are immutable lists, frozensets are immutable sets. Sets being mutable are unhashable, so they can't be used as dictionary keys which will be discussed in the next section. On the other hand, frozensets are hashable and can be used as keys to a dictionary.

Frozensets can be created using the function frozenset(). This datatype supports methods like difference(), intersection(), isdisjoint(), issubset(), issuperset(), symmetric_difference() and union(). Being immutable it does not have methods like add(), remove(), update(), difference_update(),intersection_update(),symmetric_difference_update() etc.

Example Program

```
#Demo of frozenset()
set1= frozenset({3,8,4,6})
print("Set1:",set1)
set2=frozenset({3,8})
print("Set2:",set2)
print("Result of set1.intersection(set2):", set1.
intersection(set2))
```

Output

```
Set1: frozenset({8, 3, 4, 6})
Set2: frozenset({8, 3})
Result of set1.intersection(set2): frozenset({8, 3})
```

4.6 Dictionary

Dictionary is an unordered collection of key-value pairs. It is generally used when we have a huge amount of data. We must know the key to retrieve the value. In Python, dictionaries are defined within braces {} with each item being a pair in the form key:value. Key and value can be of any type. Keys are usually numbers or strings. Values, on the other hand, can be any arbitrary Python object.

Dictionaries are enclosed by curly braces ({ }) and values can be assigned and accessed using square braces ([]).

Example Program

```
dict = {}
dict['one'] = "This is one"
dict[2]     = "This is two"
tinydict = {'name': 'john','code':6734, 'dept': 'sales'}

print(dict['one'])         # Prints value for 'one' key
print(dict[2])             # Prints value for 2 key
print(tinydict)            # Prints complete dictionary
print(tinydict.keys())     # Prints all the keys
print(tinydict.values()) # Prints all the values
```

Output

```
This is one
This is two
{'dept': 'sales', 'code': 6734, 'name': 'john'}
['dept', 'code', 'name']
['sales', 6734, 'john']
```

We can update a dictionary by adding a new key-value pair or modifying an existing entry.

Example Program

```
#Demo of updating and adding new values to dictionary
dict1= {'Name':'Tom','Age':20,'Height':160}
print(dict1)
dict1['age']=25 #updating existing value in Key-Value pair
print("Dictionary after update:",dict1)
dict1['Weight']=60 #Adding new Key-value pair
print("Dictionary after adding new Key-value pair:",dict1)
```

Output

```
{'Age': 20, 'Name': 'Tom', 'Height': 160}
Dictionary after update: {'age': 25, 'Age': 20, 'Name': 'Tom',
'Height': 160}
Dictionary after adding new Key-value pair: {'age': 25, 'Age':
20, 'Name': 'Tom', 'Weight': 60, 'Height': 160}
```

We can delete the entire dictionary elements or individual elements in a dictionary. We can use del statement to delete the dictionary completely. To remove entire elements of a dictionary, we can use the clear() method which will be discussed in the built-in methods of dictionary.

Example Program

```
#Demo of Deleting Dictionary
dict1= {'Name':'Tom','Age':20,'Height':160}
print(dict1)
del dict1['Age'] #deleting Key-value pair 'Age':20
print("Dictionary after deletion:",dict1)
dict1.clear() #Clearing entire dictionary
print(dict1)
```

Output

```
{'Age': 20, 'Name': 'Tom', 'Height': 160}
Dictionary after deletion: {'Name': 'Tom', 'Height': 160}
{}
```

Properties of Dictionary Keys

1. More than one entry per key is not allowed.ie, no duplicate key is allowed. When duplicate keys are encountered during assignment, the last assignment is taken.
2. Keys are immutable. This means keys can be numbers, strings or tuple. But it does not permit mutable objects like lists.

4.6.1 Built-in Dictionary Functions

1. **len(dict)** – Gives the length of the dictionary.

Example Program

```
#Demo of len(dict)
dict1= {'Name':'Tom','Age':20,'Height':160}
print(dict1)
print("Length of Dictionary=",len(dict1))
```

Output

```
{'Age': 20, 'Name': 'Tom', 'Height': 160}
Length of Dictionary= 3
```

2. **str(dict)** - Produces a printable string representation of the dictionary.

Example Program

```
#Demo of str(dict)
dict1= {'Name':'Tom','Age':20,'Height':160}
print(dict1)
print("Representation of Dictionary=",str(dict1))
```

Output

```
{'Age': 20, 'Name': 'Tom', 'Height': 160}
Representation of Dictionary= {'Age': 20, 'Name': 'Tom',
'Height': 160}
```

3. **type(variable)** - The method type() returns the type of the passed variable. If passed variable is dictionary then it would return a dictionary type. This function can be applied to any variable type like number, string, list, tuple etc.

Example Program

```
#Demo of type(variable)
dict1= {'Name':'Tom','Age':20,'Height':160}
print(dict1)
print("Type(variable)=",type(dict1))
s="abcde"
print("Type(variable)=",type(s))
list1= [1,'a',23,'Tom']
print("Type(variable)=",type(list1))
```

Output

```
{'Age': 20, 'Name': 'Tom', 'Height': 160}
Type(variable)= <type 'dict'>
Type(variable)= <type 'str'>
Type(variable)= <type 'list'>
```

4.6.2 Built-in Dictionary Methods

1. **dict.clear()** – Removes all elements of dictionary dict.

Example Program

```
#Demo of dict.clear()
dict1= {'Name':'Tom','Age':20,'Height':160}
print dict1
dict1.clear()
print dict1
```

Output

```
{'Age': 20, 'Name': 'Tom', 'Height': 160}
{}
```

2. **dict.copy()** – Returns a copy of the dictionary dict().

Example Program

```
#Demo of dict.copy()
dict1= {'Name':'Tom','Age':20,'Height':160}
```

```
print(dict1)
dict2=dict1.copy()
print(dict2)
```

Output

```
{'Age': 20, 'Name': 'Tom', 'Height': 160}
{'Age': 20, 'Name': 'Tom', 'Height': 160}
```

3. **dict.keys()** – Returns a list of keys in dictionary dict.

   Example Program

```
#Demo of dict.keys()
dict1= {'Name':'Tom','Age':20,'Height':160}
print(dict1)
print("Keys in Dictionary:",dict1.keys())
```

   Output

```
{'Age': 20, 'Name': 'Tom', 'Height': 160}
Keys in Dictionary: ['Age', 'Name', 'Height']
```

4. **dict.values()** – This method returns list of all values available in a dictionary.

   Example Program

```
#Demo of dict.values()
dict1= {'Name':'Tom','Age':20,'Height':160}
print(dict1)
print("Values in Dictionary:",dict1.values())
```

   Output

```
{'Age': 20, 'Name': 'Tom', 'Height': 160}
Values in Dictionary: [20, 'Tom', 160]
```

5. **dict.items()** – Returns a list of dictionary dict's(key,value) tuple pairs.

   Example Program

```
#Demo of dict.items()
dict1= {'Name':'Tom','Age':20,'Height':160}
print(dict1)
print("Items in Dictionary:",dict1.items())
```

   Output

```
{'Age': 20, 'Name': 'Tom', 'Height': 160}
Items in Dictionary: [('Age', 20), ('Name', 'Tom'), ('Height',
160)]
```

6. **dict1.update(dict2)** – The dictionary dict2's key-value pair will be updated in dictionary dict1.

Example Program

```
#Demo of dict1.update(dict2)
dict1= {'Name':'Tom','Age':20,'Height':160}
print(dict1)
dict2={'Weight': 60}
print(dict2)
dict1.update(dict2)
print("Dict1 updated Dict2 :",dict1)
```

Output

```
{'Age': 20, 'Name': 'Tom', 'Height': 160}
{'Weight': 60}
Dict1 updated Dict2 : {'Age': 20, 'Name': 'Tom', 'Weight': 60,
'Height': 160}
```

7. **dict.has_key(key)** - Returns True, if the key is in the dictionary dict, else False is returned.

Example Program

```
##Demo of dict1.has_key(key)
dict1= {'Name':'Tom','Age':20,'Height':160}
print(dict1)
print("Dict1.has_key(key) :",dict1.has_key('Age'))
print("Dict1.has_key(key) :",dict1.has_key('Phone'))
```

Output

```
{'Age': 20, 'Name': 'Tom', 'Height': 160}
Dict1.has_key(key) : True
Dict1.has_key(key) : False
```

8. **dict.get(key, default=None)** – Returns the value corresponding to the key specified and if the key specified is not in the dictionary, it returns the default value.

Example Program

```
#Demo of dict1.get(key,default='Name')
dict1= {'Name':'Tom','Age':20,'Height':160}
print(dict1)
print("Dict1.get('Age') :",dict1.get('Age'))
print("Dict1.get('Phone') :",dict1.get('Phone',0))#'Phone not a
key, hence 0 #is given as default
```

Output

```
{'Age': 20, 'Name': 'Tom', 'Height': 160}
Dict1.get(key) : 20
Dict1.get(key) : 0
```

9. **dict.setdefault(key,default=None)** – Similar to dict.get(key,default=None) but will set the key with the value passed and if key is not in the dictionary, it will set with the default value.

Example Program

```
#Demo of dict1.set(key,default='Name')
dict1= {'Name':'Tom','Age':20,'Height':160}
print(dict1)
print("Dict1.setdefault('Age') :",dict1.setdefault('Age'))
print("Dict1.setdefault('Phone') :",dict1.
setdefault('Phone',0))#'Phone not a #key, hence 0 is given as
default value.
```

Output

```
{'Age': 20, 'Name': 'Tom', 'Height': 160}
Dict1.setdefault('Age') : 20
Dict1.setdefault('Phone') : 0
```

10. **dict.fromkeys(seq,[val])** – Creates a new dictionary from sequence seq and values from val.

Example Program

```
#Demo of dict.fromkeys(seq,[val])
list= ['Name','Age','Height']
dict= dict.fromkeys(list)
print("New Dictionary:",dict)
```

Output

```
New Dictionary: {'Age': None, 'Name': None, 'Height': None}
```

4.7 Mutable and Immutable Objects

Objects whose value can change are said to be mutable and objects whose value is unchangeable once they are created are called immutable. An object's mutability is determined by its type. For instance, numbers, string and tuples are immutable, while lists, sets and dictionaries are mutable. The following example illustrates the mutability of objects.

Example Program

```
#Mutability illustration
#Numbers
```

```
a=10
print(a)#Value of a before subtraction
print(a-2)#value of a-2
print(a)#Value of a after subtraction
#Strings
str="abcde"
print(str)#Before applying upper()function
print(str).upper())#result of upper()
print(str)#After applying upper()function
#Lists
list=[1,2,3,4,5]
print(list)#Before applying remove()method
list.remove(3)
print(list)#After applying remove()method
```

Output

```
10
8
10
abcde
ABCDE
abcde
[1,2,3,4,5]
[1,2,4,5]
```

From the above example, it is clear that the values of numbers and string are not changed even after applying a function or operation. But in the case of list, the value is changed or the changes are reflected in the original variable and hence called mutable.

4.8 Data Type Conversion

We may need to perform conversions between the built-in types. To convert between different data types, use the type name as a function. There are several built-in functions to perform conversion fromone data type to another. These functions return a new object representing the converted value. Table 4.6 shows various functions and their descriptions used for data type conversion.

Table 4.6: Functions for Data Type Conversions

Function	Description
int(x [,base])	Converts x to an integer. base specifies the base if x is a string.
long(x [,base])	Converts x to a long integer. base specifies the base if x is a string.
float(x)	Converts x to a floating-point number.

Function	Description
complex(real [,imag])	Creates a complex number.
str(x)	Converts object x to a string representation.
repr(x)	Converts object x to an expression string.
eval(str)	Evaluates a string and returns an object.
tuple(s)	Converts s to a tuple.
list(s)	Converts s to a list.
set(s)	Converts s to a set.
dict(d)	Creates a dictionary. d must be a sequence of (key,value) tuples.
frozenset(s)	Converts s to a frozen set.
chr(x)	Converts an integer to a character.
unichr(x)	Converts an integer to a Unicode character.
ord(x)	Converts a single character to its integer value.
hex(x)	Converts an integer to a hexadecimal string.
oct(x)	Converts an integer to an octal string.

Example Program 1

```
# Demo of Data Type Conversions
x= 12.8
print("Integer x=",int(x))
x=12000
print("Long x=", long(x))
x=12
print("Floating Point x=", float(x))
real,img=5,2
print("Complex number =",complex(real,img))
x=12
print("String conversion of", x ,"is", str(x))
x=12
print("Expression String of", x ,"is", repr(x))
```

Output 1

```
Integer x= 12
Long x= 12000
Floating Point x= 12.0
Complex number = (5+2j)
String conversion of 12 is 12
Expression String of 12 is 12
```

Example Program 2

```
# Demo of Data Type Conversions
s='abcde'
s1={1:'a',2:'b',3:'c'}
print("Conversion of", s ,"to tuple is ",tuple(s))
print("Conversion of", s ,"to list is ",list(s))
print("Conversion of", s ,"to set is ",set(s))
print("Conversion of", s ,"to frozenset is ",frozenset(s))
print("Conversion of", s1 ,"to dictionary is ",dict(s1))
```

Output 2

```
Conversion of abcde to tuple is ('a', 'b', 'c', d', 'e')
Conversion of abcde to list is ['a', 'b', 'c','d', 'e']
Conversion of abcde to set is set(['a', 'c', 'b', 'e', 'd'])
Conversion of abcde to frozenset is frozenset(['a', 'c', 'b',
'e', 'd'])
Conversion of {1: 'a', 2: 'b', 3: 'c'} to dictionary is {1: 'a',
2: 'b', 3: 'c'}
```

Example Program 3

```
# Demo of Data Type Conversions
a=120
s='a'
print("Conversion of", a ,"to character is",chr(a) )
print("Conversion of", a ,"to unicode character is",unichr(a))
print("Conversion of", s ,"to integer is",ord(s))
print("Conversion of", a ,"to hexadecimal string is",hex(a))
print("Conversion of", a ,"to octal string is",oct(a))
```

Output 3

```
Conversion of 120 to character is x
Conversion of 120 to unicode character is x
Conversion of a to integer is 97
Conversion of 120 to hexadecimal string is 0x78
Conversion of 120 to octal string is 0170
```

4.9 Solved Lab Exercises

1. Write a Python program which accept the radius of a circle from the user and compute the area.

Program

```
import math
r = float(input("Input the radius of the circle:"))
print("The area of the circle with radius ",r,"is:",(math.pi *
r**2))
```

Output

```
Input the radius of the circle:3.5
The area of the circle with radius  3.5 is: 38.48451000647496
```

2. Program to find the biggest of three numbers.

Program

```
# Biggest of three numbers
a =int(input("Enter first number:")) #Reads First Number
b =int(input("Enter second number:")) #Reads Second Number
c =int(input("Enter third number:")) #Reads Third Number
big = max(a,b,c)#Finds the biggest
print("Biggest of", a,b,c, "is", big) #prints the biggest number
```

Output

```
Enter first number:3
Enter second number:4
Enter third number:5
Biggest of 3 4 5 is 5
```

3. Write a Python program which accepts a sequence of comma-separated numbers from user and generate a list and a tuple with those numbers.

Program

```
values = input("Input some comma seprated numbers : ")
    list = values.split(",")
    tuple = tuple(list)
    print('List : ',list)
    print('Tuple : ',tuple)
```

Output

```
Input some comma seprated numbers : 1,8,3,4,5
List :  ['1', '8', '3', '4', '5']
Tuple :  ('1', '8', '3', '4', '5')
```

4. Write a Python program to accept a filename from the user print the extension of that.

Program

```
filename = input("Input the Filename: ")
f_extns = filename.split(".")
print("The extension of the file is : ",f_extns[-1])
```

Output

```
Input the Filename: ABC.doc
The extension of the file is :  doc
```

5. Write a Python program to display the first and last colors from the following list.

Program

```
color=input("Enter colors(space between colors):")
color_list = color.split(" ")
print(color_list)
print("The first color in the list is:",color_list[0],"and last
color is:",color_list[-1])
```

Output

```
Enter colors(space between colors):red green blue white yellow
['red', 'green', 'blue', 'white', 'yellow']
The first color in the list is: red and last color is: yellow
```

6. Write a Python program that accept an integer (n) and computes the value of n+nn+nnn.

Program

```
a = int(input("Input an integer : "))
n1 = int("%s" % a)
n2 = int("%s%s" % (a,a))
n3 = int("%s%s%s" % (a,a,a))
print(n1," ", n2, " ",n3)
print("sum=",(n1+n2+n3))
```

Output

```
Input an integer : 2
2   22   222
sum= 246
```

7. Write a Python program to print out a set containing all the colors from color_list_1 which are not present in color_list_2.

Program

```
color1=input("Enter a set of colors(space separated):")
color2=input("Enter a set of colors(space separated):")
c1=set(color1.split())
c2=set(color2.split())
print("The difference between",c1, "and", c2,"is",c1.
difference(c2))
```

Output

```
Enter a set of colors(space separated):red green blue
Enter a set of colors(space separated):green blue
The difference between {'blue', 'red', 'green'} and {'blue',
'green'} is {'red'}
```

8. Write a Python program to get a string from a given string where all occurrences of its first char have been changed to '$', except the first char itself.

Program

```
str1=input("Enter a String:")
print("Original String:",str1)
char = str1[0]
str1 = str1.replace(char, '$')
str1 = char + str1[1:]
print("Replaced String:",str1)
```

Output

```
Enter a String:onion
Original String: onion
Replaced String: oni$n
```

9. Write a Python program to get a single string from two given strings, separated by a space and swap the first two characters of each string.

Program

```
str1=input("Enter first string:")
str2=input("Enter second string:")
new_a = str2[:2] + str1[2:]
new_b = str1[:2] + str2[2:]
print("The new string after swapping first two characters of both
string:",(new_a+' '+new_b))
```

Output

```
Enter first string:python
Enter second string:Programming
The new string after swapping first two characters of both
string: prthon pyogramming
```

10. Write a Python program to remove the nth index character from a non empty string.

Program

```
str1=input("Enter a string:")
n=int(input("Enter the index position of the character to be
removed:"))
first_part = str1[:n-1]
last_part = str1[n:]
print("The new string after removing the character=",(first_part
+ last_part))
```

Output

```
Enter a string:python
Enter the index position of the character to be removed:3
The new string after removing the character= pyhon
```

11. Write a Python program to change a given string to a new string where the first and last chars have been exchanged.

Program

```
str1=input("Enter a String:")
print("String after Swapping first and last
character:",(str1[-1] + str1[1:-1] + str1[0]))
```

Output

```
Enter a String:python
String after Swapping first and last character: nythop
```

12. Write a Python script that takes input from the user and displays that input back in upper and lower cases.

Program

```
str1 = input("Input a String: ")
print("String in uppercase:",str1.upper())
print("String in lowercase is:",str1.lower())
```

Output

```
Input a String: Python Programming is fun
String in uppercase: PYTHON ProgramMING IS FUN
String in lowercase is: python Programming is fun
```

13. **Write a Python program to get the largest number from a list.**

Program

```
lis=input("Enter a list(space separated):")
lis1=list(map(int,lis.split()))
print("Maximum element in a list:",max(lis1))
```

Output

```
Enter a list(space separated):1 4 65 43 23 12
Maximum element in a list: 65
```

14. **Write a Python program to clone or copy a list.**

Program

```
l=input("Enter a list(space separated):")
lis =list(l.split())
new_lis=list(lis)
print("Old list:",lis)
print("Copy of list:",new_lis)
```

Output

```
Enter a list(space separated):1 2 Bob Cat
Old list: ['1', '2', 'Bob', 'Cat']
Copy of list: ['1', '2', 'Bob', 'Cat']
```

15. **Write a Python program to shuffle and print a specified list.**

Program

```
import random
color= input("Enter a list(space separated):")
liscolor =list(color.split())
random.shuffle(liscolor)
print("List after shuffling:",end='')
print(liscolor)
```

Output

```
Enter a list(space separated):1 cat bat 3 sat 5
List after shuffling:['3', '5', '1', 'bat', 'sat', 'cat']
```

16. **Write a Python script to sort (ascending and descending) a dictionary by value.**

Program

```
import operator
d = {1: 2, 3: 4, 4: 3, 2: 1, 0: 0}
print('Original dictionary : ',d)
```

```
sorted_d = sorted(d.items(), key=operator.itemgetter(1))
print('Dictionary in ascending order by value : ',sorted_d)
sorted_d = sorted(d.items(), key=operator.itemgetter(1),reverse=True)
print('Dictionary in descending order by value : ',sorted_d)
```

Output

```
Original dictionary :  {0: 0, 1: 2, 2: 1, 3: 4, 4: 3}
Dictionary in ascending order by value :  [(0, 0), (2, 1), (1,
2), (4, 3), (3, 4)]
Dictionary in descending order by value :  [(3, 4), (4, 3), (1,
2), (2, 1), (0, 0)]
```

17. **Write a Python script to add key to a dictionary.**

Program

```
d = {0:10, 1:20}
print(d)
d.update({2:30})
print(d)
```

Output

```
{0: 10, 1: 20}
{0: 10, 1: 20, 2: 30}
```

18. **Write a Python script to merge two Python dictionaries.**

Program

```
d1 = {'a': 100, 'b': 200}
d2 = {'x': 300, 'y': 200}
print("Dictionary 1=:",d1)
print("Dictionary 2=:",d2)
d = d1.copy()
d.update(d2)
print("Merged Dictionary:",d)
```

Output

```
Dictionary 1=: {'b': 200, 'a': 100}
Dictionary 2=: {'y': 200, 'x': 300}
Merged Dictionary: {'b': 200, 'x': 300, 'y': 200, 'a': 100}
```

4.10 Conclusion

This Chapter covers all the data types in Python which includes number, strings, list, tuple, set and dictionary. The data type number includes mathematical functions, trigonometric functions and random number functions. String includes escape characters, formatting operators and formatting functions. The built-in functions and methods associated with list, tuple, set and dictionary is illustrated with examples. The review questions given in the Section 4.11 are the most frequently asked questions for Interviews and University Examinations. This help students to prepare for University Examinations, Certification Examinations and Job Interviews.

4.11 Review Questions

1. What are the data types available in Python?
2. What is the output of print str if str = 'Python Programming'?
3. What is the output of print str[0] if str = 'Python Programming'?
4. What is the output of print str[2:5] if str = 'Python Programming'?
5. What is the output of print str[2:] if str = 'Python Programming'?
6. What is the output of print str * 2 if str = 'Python Programming'?
7. What is the output of print str + "TEST" if str = 'Python Programming'?
8. What is the output of print list if list = ['abcd', 786 , 2.23, 'Tom', 70.2]?
9. What is the output of print list[0] if list = ['abcd', 786 , 2.23, 'Tom', 70.2]?
10. What is the output of print list[1:3] if list = ['abcd', 786 , 2.23, 'Tom', 70.2]?
11. What is the output of print list[2:] if list = ['abcd', 786 , 2.23, 'Tom', 70.2]?
12. What is the output of print smalllist * 2 if smalllist = ['Jack', 20]?
13. What is the output of print list + smalllist * 2 if list = ['abcd', 786 , 2.23, 'Tom', 70.2] and smalllist = ['Jack', 20]?
14. What are tuples in Python?
15. What are sets in Python?
16. What is the difference between tuples and lists in Python?
17. What is the output of print tuple if tuple = ('abcd', 786 , 2.23, 'Tom', 70.2)?
18. What is the output of print tuple[0] if tuple = ('abcd', 786 , 2.23, 'Tom', 70.2)?
19. What is the output of print tuple[1:3] if tuple = ('abcd', 786 , 2.23, 'Tom', 70.2)?
20. What is the output of print tuple[2:] if tuple = ('abcd', 786 , 2.23, 'Tom', 70.2)?
21. What is the output of print smalltuple * 2 if smalltuple = ('Jack', 20)?
22. What is the output of print tuple + smalltuple if tuple = ('abcd', 786 , 2.23, 'Tom', 70.2) and smalltuple = ('Jack', 20)?
23. What do you mean by a Python dictionary?
24. How will you create a dictionary in Python?
25. How will you get all the keys from a dictionary?
26. How will you get all the values from a dictionary?
27. How will you convert a string to an int in Python?
28. How will you convert a string to a long in Python?
29. How will you convert a string to a float in Python?
30. How will you convert a object to a string in Python?

31. How will you convert a object to a regular expression in Python?
32. How will you convert a String to an object in Python?
33. How will you convert a string to a tuple in Python?
34. How will you convert a string to a list in Python?
35. How will you convert a string to a set in Python?
36. How will you create a dictionary using tuples in Python?
37. How will you convert a string to a frozen set in Python?
38. How will you convert an integer to a character in Python?
39. How will you convert an integer to a unicode character in Python?
40. How will you convert a single character to its integer value in Python?
41. How will you convert an integer to hexadecimal string in Python?
42. How will you convert an integer to octal string in Python?
43. How can you pick a random item from a list or tuple?
44. How can you pick a random item from a range?
45. How can you get a random number in python?
46. How will you set the starting value in generating random numbers?
47. How will you randomizes the items of a list in place?
48. How will you capitalizes first letter of string?
49. How will you check in a string that all characters are alphanumeric?
50. How will you check in a string that all characters are digits?
51. How will you check in a string that all characters are in lowercase?
52. How will you check in a string that all characters are numerics?
53. How will you check in a string that all characters are whitespaces?
54. How will you check in a string that it is properly titlecased?
55. How will you check in a string that all characters are in uppercase?
56. How will you merge elements in a sequence?
57. How will you get the length of the string?
58. How will you get a space-padded string with the original string left-justified to a total of width columns?
59. How will you convert a string to all lowercase?
60. How will you remove all leading whitespace in string?
61. How will you get the max alphabetical character from the string?
62. How will you get the min alphabetical character from the string?
63. How will you replaces all occurrences of old substring in string with new string?
64. How will you remove all leading and trailing whitespace in string?
65. How will you change case for all letters in string?
66. How will you get titlecased version of string?
67. How will you convert a string to all uppercase?

68. How will you check in a string that all characters are decimal?
69. What is the difference between del() and remove() methods of list?
70. What is the output of len([1, 2, 3])?
71. What is the output of [1, 2, 3] + [4, 5, 6]?
72. What is the output of ['Hi!'] * 4?
73. What is the output of 3 in [1, 2, 3]?
74. What is the output of for x in [1, 2, 3]: print x?
75. What is the output of L[2] if L = [1,2,3]?
76. What is the output of L[-2] if L = [1,2,3]?
77. What is the output of L[1:] if L = [1,2,3]?
78. How will you get the length of a list?
79. How will you get the max valued item of a list?
80. How will you get the min valued item of a list?
81. How will you get the index of an object in a list?
82. How will you insert an object at given index in a list?
83. How will you remove last object from a list?
84. How will you remove an object from a list?
85. How will you reverse a list?
86. How will you sort a list?

05 Flow Control

CONTENTS

5.1 Decision Making

Decision making is required when we want to execute a code only if a certain condition is satisfied. The `if…elif…else` statement is used in Python for decision making.

5.1.1 *if* statement

Syntax

```
if test expression:
    statement(s)
```

The following Fig. 5.1 shows the flowchart of the `if` statement.

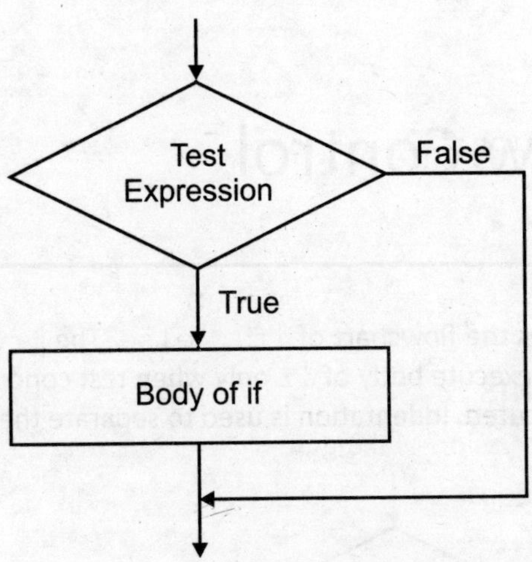

Fig. 5.1: Flowchart of *if* Statement

Here, the Program evaluates the `test expression` and will execute statement(s) only if the text expression is `True`. If the text expression is `False`, the statement(s) is not executed. In Python, the body of the `if` statement is indicated by the indentation. Body starts with an indentation and ends with the first unindented line. Python interprets non-zero values as `True`. `None` and `0` are interpreted as `False`.

Example Program

```
num =int(input("Enter a number: "))
if num == 0:
    print("Zero")
print("This is always printed")
```

Output 1

```
Enter a number: 0
Zero
This is always printed
```

Output 2

```
Enter a number: 2
This is always printed
```

In the above example, `num == 0` is the test expression. The body of `if` is executed only if this evaluates to `True`. When user enters 0, test expression is True and body inside `if` is executed. When user enters 2, test expression is False and body inside `if` is skipped. The statement `This is always printed` because the `print` statement falls outside the `if` block. The statement outside the `if` block is shown by unindentation. Hence, it is executed regardless of the test expression or it is always executed.

5.1.2 *if....else* statement

Syntax

```
if test expression:
     Body of if
else:
     Body of else
```

The following Fig. 5.2 shows the flowchart of `if.....else`. The `if..else` statement evaluates `test expression` and will execute body of `if` only when test condition is `True`. If the condition is `False`, body of `else` is executed. Indentation is used to separate the blocks.

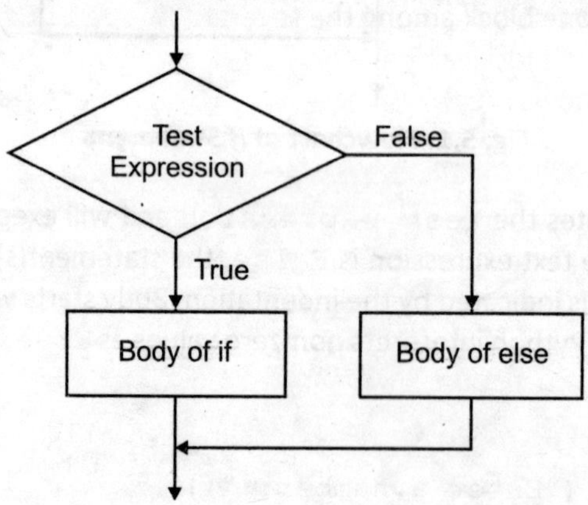

Fig. 5.2: Flow chart of `if.....else`

Example Program

```
num =int(input("Enter a number: "))
if num >= 0:
     print("Positive Number or Zero")
else:
     print("Negative Number")
```

Output 1

```
Enter a number: 5
Positive Number or Zero
```

Output 2

```
Enter a number: -2
Negative Number
```

In the above example, when user enters 5, the test expression is `True`. Hence the body of `if` is executed and body of `else` is skipped. When user enters -2, the test expression is `False` and body of `else` is executed and body of `if` is skipped.

5.1.3 *if...elif...else* statement

Syntax

```
if test expression:
    Body of if
elif test expression:
    Body of elif
else:
    Body of else
```

The `elif` is short for else if. It allows us to check for multiple expressions. If the condition for `if` is `False`, it checks the condition of the next `elif` block and so on. If all the conditions are `False`, body of else is executed. Only one block among the several `if...elif...else` blocks is executed according to the condition. A `if` block can have only one `else` block. But it can have multiple `elif` blocks. The following Fig. 5.3 shows the flow chart for `if...elif..else` statement.

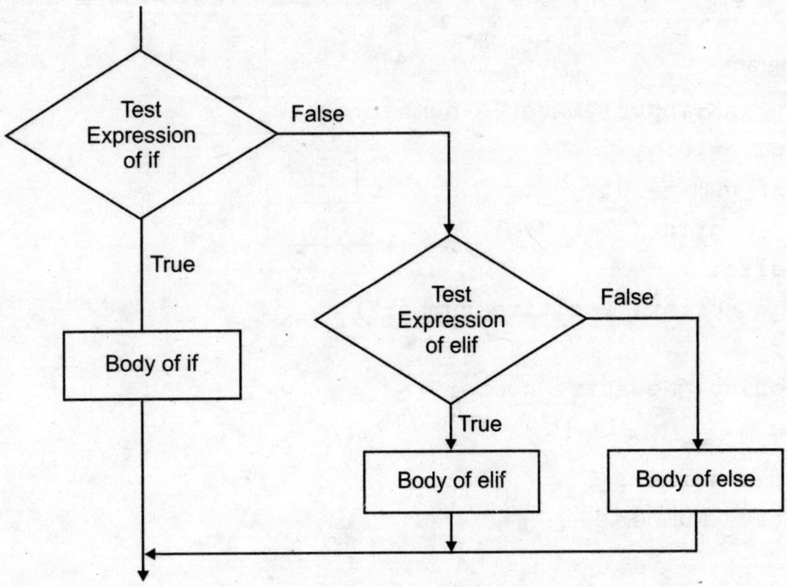

Fig. 5.3: Flow chart for `if...elif...else`

Example Program

```
num =int(input("Enter a number: "))
if num > 0:
    print("Positive number")
elif num == 0:
    print("Zero")
else:
    print("Negative number")
```

Output 1

```
Enter a number: 5
Positive Number
```

Output 2

```
Enter a number: 0
Zero
```

Output 3

```
Enter a number: -2
Negative Number
```

5.1.4 Nested *if* statement

We can have a `if...elif...else` statement inside another `if...elif...else` statement. This is called nesting in computer programming. Indentation is the only way to identify the level of nesting.

Example Program

```
num = int(input("Enter a number: "))
if num >= 0:
    if num == 0:
        print("Zero")
    else:
        print("Positive number")
else:
    print("Negative number")
```

Output 1

```
Enter a number: 5
Positive Number
```

Output 2

```
Enter a number: 0
Zero
```

Output 3

```
Enter a number: -2
Negative Number
```

5.2 Loops

Generally, statements are executed sequentially. The first statement in a function is executed first, followed by the second, and so on. There will be situations when we need to execute a block of code several number of times. Python provides various control structures that allow for repeated execution. A loop statement allows us to execute a statement or group of statements multiple times.

5.2.1 *for* loop

The `for` loop in Python is used to iterate over a sequence (list, tuple, string) or other objects that can be iterated. Iterating over a sequence is called traversal. Fig. 5.4 shows the flow chart of `for` loop.

Syntax

```
for item in sequence:
    Body of for
```

Here, `item` is the variable that takes the value of the item inside the sequence of each iteration. The sequence can be list, tuple, string, set etc. Loop continues until we reach the last item in the sequence. The body of `for` loop is separated from the rest of the code using indentation.

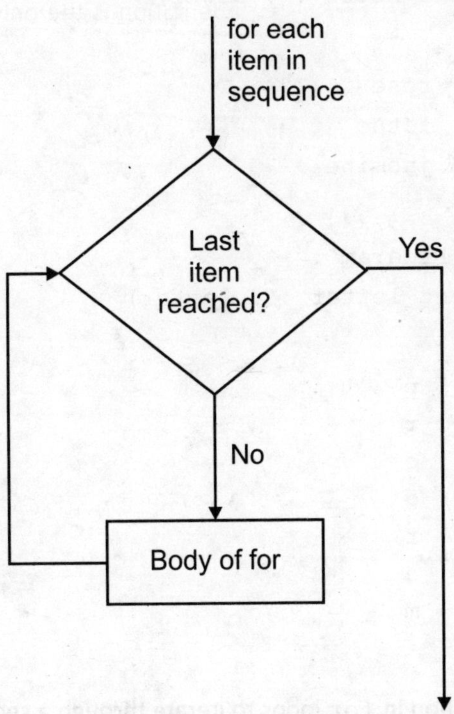

Fig. 5.4: Flow chart of `for` loop

Example Program 1

```
#Program to find the sum of all numbers stored in a list
# List of numbers
numbers = [2,4,6,8,10]
# variable to store the sum
```

```
sum = 0
# iterate over the list
for item in numbers:
    sum = sum+item
# print the sum
print("The sum is",sum)
```

Output 1

```
The sum is 30
```

Example Program 2

```
flowers = ['rose', 'lotus', 'jasmine']
for flower in flowers:
   print('Current flower :', flower)
```

Output 2

```
Current flower : rose
Current flower : lotus
Current flower : jasmine
```

Example Program 3

```
for letter in 'Program':
   print('Current letter :', letter)
```

Output 3

```
Current letter : p
Current letter : r
Current letter : o
Current letter : g
Current letter : r
Current letter : a
Current letter : m
```

range() function

We can use the `range()` function in `for` loops to iterate through a sequence of numbers. It can be combined with the `len()` function to iterate though a sequence using indexing. `len()` function is used to find the length of a string or number of elements in a list, tuple, set etc.

Example Program

```
flowers = ['rose', 'lotus', 'jasmine']
for i in range(len(flowers)):
 print('Current flower :', flowers[i])
```

Output

```
Current flower : rose
Current flower : lotus
Current flower : jasmine
```

We can generate a sequence of numbers using `range()` function. `range(10)` will generate numbers from 0 to 9 (10 numbers). We can also define the `start`, `stop` and `step_size` as `range(start,stop,step_size)`. The default value of `step_size` is 1, if not provided. This function does not store all the values in memory. It keeps track of the the `start`, `stop`, `step_size` and generates the next number.

Example Program

```
for num in range(2, 10, 2):print("Number = ", num)
```

Output

```
Number = 2
Number = 4
Number = 6
Number = 8
```

5.2.2 *for* loop with *else*

Python supports to have an else statement associated with a loop statement. If the **else** statement is used with a **for** loop, the **else** statement is executed when the loop has finished iterating the list. A `break` statement can be used to stop a `for` loop. In this case, the `else` part is ignored. Hence, a `for` loop's `else` part runs if no break occurs. Break statement is discussed in the Section 5.4 Control Statements.

Example Program

```
#Program to find whether an item is present in the list
list=[10,12,13,34,27,98]
num = int(input("Enter the number to be searched in the list:
"))
for item in range(len(list)):
 if list[item] == num:
   print("Item found at: ",(item+1))
   break
else:
   print("Item not found in the list")
```

Output 1

```
Enter the number to be searched in the list:34
Item found at:4
```

Output 2

```
Enter the number to be searched in the list:99
Item not found in the list
```

5.2.3 *while* loop

The `while` loop in Python is used to iterate over a block of code as long as the test expression (condition) is true. We generally use this loop when we don't know the number of times to iterate in advance. Fig. 5.5 shows the flow chart of a `while` loop.

Syntax

```
while test_expression:
    Body of while
```

In `while` loop, test expression is checked first. The body of the loop is entered only if the `test_expression` evaluates to `True`. After one iteration, the test expression is checked again. This process is continued until the `test_expression` evaluates to `False`. In Python, the body of the `while` loop is determined through indentation. Body starts with indentation and the first unindented line shows the end. When the condition is tested and the result is false, the loop body will be skipped and the first statement after the while loop will be executed.

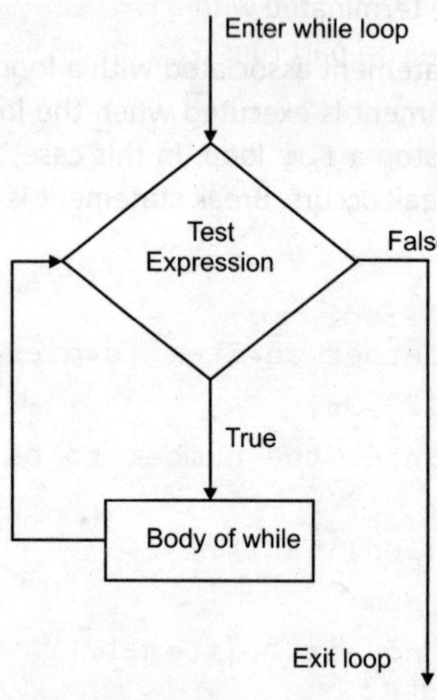

Fig. 5.5: Flow chart for while loop

Example Program

```
# Program to find the sum of first N natural numbers
n =int(input("Enter the limit: "))
sum=0
i=1
```

```
while i<=n:
    sum=sum+i
    i=i+1
print("Sum of first", n, "natural numbers is ", sum)
```

Output

```
Enter the limit: 5
Sum of first 5 natural numbers is 15
```

Illustration

In the above program, when the text `Enter the limit` appears, 5 is given as the input. ie. n=5. Initially, a counter i is set to 1 and sum is set to 0. When the condition is checked for the first time i<=n, it is True. Hence the execution enters the body of while loop. Sum is added with i and i is incremented. Since the next statement is unindented, it assumes the end of while block. This process is repeated when the condition given in the while loop is False and the control goes to the next print statement to print the sum.

5.2.4 *while* loop with *else* statement

If the `else` statement is used with a `while` loop, the `else` statement is executed when the condition becomes False. `while` loop can be terminated with a `break` statement. In such case, the `else` part is ignored. Hence, a `while` loop's `else` part runs if no break occurs and the condition is False.

Example Program 1

```
# Demo of While with else
count=1
while count<=3:
    print("Python Programming")
    count=count+1
else:
    print("Exit")
print("End of Program")
```

Output 1

```
Python Programming
Python Programming
Python Programming
Exit
End of Program
```

Illustration

In this example, initially the count is 1. The condition in the while loop is checked and since it is True, the body of the while loop is executed. The loop is terminated when the condition is False and it goes to the else statement. After executing the else block it will move on to the rest of the Program statements. In this example the print statement after the else block is executed.

Example Program 2

```
# Demo of While with else
count=1
while count<=3:
    print("Python Programming")
    count=count+1
    if count==2:break
else:
    print("Exit")
print("End of Program")
```

Output 2

```
Python Programming
End of Program
```

Illustration

In this example, initially the count is 1. The condition in the `while` loop is checked and since it is True, the body of the `while` loop is executed. When the `if` condition inside the `while` loop is True, ie. when count becomes 2, the control is exited from the `while` loop. It will not execute the `else` part of the loop. The control will moves on to the next statement after the `else`. Hence the print statement `End of Program` is executed.

5.3 Nested Loops

Sometimes we need to place a loop inside another loop. This is called nested loop. We can have nested loops for both `while` and `for`.

Syntax for nested for loop

```
for iterating_variable in sequence:
   for iterating_variable in sequence:
      statements(s)
   statements(s)
```

Syntax for nested while loop

```
while expression:
   while expression:
      statement(s)
   statement(s)
```

Q: Write a program to print the prime numbers starting from 1 upto a limit entered by the user.

Program using **nested `for`**

```
#Program to generate prime numbers between 2 Limits
import math
n =int(input("Enter a Limit:"))
for i in range(1,n):
  k=int(math.sqrt(i))
  for j in range(2,k+1):
   if i%j==0:break
  else: print(i)
```

Output

```
Enter a Limit:12
1
2
3
5
7
11
```

The limit entered by the user is stored in n. To find whether a number is prime, the logic used is to divide that number from 2 to square root of that number (Since all numbers are completely divisible by 1, we started from 2). If the remainder of this division is zero at any time, that number is skipped and moved to next number. A complete division shows that the number is not prime. If the remainder is not zero at any time, it shows that it is a prime number.

The outer `for` loop starts from 1 to the input entered by the user. Initially i=1. A variable k is used to store the square root of the number. The inner `for` loop is used to find whether the number is completely divisible by any number between 2 and square root of that number(k). If it is completely divisible by any number between 2 and k, the number is not prime, else the number is considered prime. The same steps are repeated until the limit entered by the user is reached.

The above program is rewritten using nested while and is given below.

Program using **nested `while`**

```
#Program to generate prime numbers between 2 Limits
import math
n =int(input("Enter a Limit:"))
i=1
while i<=n:
  k=int(math.sqrt(i))
  j=2
  while j<=k:
```

```
        if i%j==0:break
        j+=1
      else: print(i)
      i+=1
```

Output

```
Enter a Limit:12
1
2
3
5
7
11
```

5.4 Control Statements

Control statements change the execution from normal sequence. Loops iterate over a block of code until test expression is False, but sometimes we wish to terminate the current iteration or even the whole loop without checking test expression. The `break` and `continue` statements are used in these cases. Python supports the following three control statements.

1. `break`
2. `continue`
3. `pass`

5.4.1 *break* statement

The `break` statement terminates the loop containing it. Control of the Program flows to the statement immediately after the body of the loop. If it is inside a nested loop (loop inside another loop), `break` will terminate the innermost loop. It can be used with both `for` and `while` loops. Fig. 5.6 shows the flow chart of `break` statement.

Example Program 1

```
#Demo of break statement in Python
for i in range(2,10,2):
 if i==6: break
 print(i)
print("End of Program")
```

Output 1

```
2
4
End of Program
```

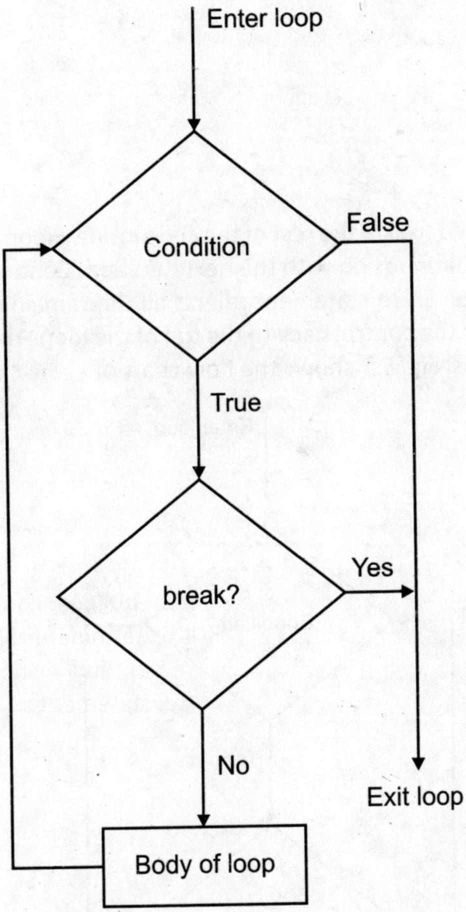

Fig 5.6: Flow chart of **`break`** statement

Illustration

In this the `for` loop is intended to print the even numbers from 2 to 10. The `if` condition checks whether i=6. If it is 6, the control goes to the next statement after the `for` loop. Hence it goes to the print statement `End of Program.`

Example Program 2

```
#Demo of break statement in Python
i=5
while i>0:
 if i==3: break
 print(i)
 i=i-1
print("End of Program")
```

Output 2

```
5
4
End of Program
```

5.4.2 *continue* statement

The `continue` statement is used to skip the rest of the code inside a loop for the current iteration only. Loop does not terminate but continues on with the next iteration. Continue returns the control to the beginning of the loop. The `continue` statement rejects all the remaining statements in the current iteration of the loop and moves the control back to the top of the loop. The **continue** statement can be used in both *while* and *for* loops. Fig. 5.7 shows the flow chart of `continue` statement.

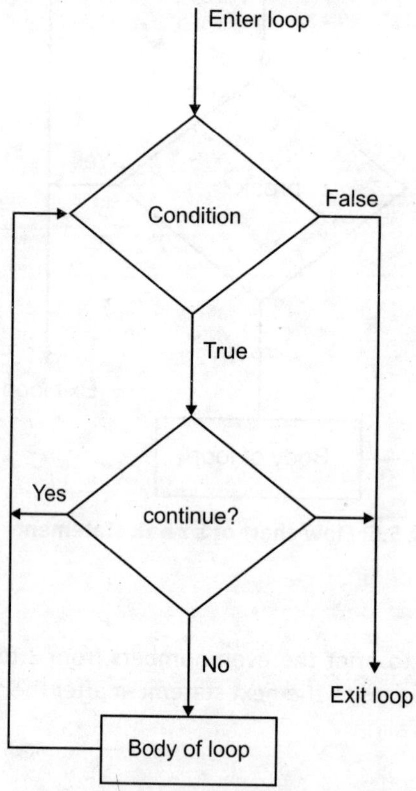

Fig. 5.7: Flow chart of `continue`

Example Program

```
# Demo of continue in Python
for letter in 'abcd':
 if letter =='c': continue
 print(letter)
```

Output

```
a
b
d
```

Illustration

When the letter=c, the continue statement is executed and the control goes to the beginning of the loop, bypasses the rest of the statements in the body of the loop. In the output the letters from "a" to "d" except "c" gets printed.

5.4.3 *pass* statement

In Python Programming, `pass` is a null statement. The difference between a comment and `pass` statement in Python is that, while the interpreter ignores a comment entirely, `pass` is not ignored. But nothing happens when it is executed. It results in no operation.

It is used as a placeholder. Suppose we have a loop or a function that is not implemented yet, but we want to implement it in the future. The function or loop cannot have an empty body. The interpreter will not allow this. So, we use the `pass` statement to construct a body that does nothing.

Example

```
for val in sequence:
    pass
```

5.5 Types of Loops

There are different types of loops depending on the position at which condition is checked.

5.5.1 Infinite Loop

A loop becomes infinite loop if a condition never becomes `False`. This results in a loop that never ends. Such a loop is called an infinite loop. We can create an infinite loop using `while` statement. If the condition of `while` loop is always `True`, we get an infinite loop. We must use `while` loops with caution because of the possibility that the condition may never resolves to a `False` value.

Example Program

```
count=1
while count==1:
  n=input("Enter a Number:")
  print("Number=", n)
```

This will continue running unless you give CTRL+C to exit from the loop.

5.5.2 Loops with condition at the top

This is a normal `while` loop without `break` statements. The condition of the `while` loop is at the top and the loop terminates when this condition is `False`. This loop is already explained in Section 5.2.3

5.5.3 Loop with condition in the middle

This kind of loop can be implemented using an infinite loop along with a conditional break in between the body of the loop. Fig. 5.8 shows the flow chart of a loop with condition in the middle.

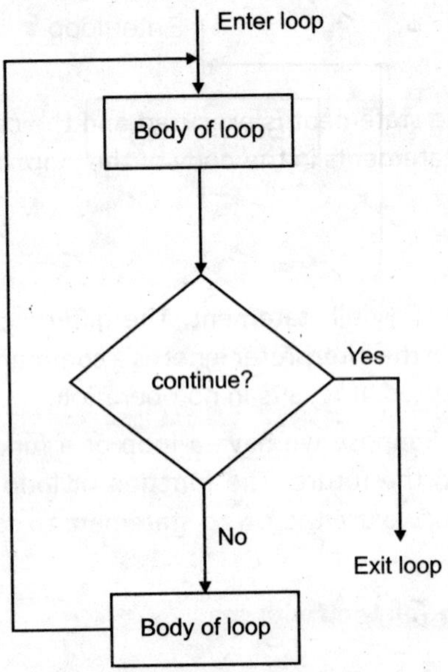

Fig. 5.8: Loop with condition in the middle

Example Program

```
vowels='aeiou'
# Infinite Loop
while True:
    v = input ("Enter a letter:")
    if v in vowels:
        print(v, "is a vowel")
        break
    print("This is not a vowel, Enter another letter")
print("End of Program")
```

Output

```
Enter a letter:t
This is not a vowel, Enter another letter
Enter a letter:o
o is a vowel
End of Program
```

5.5.4 Loop with condition at the bottom

This kind of loop ensures that the body of the loop is executed at least once. It can be implemented using an infinite loop along with a conditional break at the end. This is similar to the `do...while` loop in C. Fig. 5.9 shows the flow chart of loop with condition at the bottom.

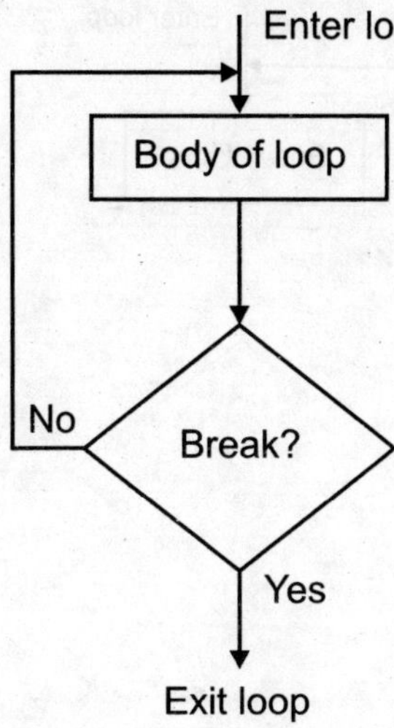

Fig 5.9: Loop with condition at the bottom

Example Program

```
# Demo of loop with condition at the bottom
choice=0
a,b=6,3
while choice !=5:
 print("Menu")
 print("1. Addition")
 print("2. Subtraction")
 print("3. Multiplication")
 print("4. Division")
 print("5. Exit")
 choice =int(input("Enter your choice:"))
 if choice==1: print("Sum=",(a+b))
 if choice==2: print("Difference=", (a-b))
 if choice==3: print("Product=",(a*b))
 if choice==4: print("Quotient=", (a/b))
 if choice==5: break
print("End of Program")
```

Output

```
Menu
1. Addition
2. Subtraction
3. Multiplication
4. Division
5. Exit
Enter your choice:2
Difference= 3
Menu
1. Addition
2. Subtraction
3. Multiplication
4. Division
5. Exit
Enter your choice:5
End of Program
```

5.6 Solved Lab Exercises

1. **Program to find the GCD of 2 numbers.**

Program

```
# GCD of two numbers
a =int(input("Enter first number:")) #Reads First Number
b =int(input ("Enter second number:")) #Reads Second Number
for i in range (1, min(a,b)+1):
 if a%i==0 and b%i==0: gcd=i
print("GCD of",a ,"and",b, "is",gcd)
```

Output

```
Enter first number:12
Enter second number:18
6
```

2. **Program to find the factorial of a number.**

Program

```
# Factorial of a number
a =int(input("Enter the number:")) #Reads Number
fact=1
```

```
for i in range (1, a+1):
 fact=fact*i
print("Factorial of", a, "is", fact)
```

Output

```
Enter the number:5
Factorial of 5 is 120
```

3. **Program to generate fibonacci series of N terms.**

Program

```
# Fibonacci series of first N numbers
n =int(input("Enter the number of terms:")) #Reads the limit
f1,f2=0,1
f3=f1+f2
print("Fibonacci series of first", n, "terms")
print(f1)
print(f2)
for i in range (3, n+1):
 print(f3)
 f1=f2
 f2=f3
 f3=f1+f2
```

Output

```
Enter the number of terms:5
Fibonacci series of first 5 terms
0
1
1
2
3
```

4. **Program to count the number of vowels.**

Program

```
# Count the number of vowels
s = input("Enter a String:")#Reads the String
count=0
for i in s:
 if i in 'aeiouAEIOU':
   count+=1
print("The number of vowels in ", s, "is", count)
```

Output

```
Enter a String:Python Programming
The number of vowels in Python Programming is 4
```

5. **Program to find the sum of all items in a list.**

Program

```
# Sum of all elements in a list
list = input("Enter a list:")#Reads the List from the keyboard
list1=map(int,list.split())# Convert the items in it to integers
sum=0 #initialize sum to 0
for i in list1:sum+=i
print("The sum of all items in list", list, "is", sum)
```

Output

```
Enter a list:1 2 3 4
The sum of all items in list 1 2 3 4 is 10
```

6. **Write a program that prints the numbers from 1 to 20. But for multiples of three print "Fizz" instead of the number and for the multiples of five print "Buzz". For numbers which are multiples of both three and five print "FizzBuzz". This is famously known as the FizzBuzz test.**

Program

```
#Program for FizzBuzz Test
for i in range(1,20):
    if i%3==0 and i%5==0: print("FizzBuzz")
    elif i%3==0:print("Fizz")
    elif i%5==0:print("Buzz")
    else: print(i)
```

Output

```
1
2
Fizz
4
Buzz
Fizz
7
8
Fizz
Buzz
11
```

```
Fizz
13
14
FizzBuzz
16
17
Fizz
19
```

7. **Write a program that prints the following pyramid on the screen. The number of lines must be obtained from the user as input.**

```
1
2 2
3 3 3
4 4 4 4
```

Program

```
#Program for Pyramid
n=int(input("Enter the step size:"))
for i in range(1,n+1):
    for j in range(1,i+1):
        print(i,end=' ')
    print()
```

Output

```
Enter the step size:5
1
2 2
3 3 3
4 4 4 4
5 5 5 5 5
```

8. **Write a program to find Primitive Pythagorean Triads A pythagorean triad has the property $a^2 + b^2 = c^2$. By primitive we mean triads that do not 'depend' on others. For example, (4,3,5) is a variant of (3,4,5) and hence is not primitive. And (10,24,26) is easily derived from (5,12,13) and should not be displayed by our Program. Write a Program to print primitive pythagorean triads. The Program should generate all triads with a, b values in the range 0—50.**

Program

```
#Pythagorean Triad
for i in range(1,50):
    for j in range(1,i):
```

```
        for k in range(1,j):
            if k*k+j*j==i*i:
                flag=0
                for l in range(2,i):
                    if i%l==0 and j%l==0 and k%l==0:
                        flag=1
                        break
                if flag:continue
                print("a=",k,"b=",j,"c=",i)
```

Output

```
a= 3 b= 4 c= 5
a= 5 b= 12 c= 13
a= 8 b= 15 c= 17
a= 7 b= 24 c= 25
a= 20 b= 21 c= 29
a= 12 b= 35 c= 37
a= 9 b= 40 c= 41
a= 28 b= 45 c= 53
a= 11 b= 60 c= 61
a= 33 b= 56 c= 65
a= 16 b= 63 c= 65
a= 48 b= 55 c= 73
a= 36 b= 77 c= 85
a= 13 b= 84 c= 85
a= 39 b= 80 c= 89
a= 65 b= 72 c= 97
```

9. Write a program that generates a list of all four digit numbers that have all their digits even and are perfect squares. For example, the output should include 6400 but not 8100 (one digit is odd) or 4248 (not a perfect square).

Program

```
#Four digit perfect square with even digits
import math
for i in range(1000,10000):
    num=int(math.sqrt(i))
    if num*num==i:
        n=i
        while n!=0:
            r=n%10
```

```
            n=n//10
            if r%2!=0:break
        else:print(i)
```

Output

```
4624
6084
6400
8464
```

10. Write a program to display the following pyramid. The number of lines has to be a parameter obtained from the user. The pyramid must appear aligned to the left edge of the screen.

```
1
2 4
3 6 9
4 8 12 16
5 10 15 20 25
```

Program

```
#Program for Pyramid
n=int(input("Enter the step size:"))
for i in range(1,n+1):
    k=i
    for j in range(1,i+1):
        print(k,end=' ')
        k+=i
    print()
```

Output

```
Enter the step size:5
1
2 4
3 6 9
4 8 12 16
5 10 15 20 25
```

11. Write a program to display the following output. The last number where the Program will stop printing has to be a parameter obtained from the user. The pyramid must appear aligned to the left edge of the screen. Note that depending on the last number, the base of the pyramid may be smaller than the line above it.

```
1
2 3
```

```
4 5 6
7 8 9 10
11 12
```

Program

```
#Program for Pyramid
n=int(input("Enter the limit for the pyramid:"))
k=1
for i in range(1,n+1):
        for j in range(1,i+1):
          if k==n+1: break
          print(k,end=' ')
          k+=1
        print()
        if k==n+1: break
```

Output

```
Enter the limit for the pyramid:12
1
2 3
4 5 6
7 8 9 10
11 12
```

12. Given an empty chessboard and one Bishop placed in any square, say (r, c), generate the list of all squares the Bishop could move to.

Program

```
# Movement of Bishop in Chess
r = int(input("Enter row number:"))
c = int(input("Enter column number:"))
while (c in range(1,9) and r in range(1,9)):
        print("Possible Movements in (row, col)")
        if r==1 and c==1:
          print(r,c+1)
          print(r+1,c)
          break
        elif r==1 and c==8:
          print(r,c-1)
          print(r+1,c)
```

```
            break
          elif c==1 and r==8:
            print(r-1,c)
            print(r,c+1)
            break
          elif c==8 and r==8:
            print(r-1,c)
            print(r,c-1)
            break
          elif c==1 and r<8:
            print(r,c+1)
            print(r+1,c)
            print(r-1,c)
            break
          elif r==1:
            print(r+1,c)
            print(r,c+1)
            print(r,c-1)
            break
          elif c==8:
            print(r-1,c)
            print(r+1,c)
            print(r,c-1)
            break
          elif r==8:
            print(r-1,c)
            print(r, c+1)
            print(r,c-1)
            break
        else:
            print(r,c-1)
            print(r, c+1)
            print(r+1, c)
            print(r-1, c)
            break
else:
          print("Invalid range for row or column")
```

Output

```
Enter row number:3
Enter column number:4
Possible Movements in (row, col)
3 3
3 5
4 4
2 4
```

13. Write a Python program which accept the user's name and print them in reverse order with a space between them.

Program

```
name = input("Input your Name : ")
l=name.split()
l.reverse()
print("Reversed name:",end=' ')
for i in l:
print(i,end=' ')
```

Output

```
Input your Name : Sam Charles Alexander
Reversed name: Alexander Charles Sam
```

14. Write a Python program to count a number in a given list.

Program

```
str=input("Enter a list(values space separated):")
lis=list(map(int,str.split()))
n=int(input("Enter the number to search for the number of
occurrences:"))
print(lis)
print("Number of occurrences of",n,"is",lis.count(n),"times")
```

Output

```
Enter a list(values space separated):1 4 5 2 3 5 2 5 2 6 2
Enter the number to search for the number of occurrences:2
[1, 4, 5, 2, 3, 5, 2, 5, 2, 6, 2]
Number of occurrences of 2 is 4 times
```

15. Write a Python program to get the n (non-negative integer) copies of the first 2 characters of a given string. Print n copies of the whole string if the length is less than 2.

Program

```
str1=input("Enter a String:")
n=int(input("Enter the number of copies of first two
characters:"))
flen = 2
if flen > len(str1):
    flen = len(str1)
substr = str1[:flen]
result = ""
for i in range(n):
      result = result + substr
print("Copy of the substring:",result)
```

Output

```
Enter a String:Python Programming
Enter the number of copies of first two characters:4
Copy of the substring: PyPyPyPy
```

16. **Write a Python program to check whether a specified value is contained in a group of values.**

Program

```
lis=input("Enter a list(values space separated):")
n=int(input("Enter the number to be searched:"))
lis1=list(map(int,lis.split()))
print(lis1)
for value in lis1:
  if n == value:

    print("The number", n ,"is found in the list.")
    break
else:
    print("The number", n ,"is not found in the list")
```

Output

```
Enter a list(values space separated):1 2 3
Enter the number to be searched:4
[1, 2, 3]
The number 4 is not found in the list
```

17. **Write a Python program to concatenate all elements in a list into a string and return it.**

Program

```
lis=input("Enter a list(space separated):")
s1=lis.split()
print(s1)
result= ''
for element in s1:
  result += str(element)
print("Concatenated elements in the list:",result)
```

Output

```
Enter a list(space separated):1 2 3 4
['1', '2', '3', '4']
Concatenated elements in the list: 1234
```

18. **Write a Python program to print all even numbers from a given numbers list in the same order and stop the printing if any numbers that come after 237 in the sequence.**

Program

```
lis=input("Enter a list(elements space separated):")
lis1=list(map(int,lis.split()))
print(lis1)
print("Even Numbers upto 237")
for x in lis1:
    if x == 237:
        break
    elif x % 2 == 0:
        print(x, end=' ')
```

Output

```
Enter a list(elements space separated):12 3 34 21 56 78 21 90
237 12 23 45
[12, 3, 34, 21, 56, 78, 21, 90, 237, 12, 23, 45]
Even Numbers upto 237
12 34 56 78 90
```

19. **Write a Python program to get the least common multiple (LCM) of two positive integers.**

Program

```
x=int(input("Enter first positive integer:"))
y=int(input("Enter second positive integer:"))
if x > y:
```

```
    z = x
else:
    z = y
while True:
        if (z % x == 0) and (z % y == 0):
            lcm = z
            break
        z += 1
print("LCM of",x, "and",y,"is",lcm)
```

Output

```
Enter first positive integer:6
Enter second positive integer:10
LCM of 6 and 10 is 30
```

20. Write a Python program to count the number of characters (character frequency) in a string.

Program

```
dict = {}
str1=input("Enter a string:")
for n in str1:
        if n in dict:
            dict[n] += 1
        else:
            dict[n] = 1
print("Character frequency")
for k,v in dict.items():
    print(k,v)
```

Output

```
Enter a string:pythonprogramming
Character frequency
r 2
m 2
h 1
n 2
t 1
i 1
a 1
y 1
```

```
g 2
p 2
o 2
```

21. **Write a Python program to get a string made of the first 2 and the last 2 chars from a given a string. If the string length is less than 2, return instead the empty string.**

Program

```
str1=input("Enter a string:")
if len(str1) < 2:
    print(None)
else:
    print("String made from last two characters of both
ends:",(str1[0:2] + str1[-2:]))
```

Output

```
Enter a string:Python Programming
String made from last two characters of both ends: Pyng
```

22. **Write a Python program to add 'ing' at the end of a given string (length should be at least 3). If the given string is already ends with 'ing' then add 'ly' instead. If the string length of the given string is less than 3, leave it unchanged.**

Program

```
str1=input("Enter a String:")
length = len(str1)
if length > 2:
    if str1[-3:] == 'ing':
      str1 += 'ly'
    else:
      str1 += 'ing'
print("New String:",str1)
```

Output

```
Enter a String:Python Programm
New String: Python Programming
```

23. **Write a Python program to find the first appearance of the substring 'not' and 'poor' from a given string, if 'not' follows the 'poor', replace the whole 'not'...'poor' substring with 'good'. Return the resulting string.**

Program

```
str1=input("Enter a string:")
snot = str1.find('not')
sbad = str1.find('poor')
```

```
if sbad > snot:
    str1 = str1.replace(str1[snot:(sbad+4)], 'good')
print(str1)
```

Output

```
Enter a string:It is not that poor
It is good
```

24. Write a Python function that takes a list of words and returns the length of the longest one.

Program

```
lis=input("Enter a list with some strings (space separated):")
words_list=lis.split()
word_len = []
for n in words_list:
    word_len.append((len(n), n))
    print(word_len)
    word_len.sort()
    print(word_len)
print("Longest Word:",word_len[-1][1])
```

Output

```
Enter a list with some strings (space separated):apple orange
pear kiwi
[(5, 'apple')]
[(5, 'apple')]
[(5, 'apple'), (6, 'orange')]
[(5, 'apple'), (6, 'orange')]
[(5, 'apple'), (6, 'orange'), (4, 'pear')]
[(4, 'pear'), (5, 'apple'), (6, 'orange')]
[(4, 'pear'), (5, 'apple'), (6, 'orange'), (4, 'kiwi')]
[(4, 'kiwi'), (4, 'pear'), (5, 'apple'), (6, 'orange')]
Longest Word: orange
```

25. Write a Python program to remove the characters which have odd index values of a given string.

Program

```
str1=input("Enter a String:")
result = ""
for i in range(0,len(str1),2):
    if i % 2 == 0:
      result = result + str1[i]
```

```
print("String after removing characters in odd
positions:",result)
```

Output

```
Enter a String:Python programming
String after removing characters in odd positions: Pto rgamn
```

26. **Write a Python program to count the occurrences of each word in a given sentence.**

Program

```
str1=input("Enter a String:")
counts = {}
words = str1.split()
for word in words:
        if word in counts:
            counts[word] += 1
        else:
            counts[word] = 1
for k,v in counts.items():
    print(k,v)
```

Output

```
Enter a String:Learning Python is fun and Python is powerful
powerful 1
Python 2
fun 1
and 1
is 2
Learning 1
```

27. **Write a Python program that accepts a comma separated sequence of words as input and prints the unique words in sorted form (alphanumerically).**

Program

```
items = input("Input comma separated sequence of words:")
words=items.split(",")
for word in words:
   lis=(",".join(sorted(list(set(words)))))
print(lis)
```

Output

```
Input comma separated sequence of words:yellow,white,blue,red,gr
een,blue,red,black
black,blue,green,red,white,yellow
```

28. **Write a Python program to count the number of strings where the string length is 2 or more and the first and last character are same from a given list of strings.**

Program

```
lis=input("Enter a list(space separated):")
words=list(lis.split())
ctr = 0
for word in words:
    if len(word) > 1 and word[0] == word[-1]:
        ctr += 1
print("Count=",ctr)
```

Output

```
Enter a list(space separated):cat bob pop dog am pat abba
Count= 3
```

29. **Write a Python program to remove duplicates from a list.**

Program

```
lis=input("Enter a list(space separated):")
lis1=list(lis.split())
uniq_items = []
for x in lis1:
    if x not in uniq_items:
        uniq_items.append(x)
print(uniq_items)
```

Output

```
Enter a list(space separated):1 2 bat 12 bat 3 1 2
['1', '2', 'bat', '12', '3']
```

30. **Write a Python program to check a list is empty or not.**

Program

```
l=input("Enter a list(space separated):")
lis =list(l.split())
if not lis:
  print("List is empty")
else:
  print("List is non-empty")
  print(lis)
```

Output

```
Enter a list(space separated):1 2 3 4 5
List is non-empty
['1', '2', '3', '4', '5']
```

31. Write a Python program to find the list of words that are longer than n from a given list of words.

Program

```
str=input("Enter a list of words(space separated):")
n=int(input("Enter a length:"))
txt=str.split()
word_len=[]
for x in txt:
    if len(x) > n:
        word_len.append(x)
print("Words with length greater than", n,"=",word_len)
```

Output

```
Enter a list of words(space separated):bat apple mango rabbit
rat
Enter a length:3
Words with length greater than 3 = ['apple', 'mango', 'rabbit']
```

32. Write a Python program to print a specified list after removing the 0th, 2nd, 4th and 5th elements.

Program

```
list1=input("Enter a list(space separated):")
lis1=list(list1.split())
lis1= [x for (i,x) in enumerate(lis1) if i not in (0,2,4,5)]
print(lis1)
```

Output

```
Enter a list(space separated):mango banana orange kiwi pear
apple
['banana', 'kiwi']
```

33. Write a Python program to generate a 3*4*6 3D array whose each element is *.

Program

```
array = [[ ['*' for col in range(6)] for col in range(4)] for
row in range(3)]
print(array)
```

Output

```
[[['*', '*', '*', '*', '*', '*'], ['*', '*', '*', '*', '*',
'*'], ['*', '*', '*', '*', '*', '*'], ['*', '*', '*', '*', '*',
'*']], [['*', '*', '*', '*', '*', '*'], ['*', '*', '*', '*',
'*', '*'], ['*', '*', '*', '*', '*', '*'], ['*', '*', '*', '*',
'*', '*']], [['*', '*', '*', '*', '*', '*'], ['*', '*', '*',
'*', '*', '*'], ['*', '*', '*', '*', '*', '*'], ['*', '*', '*',
'*', '*', '*']]]
```

34. Write a Python program to print the numbers of a specified list after removing even numbers from it.

Program

```
num1 =input("Enter an integer list(space separated):")
num =list(map(int,num1.split()))
num=[x for x in num if x%2!=0]
print("List after removing even numbers",end=' ')
print(num)
```

Output

```
Enter an integer list(space separated):1 2 4 21 4 56 3
List after removing even numbers [1, 21, 3]
```

35. Write a Python program to generate and print a list of first and last 5 elements where the values are square of numbers between 1 and 30 (both included).

Program

```
l = list()
for i in range(1,21):
        l.append(i**2)
print(l[:5])
print(l[-5:])
```

Output

```
[1, 4, 9, 16, 25]
[256, 289, 324, 361, 400]
```

36. Write a Python script to concatenate following dictionaries to create a new one.

Program

```
dic1={1:10, 2:20}
dic2={3:30, 4:40}
dic3={5:50,6:60}
dic4 = {}
print("Dictionary 1:",dic1)
print("Dictionary 2:",dic2)
```

```
print("Dictionary 3:",dic3)
print("Concatenated Dictionary:",end=' ')
for d in (dic1, dic2, dic3): dic4.update(d)
print(dic4)
```

Output

```
Dictionary 1: {1: 10, 2: 20}
Dictionary 2: {3: 30, 4: 40}
Dictionary 3: {5: 50, 6: 60}
Concatenated Dictionary: {1: 10, 2: 20, 3: 30, 4: 40, 5: 50, 6:
60}
```

37. Write a Python script to check if a given key already exists in a dictionary.

Program

```
d = {1: 10, 2: 20, 3: 30, 4: 40, 5: 50, 6: 60}
x=int(input("Enter a key value:"))
if x in d:
        print('Key is present in the dictionary')
else:
        print('Key is not present in the dictionary')
```

Output

```
Enter a key value:2
Key is present in the dictionary
```

38. Write a Python script to generate and print a dictionary that contains number (between 1 and n) in the form (x, x*x).

Program

```
n=int(input("Enter a limit:"))
d = dict()
for x in range(1,n+1):
    d[x]=x*x
print(d)
```

Output

```
Enter a limit:4
{1: 1, 2: 4, 3: 9, 4: 16}
```

39. Write a Python script to print a dictionary where the keys are numbers between m and n (both included) and the values are square of keys.

Program

```
m=int(input("Enter a lower limit:"))
n=int(input("Enter an upper limit:"))
d={}
for x in range(m,n+1):
    d[x]=x**2
print(d)
```

Output

```
Enter a lower limit:2
Enter an upper limit:10
{2: 4, 3: 9, 4: 16, 5: 25, 6: 36, 7: 49, 8: 64, 9: 81, 10: 100}
```

40. **Write a Python program to find those numbers which are divisible by 7 and multiple of 5, between 1500 and 2000 (both included).**

Program

```
nl=[]
for x in range(1500, 2000):
    if x%7==0 and x%5==0:
        nl.append(str(x))
print (','.join(nl))
```

Output

```
1505,1540,1575,1610,1645,1680,1715,1750,1785,1820,1855,1890,1925
,1960,1995
```

41. **Write a Python program to convert temperatures to and from celsius, fahrenheit.**

Program

```
temp = input("Input the  temperature you like to convert? (e.g.,
45F, 102C etc.) : ")
degree = int(temp[:-1])
i_convention = temp[-1]
if i_convention.upper() == "C":
  result = int(round((9 * degree) / 5 + 32))
  o_convention = "Fahrenheit"
elif i_convention.upper() == "F":
  result = int(round((degree - 32) * 5 / 9))
  o_convention = "Celsius"
else:
  print("Input proper convention.")
```

```
print("The temperature in", o_convention, "is", result,
"degrees.")
```

Output

```
Input the  temperature you like to convert? (e.g., 45F, 102C
etc.) : 37C
The temperature in Fahrenheit is 99 degrees.
```

42. **Write a Python program to construct the following pattern, using a nested for loop.**

```
*
* *
* * *
* * * *
* * * * *
* * * *
* * *
* *
*
```

Program

```
n=5
for i in range(n):
    for j in range(i):
        print ('* ', end="")
    print('')
for i in range(n,0,-1):
    for j in range(i):
        print('* ', end="")
    print('')
```

Output

```
*
* *
* * *
* * * *
* * * * *
* * * *
* * *
* *
*
```

43. Write a Python program that accept a word from the user and reverse it.

Program

```
word = input("Input a word to reverse:")
for char in range(len(word)- 1, -1, -1):
  print(word[char], end="")
```

Output

```
Input a word to reverse:Python
nohtyP
```

44. Write a Python program that counts odd and even numbers from a list.

Program

```
lis=input("Enter some positive integers(space separated):")
numbers=list(map(int,lis.split()))
count_odd = 0
count_even = 0
for x in numbers:
        if not x % 2:
          count_even+=1
        else:
          count_odd+=1
print("Number of even numbers :",count_even)
print("Number of odd numbers :",count_odd)
```

Output

```
Enter some positive integers(space separated):1 2 3 4 5 6 7 8
Number of even numbers : 4
Number of odd numbers : 4
```

45. Write a Python program which takes two digits m (row) and n (column) as input and generates a two dimensional array. Read the elements and display the array.

Program

```
row_num = int(input("Input number of rows: "))
col_num = int(input("Input number of columns: "))
multi_list = [[0 for col in range(col_num)] for row in
range(row_num)]
for row in range(row_num):
    for col in range(col_num):
        multi_list[row][col]= int(input("Enter the value:"))
print(multi_list)
```

Output

```
Input number of rows: 2
Input number of columns: 2
Enter the value:1
Enter the value:2
Enter the value:3
Enter the value:4
[[1, 2], [3, 4]]
```

46. Write a Python program that accepts sequence of lines (blank line to terminate) as input and prints the lines as output (all characters in lower case).

Program

```
lines = []
while True:
    l = input("Enter a line:")
    if l:
        lines.append(l.lower())
    else:
        break
for l in lines:
    print(l)
```

Output

```
Enter a line:python
Enter a line:Programming
Enter a line:Is
Enter a line:Fun
Enter a line:
python
Programming
is
fun
```

47. Write a Python program which accepts a sequence of comma separated 4 digit binary numbers as its input and print the numbers that are divisible by 5 in a comma separated sequence.

Program

```
items = []
num=input("Enter some binary numbers(comma separated):")
num1=list(num.split(','))
```

```
for p in num1:
    x = int(p,2)
    if not x%5:
        items.append(p)
print(','.join(items))
```

Output

```
Enter some binary numbers(comma separated):0101,1100,1111,1010
0101,1111,1010
```

48. **Write a Python program that accepts a string and calculate the number of digits, letters and other characters.**

Program

```
s = input("Input a string:")
d=l=a=0
for c in s:
    if c.isdigit():
        d=d+1
    elif c.isalpha():
        l=l+1
    else:
        a+=1
print("Letters:", l)
print("Digits:", d)
print("Other Characters:",a)
```

Output

```
Input a string:**python Programming123#
Letters: 17
Digits: 3
Other Characters: 4
```

49. **Write a Python program to find numbers between 100 and 400 (both included) where each digit of a number is an even number. The numbers obtained should be printed in a comma-separated sequence.**

Program

```
items = []
for i in range(100, 401):
  s = str(i)
```

```
        if (int(s[0])%2==0) and (int(s[1])%2==0) and (int(s[2])%2==0):
          items.append(s)
    print(",".join(items))
```

Output

```
200,202,204,206,208,220,222,224,226,228,240,242,244,246,248,260,
262,264,266,268,280,282,284,286,288,400
```

5.7 Conclusion

This Chapter explains various types of decision making in Python which includes the `if`, `if …else`, `if…elif…else`, nested loops with the flow charts and illustrated examples. Python's looping constructs which includes `for loop`, `for loop with else`, `while loop` and `while loop with else` are explained in detail. The two looping constructs `for loop with else` and `while loop with else` are absent in other programming languages like C, C++, Java etc. Similarly Python's control statements `break`, `continue` and `pass` are explained with illustrated examples. In this `pass` is a new type of control statement available only in Python. Various types of loops like infinite loops, loops with condition at the top, loops with condition in the middle and loops with condition at the bottom is also covered in this Chapter. This Chapter has provided solved programs which aid a user in Python programming.

5.8 Review Questions

1. Explain various decision making statements in Python.
2. Explain for loop with else with an example.
3. What is the purpose of break statement?
4. Differentiate while loop and while loop with else with examples.
5. What is the purpose of continue statement?
6. What is the purpose of pass statement in Python?
7. Differentiate break and continue statements.
8. Explain different types of loops with examples.

06 Functions

CONTENTS

A group of related statements to perform a specific task is known as a function. Functions help to break the program into smaller units. Functions avoid repetition and enhance code reusability. Functions provide better modularity in programming. Python provides two types of functions.

a) Built-in functions
b) User-defined functions

Functions like input(), print() etc. are examples of built-in functions. The code of these functions will be already defined. We can create our own functions to perform a particular task. These functions are called user-defined functions.

6.1 Function Definition

The following specifies simple rules for defining a function.

- Function block or Function header begins with the keyword def followed by the function name and parentheses (( )).
- Any input parameters or arguments should be placed within these parentheses. We can also define parameters inside these parentheses.

- The first string after the function header is called the `docstring` and is short for documentation string. It is used to explain in brief, what a function does. Although optional, documentation is a good programming practice.
- The code block within every function starts with a colon (:) and is indented.
- The `return` statement [expression] exits a function, optionally passing back an expression to the caller. A `return` statement with no arguments is the same as `return None`.

Syntax

```
def functionname( parameters ):
   "function_docstring"
   function_suite
   return [expression]
```

Example Program

```
def sum_of_two_numbers(a,b): #Function Header with 2 parameters
a and b
 "This Function is to find the sum of two numbers" #Docstring
 sum=a+b
 return sum
```

6.2 Function Calling

After defining a function, we can call the function from another function or directly from the Python prompt. The order of the parameters specified in the function definition should be preserved in function call also.

Example Program

```
#Main Program Code
a = int(input("Enter the first number:"))
b = int(input("Enter the second number:"))
s = sum_of_two_numbers(a,b)#Function calling
print("Sum of",a,"and",b,"is", s)
```

Output

```
Enter the first number:4
Enter the second number:3
Sum of 4 and 3 is 7
```

All the parameters in Python are passed by reference. It means if we change a parameter which refers to within a function, the change also reflects back in the calling function. Parameters and variables defined inside a function is not visible from outside. Hence, they have a local scope. Lifetime of a variable is the period throughout which the variable exists in the memory. The lifetime of variables inside a function is as long as the function executes. All variables in a program may not be accessible at all locations in that program. This depends on where we have declared a variable. The scope of a variable determines the portion of the program where we can access a particular identifier. They are destroyed once we return from the function. Hence, a function does not remember the value of a variable from its previous calls.

Example Program

```
def value_change(a): #Function Header
    a=10
    print("Value inside function=",a) #prints the value of a inside function
    return
#Main Program Code
a =int(input("Enter a number:"))
value_change(a)#Function calling
print("Value outside function=",a) #prints value of a outside function
```

Output

```
Enter a number:3
Value inside function = 10
Value outside function = 3
```

Here in the main program a number is read and stored in variable a. Even though this value is passed to the function value_change, a is assigned another value inside the function. This value is displayed inside the function. After returning from the function, it will display the value read from the main function. The variable a declared inside function value_change is local to that function and hence after returning to the main program, a will display the value stored in the main program.

6.3 Function Arguments

We can call the function by any of the following 4 arguments.

- Required arguments
- Keyword arguments
- Default arguments
- Variable-length arguments

6.3.1 Required Arguments

Required arguments are the arguments passed to a function in correct positional order. Here, the number of arguments in the function call should match exactly with the function definition. Consider the following example.

Example Program

```
def value_change(a): #Function Header
    a=10
```

```
  print("Value inside function=",a) #prints the value of a inside
function
  return
#Main Program Code
a =int(input("Enter a number:"))
value_change()#Function calling without passing parameter
print("Value outside function=",a) #prints value of a outside
function
```

Output

```
Enter a number:4
Traceback (most recent call last):
  File "main.py", line 7, in <module>
    value_change()#Function calling without passing parameter
TypeError: value_change() takes exactly 1 argument (0 given)
```

The above example contains a function which requires 1 parameter. In the main program code, the function is called without passing the parameter. Hence it resulted in an error.

6.3.2 Keyword Arguments

When we use keyword arguments in a function call, the caller identifies the arguments by the parameter name. This allows us to skip arguments or place them out of order because the Python interpreter is able to use the keywords provided to match the values with parameters.

Example Program

```
# Function definition
def studentinfo(rollno,name,course):
   print("Roll Number:",rollno)
   print("Name:",name)
   print("Course:",course)
#Function calling
#order of parameters in function call is shuffled
studentinfo(course="UG",rollno=50,name="Jack")
```

Output

```
Roll Number: 50
Name: Jack
Course: UG
```

6.3.3 Default Arguments

A default argument is an argument that assumes a default value if a value is not provided in the function call for that argument. The following example shows how default arguments are invoked.

Example Program

```
# Function definition
def studentinfo(rollno,name,course="UG"):
   "This prints a passed info into this function"
   print("Roll Number:",rollno)
   print("Name:",name)
   print("Course:",course)
#Function calling
#Order of parameters is shuffled
studentinfo(course="UG", rollno=50, name="Jack")
#The parameter course is omitted
studentinfo(rollno=51,name="Tom")
```

Output

```
Roll Number: 50
Name: Jack
Course: UG
Roll Number: 51
Name: Tom
Course: UG
```

In the above example, the first function call to `studentinfo` passes the three parameters. In the case of second function call to `studentinfo`, the parameter `course` is omitted. Hence it takes the default value "UG" given to `course` in the function definition.

6.3.4 Variable-Length Arguments

In some cases we may need to process a function for more arguments than specified while defining the function. These arguments are called *variable-length* arguments and are not named in the function definition, unlike required and default arguments. An asterisk (*) is placed before the variable name that holds the values of all non-keyword variable arguments. This tuple remains empty if no additional arguments are specified during the function call. The following shows the syntax of a function definition with *variable-length* arguments.

Syntax

```
def functionname([formal_arguments,] *variable_arguments_tuple
):
   "function_docstring"
   function_statements
   return [expression]
```

Example Program

```
# Function definition
def variablelengthfunction(*argument):
```

```
    print("Result:",)
    for i in argument: print(i)
#Function call with 1 argument
variablelengthfunction(10)
#Function call with 4 arguments
variablelengthfunction(10,30,50,80)
```

Output

```
Result: 10 #Result of function call with 1 argument
Result: 10 #Result of function call with 4 arguments
30
50
80
```

6.4 Anonymous Functions (Lambda Functions)

In Python, anonymous function is a function that is defined without a name. While normal functions are defined using the def keyword, in Python anonymous functions are defined using the lambda keyword. Hence, anonymous functions are also called lambda functions. The following are the characteristics of lambda functions.

1. Lambda functions can take any number of arguments but return only one value in the form of an expression.
2. It cannot contain multiple expressions.
3. It cannot have comments.
4. A lambda function cannot be a direct call to print because lambda requires an expression.
5. Lambda functions have their own local namespace and cannot access variables other than those in their parameter list and those in the global namespace.
6. Lambda functions are not equivalent to inline functions in C or C++.

Syntax

```
lambda [arg1 [,arg2,.....argn]]:expression
```

Example Program

```
# Lambda Function definition
square=lambda x : x*x
# Usage of lambda function
n=int(input("Enter a number:"))
print("Square of", n,"is", square(n)) #Lambda function call
```

Output

```
Enter a number:5
Square of 5 is 25
```

In the above example, lambda is the keyword, x shows the argument passed, and x*x is the expression to be evaluated and stored in the variable square. In the case of calculating the square of a number, only one argument is passed. More than one argument is possible for lambda functions. The following example shows a lambda function which takes two arguments and returns the sum.

Example Program

```
# Lambda Function definition
sum=lambda x,y : x+y
# Usage of lambda function
m=int(input("Enter first number:"))
n=int(input("Enter second number:"))
print("Sum of", m, "and", n,"is", sum(m,n))#Lambda function call
```

Output

```
Enter first number:10
Enter second number:20
Sum of 10 and 20 is 30
```

6.4.1 Uses of lambda function

We use lambda functions when we require a nameless function for a short period of time. In Python, we generally use it as an argument to a higher-order function (a function that takes in other functions as arguments). Lambda functions are used along with built-in functions like filter(), map() etc.

Example Program with filter()

The filter() function in Python takes in a function and a list as arguments. The function is called with all the items in the list and a new list is returned which contains items for which the function evaluates to True.

```
# Lambda Function to filter out only the odd numbers from a list
oldlist=[2,31,42,11,6,5,23,44]
# Usage of lambda function
newlist=list(filter(lambda x: (x%2!=0),oldlist))
print(oldlist)
print(newlist)
```

Output

```
[2, 31, 42, 11, 6, 5, 23, 44]
[31, 11, 5, 23]
```

Example Program with map()

The map() function in Python takes in a function and a list. The function is called with all the items in the list and a new list is returned which contains items returned by that function for each item.

```
# Lambda Function to increment the items in list by 2
oldlist=[2,31,42,11,6,5,23,44]
```

```
print(oldlist)
# Usage of lambda function
newlist=list(map(lambda x: x+2,oldlist))
print("List after incrementation by 2")
print(newlist)
```

Output

```
[2, 31, 42, 11, 6, 5, 23, 44]
List after incrementation by 2
[4, 33, 44, 13, 8, 7, 25, 46]
```

6.5 Recursive Functions

Recursion is the process of defining something in terms of itself. A function can call other functions. It is possible for a function to call itself. This is known as recursion. The following example shows a recursive function to find the factorial of a number.

Example Program

```
def recursion_fact(x):
 #This is a recursive function to find the factorial of an
integer
  if x == 1: return 1
   else: return (x * recursion_fact(x-1))#Recursive calling
 num = int(input("Enter a number: "))
 if num >= 1:
   print("The factorial of", num, "is", recursion_fact(num))
```

Output

```
Enter a number: 5
The factorial of 5 is 120
```

Explanation

In the above example, recursion_fact() is a recursive function as it calls itself. When we call this function with a positive integer, it will recursively call itself by decreasing the number. Each function call multiplies the number with the factorial of number-1 until the number is equal to one. This recursive call can be explained in the following steps. Our recursion ends when the number reduces to 1. This is called the base condition. Every recursive function must have a base condition that stops the recursion or else the function calls itself infinitely. We must avoid infinite recursion.

```
recursion_fact(5)                   # 1st call with 5
5 * recursion_fact(4)               # 2nd call with 4
5 * 4 * recursion_fact(3)           # 3rd call with 3
5 * 4 * 3 *  recursion_fact(2)      # 4th call with 2
```

```
5 * 4 * 3 * 2 * recursion_fact(1)  # 5th call with 1
5 * 4 * 3 * 2 * 1                   # return from 5th call as
number=1
5 *4 * 3 * 2                       # return from 4th call
5 * 4 * 6                           # return from 3rd call
5*24                               # return from 2nd call
120                                 #return from 1st call
```

6.6 Function with more than one return value

Python has a strong mechanism of returning more than one value at a time. This is very flexible when the function needs to return more than one value. Instead of writing separate functions for returning individual values, we can return all the values within same function. The following shows an example for function returning more than one value.

Example Program

```
#Python Function Returning more than One value
def calc(a,b):
    sum=a+b
    diff=a-b
    prod=a*b
    quotient=a/b
    return sum, diff, prod, quotient
a=int(input("Enter first number:"))
b=int(input("Enter second number:"))
s,d,p,q=calc(a,b)
print("Sum=",s)
print("Difference=",d)
print("Product=",p)
print("Quotient=",q)
```

Output

```
Enter first number:10
Enter second number:5
Sum= 15
Difference= 5
Product= 50
Quotient= 2
```

6.7 Solved Lab Exercises

1. Write a Python function to check whether a number is even or odd.

Program

```
#Function to Check whether a number is even or odd.
def oddeven(x):
  if x%2==0: print("The Number", x, "is even")
  else: print("The Number", x, "is odd")
num = int(input("Enter a number: "))
oddeven(num)#Function calling
```

Output

```
Enter a number: 4
The Number 4 is even
```

2. **Write a Python function to test whether a number is within 100 of 1000 or 2000.**

Program

```
 def near_thousand(n):
    if abs(1000 - n) <= 100: th= True
    else: th=False
    if abs(2000 - n) <= 100: twoth=True
    else: twoth=False
    return th,twoth
#Main Program
n=int(input("Enter a number:"))
k,m = near_thousand(n)
if k==True:
  print("The number is within 100 of 1000")
elif m==True:
  print("The number is within 100 of 2000")
else:print("The number is  not within 100 of 1000 or 100 of
2000")
```

Output

```
Enter a number:1950
The number is within 100 of 2000
```

3. **Write a Python program to calculate the sum of three given numbers, if the values are equal then return thrice of their sum.**

Program

```
def sum_thrice(x, y, z):
   sum = x + y + z
   if x == y == z:
```

```
        sum = sum * 3
        return sum
#Main Program
a=int(input("Enter First Number:"))
b=int(input("Enter Second Number:"))
c=int(input("Enter Third Number:"))
print("Sum_Thrice:",sum_thrice(a,b,c))
```

Output

```
Enter First Number:3
Enter Second Number:3
Enter Third Number:3
Sum_Thrice: 27
```

4. **Write a Python function to get a new string from a given string where "Is" has been added to the front. If the given string already begins with "Is" then return the string unchanged.**

Program

```
def new_string(str):
  if len(str) >= 2 and str[:2] == "Is":
    return str
  return "Is " + str
#Main Program
str1=input("Enter a String:")
print("New String:",new_string(str1))
```

Output

```
Enter a String:Good Morning
New String: Is Good Morning
```

5. **Write a Python program to get a string which is n (non-negative integer) copies of a given string.**

Program

```
def larger_string(str, n):
result = " "
for i in range(n):
result = result + " " + str
return result
#Main Program
str1=input("Enter a String:")
n=int(input("Number of Copies:"))
print("Final String:",larger_string(str1,n))
```

Output

```
Enter a String:Python Program
Number of Copies:3
Final String:   Python Program Python Program Python Program
```

6. **Write a Python function that will return true if the two given integer values are equal or their sum or difference is 5.**

Program

```
def test_number5(x, y):
    eq,differ5,sum5,no=False,False,False,False
    if x == 5 or y == 5:
        eq = True
    elif abs(x-y) == 5:
        differ5 = True
    elif (x+y) == 5:
        sum5 = True
    else:
        no = True
    return eq,differ5,sum5,no
a=int(input("Enter first integer:"))
b=int(input("Enter second integer:"))
e,d,s,n = test_number5(a,b)
if e:print(a,"and",b, "are equal:",e)
if d: print("Difference of", a, "and", b,"is",5, "is",d)
if s:print("Sum of ", a, "and", b, "is", 5, "is",s)
if n: print("Sum of numbers is not 5\n Difference of numbers is
not 5\n Numbers are not equal")
```

Output

```
Enter first integer:6
Enter second integer:8
Sum of numbers is not 5
Difference of numbers is not 5
Numbers are not equal
```

7. **Write a Python function that takes two lists and returns True if they have at least one common member.**

Program

```
def common_data(list1, list2):
 result = False
```

```
 for x in list1:
  for y in list2:
        if x == y:
            result = True
 return result
#main Program
list1=input("Enter first list(space separated):")
lis1=list(list1.split())
list2=input("Enter second list(space separated):")
lis2=list(list2.split())
r=common_data(lis1,lis2)
if r:
 print(lis1,"and", lis2,"has at least common member:",r)
else:
 print(lis1,"and", lis2,"has at least common member:",r)
```

Output

```
Enter first list(space separated):1 2 cat rat
Enter second list(space separated):2 3 tiger lion
['1', '2', 'cat', 'rat'] and ['2', '3', 'tiger', 'lion'] has at
least common member: True
```

8. **Write a Python function to find the GCD of 2 numbers.**

Program

```
#Function to find the GCD of two numbers
def gcd(a,b):
 for i in range (1, min(a,b)+1):
  if a%i==0 and b%i==0: gcd=i
 print(gcd)
#Main Function
a=int(input("Enter First Number:"))
b=int(input("Enter Second Number:"))
gcd(a,b)#Function calling
```

Output

```
Enter First Number:12
Enter Second Number:18
6
```

9. **Write a Python function to generate all the factors of a number.**

Program

```
#Function to find all the factors of a number
def factors(a):
 for i in range (1,(a+1)):
  if a%i==0 : print(i)
#Main Function
a=int(input("Enter a Number:"))
factors(a)#Function calling
```

Output

```
Enter a Number:12
1
2
3
4
6
12
```

10. **Write a Python function to find the sum of digits of a number.**

Program

```
#Function to find sumofdigits of a number
def sumofdigits(n):
 sum=0
 while(n>0):
  digit=n%10
  sum+=digit
  n=n//10
 print("Sum of digits is",sum)
#Main Function
a=int(input("Enter a Number:"))
sumofdigits(a)#Function calling
```

Output

```
Enter a Number:1234
Sum of digits is 10
```

11. **Write a Python function to concatenate two strings.**

Program

```
#Function to concatenate two strings
def concatenate(s1,s2):
```

```
print("First String:",s1)
print("Second String:",s2).
print("Concatenated String:",(s1+s2))
#Main Function
s1=input("Enter first string:")
s2=input("Enter second string:")
concatenate(s1,s2)#Function calling
```

Output

```
Enter first string:Hello
Enter second string: Python
First String: Hello
Second String:  Python
Concatenated String: Hello Python
```

12. **Write a Python function called compare which takes two strings s1 and s2 and an integer n as arguments. The function should return True if first n characters of both the strings are same else the function should return False.**

Program

```
#Function to find similar substrings
def substring(s1,s2,n):
  for i in range(0,n):
   if s1[i]!= s2[i]:return False
  else : return True
#Main Function
s1=input("Enter first string:")
s2=input("Enter second string:")
n=int(input("Enter a number:"))
#substring(s1,s2,n)#Function calling
if substring(s1,s2,n):
  print("The substrings are equal:")
else:
  print("The substrings are not equal")
```

Output

```
Enter first string: Programming
Enter second string: Program
Enter a number:4
The substrings are equal
```

13. Write a Python function to find whether a number is completely divisible by another number.

Program

```
#Function to find whether a number is completely divisible by
another
def divisible(x,y):
    if x%y==0:
        print(x, "is completely divisible by", y)
    else :
        print(x, "is not completely divisible by", y)
#Main Function
x=int(input("First Number:"))
y=int(input("Second Number:"))
divisible(x,y)
```

Output

```
First Number:12
Second Number:5
12 is not completely divisible by 5
```

14. Write a Python program to display Fibonacci series using recursion.

Program

```
"""Recursive function to
   print Fibonacci sequence"""
def recursive_fibo(n):
   if n <= 1:
       return n
   else:
       return(recursive_fibo(n-1) + recursive_fibo(n-2))
# Main function
n = int(input("How many terms? "))
# check if the number of terms is valid
if n <= 0:
   print("Please enter a positive integer")
else:
   print("Fibonacci sequence:")
   for i in range(n):
       print(recursive_fibo(i))
```

Output

```
How many terms? 5
Fibonacci sequence:
0
1
1
2
3
```

15. Write a Python program to find the sum of n natural numbers using recursion.

Program

```
"""Function to return the sum
   of natural numbers using recursion"""
def recursive_sum(n):
    if n <= 1:
        return n
    else:
        return n + recursive_sum(n-1)
#Main function
num = int(input("Enter a number: "))
if num < 0:
   print("Enter a positive number:")
else:
   print("The sum of first",num, "natural numbers is",recursive_
sum(num))
```

Output

```
Enter a number: 5
The sum of first 5 natural numbers is 15
```

16. Write a Python program to convert decimal to binary using recursion.

Program

```
"""Function to print binary number
   for the input decimal using recursion"""
def binary(n):
     if n >= 1:
       binary(n//2)
       print(n%2, end=' ')
```

```
#Main function
dec = int(input("Enter an integer: "))
binary(dec)
```

Output

```
Enter an integer: 5
1 0 1
```

6.8 Conclusion

This Chapter covers a detailed explanation of function definition, function calling, return statement, scope of variables, different types of arguments like required arguments, default arguments, keyword arguments and variable-length arguments. A new type of function known as anonymous function (lambda functions) is explained with its characteristics and uses. Recursive functions are explained and illustrated with examples.

6.9 Review Questions

1. Briefly explain the function definition and function calling in Python.
2. What is the purpose of a return statement?
3. What are keyword arguments?
4. What do you mean by default arguments?
5. What do you mean by required arguments?
6. Explain with an example the execution of variable-length arguments.
7. What are lambda functions?
8. What are the characteristics of anonymous functions?
9. What are the applications of lambda functions?
10. Illustrate with an example, the working of recursive functions.
11. Discuss the different argument passing mechanism in Python with suitable examples.

07 Modules and Packages

CONTENTS

Modules refer to a file containing Python statements and definitions. A module is a Python object with arbitrarily named attributes that we can bind and reference. We use modules to break down large programs into small manageable and organized files. Further, modules provide reusability of code. A module can define functions, classes and variables. A module can also include runnable code. Python has a lot of standard modules (built-in modules) available. A full list of Python standard modules is available in the Lib directory inside the location where you installed Python.

7.1 Built-in Modules

We have already seen the built-in module `math`. The following Table 7.1 shows the list of various built-in modules and their description.

Table 7.1: Built-in modules and their description

a	
abc	Abstract base classes according to PEP 3119.
aifc	Read and write audio files in AIFF or AIFC format.
argparse	Command-line option and argument parsing library.
array	Space efficient arrays of uniformly typed numeric values.
ast	Abstract Syntax Tree classes and manipulation.
asynchat	Support for asynchronous command/response protocols.
asyncio	Asynchronous I/O, event loop, coroutines and tasks.
asyncore	A base class for developing asynchronous socket handling services.
atexit	Register and execute cleanup functions.
audioop	Manipulate raw audio data.
b	
base64	RFC 3548: Base16, Base32, Base64 Data Encodings; Base85 and Ascii85
bdb	Debugger framework.
binascii	Tools for converting between binary and various ASCII-encoded binary representations.
binhex	Encode and decode files in binhex4 format.
bisect	Array bisection algorithms for binary searching.
builtins	The module that provides the built-in namespace.
bz2	Interfaces for bzip2 compression and decompression.
c	
calendar	Functions for working with calendars, including some emulation of the Unix cal Program.
cgi	Helpers for running Python scripts via the Common Gateway Interface.
cgitb	Configurable traceback handler for CGI scripts.
chunk	Module to read IFF chunks.
cmath	Mathematical functions for complex numbers.
cmd	Build line-oriented command interpreters.
code	Facilities to implement read-eval-print loops.
codecs	Encode and decode data and streams.
codeop	Compile (possibly incomplete) Python code.
collections	Container datatypes
colorsys	Conversion functions between RGB and other color systems.
compileall	Tools for byte-compiling all Python source files in a directory tree.
concurrent	

configparser	Configuration file parser.
contextlib	Utilities for with-statement contexts.
copy	Shallow and deep copy operations.
copyreg	Register pickle support functions.
cProfile	
crypt (Unix)	The crypt() function used to check Unix passwords.
csv	Write and read tabular data to and from delimited files.
ctypes	A foreign function library for Python.
curses (Unix)	An interface to the curses library, providing portable terminal handling.
d	
datetime	Basic date and time types.
dbm	Interfaces to various Unix "database" formats.
decimal	Implementation of the General Decimal Arithmetic Specification.
difflib	Helpers for computing differences between objects.
dis	Disassembler for Python bytecode.
distutils	Support for building and installing Python modules into an existing Python installation.
doctest	Test pieces of code within docstrings.
dummy_threading	Drop-in replacement for the threading module.
e	
email	Package supporting the parsing, manipulating, and generating email messages, including MIME documents.
encodings	
ensurepip	Bootstrapping the "pip" installer into an existing Python installation or virtual environment.
enum	Implementation of an enumeration class.
errno	Standard errno system symbols.
f	
faulthandler	Dump the Python traceback.
fcntl (Unix)	The fcntl() and ioctl() system calls.
filecmp	Compare files efficiently.
fileinput	Loop over standard input or a list of files.
fnmatch	Unix shell style filename pattern matching.
formatter	Deprecated: Generic output formatter and device interface.
fpectl (Unix)	Provide control for floating point exception handling.
fractions	Rational numbers.

ftplib	FTP protocol client (requires sockets).
functools	Higher-order functions and operations on callable objects.
g	
gc	Interface to the cycle-detecting garbage collector.
getopt	Portable parser for command line options; support both short and long option names.
getpass	Portable reading of passwords and retrieval of the userid.
gettext	Multilingual internationalization services.
glob	Unix shell style pathname pattern expansion.
grp (Unix)	The group database (getgrnam() and friends).
gzip	Interfaces for gzip compression and decompression using file objects.
h	
hashlib	Secure hash and message digest algorithms.
heapq	Heap queue algorithm (a.k.a. priority queue).
hmac	Keyed-Hashing for Message Authentication (HMAC) implementation
html	Helpers for manipulating HTML.
http	HTTP status codes and messages
i	
imaplib	IMAP4 protocol client (requires sockets).
imghdr	Determine the type of image contained in a file or byte stream.
imp	**Deprecated:** *Access the implementation of the import statement.*
importlib	The implementation of the import machinery.
inspect	Extract information and source code from live objects.
io	Core tools for working with streams.
ipaddress	IPv4/IPv6 manipulation library.
itertools	Functions creating iterators for efficient looping.
j	
json	Encode and decode the JSON format.
k	
keyword	Test whether a string is a keyword in Python.
l	
lib2to3	the 2 to 3 library
linecache	This module provides random access to individual lines from text files.
locale	Internationalization services.
logging	Flexible event logging system for applications.
lzma	A Python wrapper for the liblzma compression library.

m	
macpath	Mac OS 9 path manipulation functions.
mailbox	Manipulate mailboxes in various formats
mailcap	Mailcap file handling.
marshal	Convert Python objects to streams of bytes and back (with different constraints).
math	Mathematical functions (sin() etc.).
mimetypes	Mapping of filename extensions to MIME types.
mmap	Interface to memory-mapped files for Unix and Windows.
modulefinder	Find modules used by a script.
msilib (Windows)	Creation of Microsoft Installer files, and CAB files.
msvcrt (Windows)	Miscellaneous useful routines from the MS VC++ runtime.
multiprocessing	Process-based parallelism.
n	
netrc	Loading of .netrc files.
nis (Unix)	Interface to Sun's NIS (Yellow Pages) library.
nntplib	NNTP protocol client (requires sockets).
numbers	Numeric abstract base classes (Complex, Real, Integral, etc.).
o	
operator	Functions corresponding to the standard operators.
optparse	**Deprecated:** *Command-line option parsing library.*
os	Miscellaneous operating system interfaces.
ossaudiodev (Linux, FreeBSD)	Access to OSS-compatible audio devices.
p	
parser	Access parse trees for Python source code.
pathlib	Object-oriented filesystem paths
pdb	The Python debugger for interactive interpreters.
pickle	Convert Python objects to streams of bytes and back.
pickletools	Contains extensive comments about the pickle protocols and pickle-machine opcodes, as well as some useful functions.
pipes (Unix)	A Python interface to Unix shell pipelines.
pkgutil	Utilities for the import system.
platform	Retrieves as much platform identifying data as possible.
plistlib	Generate and parse Mac OS X plist files.
poplib	POP3 protocol client (requires sockets).
posix (Unix)	The most common POSIX system calls (normally used via module os).

pprint	Data pretty printer.
profile	Python source profiler.
pstats	Statistics object for use with the profiler.
pty (Linux)	Pseudo-Terminal Handling for Linux.
pwd (Unix)	The password database (getpwnam() and friends).
py_compile	Generate byte-code files from Python source files.
pyclbr	Supports information extraction for a Python class browser.
pydoc	Documentation generator and online help system.
q	
queue	A synchronized queue class.
quopri	Encode and decode files using the MIME quoted-printable encoding.
r	
random	Generate pseudo-random numbers with various common distributions.
re	Regular expression operations.
readline (Unix)	GNU readline support for Python.
reprlib	Alternate repr() implementation with size limits.
resource (Unix)	An interface to provide resource usage information on the current process.
rlcompleter	Python identifier completion, suitable for the GNU readline library.
runpy	Locate and run Python modules without importing them first.
s	
sched	General purpose event scheduler.
select	Wait for I/O completion on multiple streams.
selectors	High-level I/O multiplexing.
shelve	Python object persistence.
shlex	Simple lexical analysis for Unix shell-like languages.
shutil	High-level file operations, including copying.
signal	Set handlers for asynchronous events.
site	Module responsible for site-specific configuration.
smtpd	A SMTP server implementation in Python.
smtplib	SMTP protocol client (requires sockets).
sndhdr	Determine type of a sound file.
socket	Low-level networking interface.
socketserver	A framework for network servers.
spwd (Unix)	The shadow password database (getspnam() and friends).
sqlite3	A DB-API 2.0 implementation using SQLite 3.x.
ssl	TLS/SSL wrapper for socket objects

stat	Utilities for interpreting the results of os.stat(), os.lstat() and os.fstat().
statistics	mathematical statistics functions
string	Common string operations.
stringprep	String preparation, as per RFC 3453
struct	Interpret bytes as packed binary data.
subprocess	Subprocess management.
sunau	Provide an interface to the Sun AU sound format.
symbol	Constants representing internal nodes of the parse tree.
symtable	Interface to the compiler's internal symbol tables.
sys	Access system-specific parameters and functions.
sysconfig	Python's configuration information
syslog (Unix)	An interface to the Unix syslog library routines.
t	
tabnanny	Tool for detecting white space related problems in Python source files in a directory tree.
tarfile	Read and write tar-format archive files.
telnetlib	Telnet client class.
tempfile	Generate temporary files and directories.
termios (Unix)	POSIX style tty control.
test	Regression tests package containing the testing suite for Python.
textwrap	Text wrapping and filling
threading	Thread-based parallelism.
time	Time access and conversions.
timeit	Measure the execution time of small code snippets.
tkinter	Interface to Tcl/Tk for graphical user interfaces
token	Constants representing terminal nodes of the parse tree.
tokenize	Lexical scanner for Python source code.
trace	Trace or track Python statement execution.
traceback	Print or retrieve a stack traceback.
tracemalloc	Trace memory allocations.
tty (Unix)	Utility functions that perform common terminal control operations.
turtle	An educational framework for simple graphics applications
turtledemo	A viewer for example turtle scripts
types	Names for built-in types.
typing	Support for type hints (see PEP 484).

u	
unicodedata	Access the Unicode Database.
unittest	Unit testing framework for Python.
urllib	
uu	Encode and decode files in uuencode format.
uuid	UUID objects (universally unique identifiers) according to RFC 4122
v	
venv	Creation of virtual environments.
w	
warnings	Issue warning messages and control their disposition.
wave	Provide an interface to the WAV sound format.
weakref	Support for weak references and weak dictionaries.
webbrowser	Easy-to-use controller for Web browsers.
winreg (Windows)	Routines and objects for manipulating the Windows registry.
winsound (Windows)	Access to the sound-playing machinery for Windows.
wsgiref	WSGI Utilities and Reference Implementation.
x	
xdrlib	Encoders and decoders for the External Data Representation (XDR).
xml	Package containing XML processing modules
xmlrpc	
z	
zipapp	Manage executable python zip archives
zipfile	Read and write ZIP-format archive files.
zipimport	support for importing Python modules from ZIP archives.
zlib	Low-level interface to compression and decompression routines compatible with gzip.

7.2 Creating Modules

We can define our most used functions in a module and import it, instead of copying their definitions into different programs. A file containing Python code, for e.g.: `prime.py`, is called a module and its module name would be `prime`. The Python code for a module named `test` normally resides in a file named `test.py`.

Let us create a module for finding the sum of two numbers. The following code creates a module in Python. Type the code and save it as test.py.

Example

```
# Python Module example
```

```
"""This Program adds two
    numbers and return the result"""
def sum(a, b):
    result = a + b
    return result
```

Here we have a function `sum()` inside a module named `test`. The function takes in two numbers and returns their sum.

7.3 *import* Statement

We can use any Python source file as a module by executing an import statement in some other Python source file. User-defined modules can be imported the same way as we import built-in modules.

We use the `import` keyword to do this. The import has the following syntax.

```
import module1[, module2[,... moduleN]
```

When the interpreter encounters an import statement, it imports the module if the module is present in the search path. A search path is a list of directories that the interpreter searches before importing a module. For example, to import the module `test.py`, you need to put the following command at the top of the script.

Example

```
import test
print(test.sum(2,3))
```

Output

```
5
```

When the above code in the example is executed, we get the result 5.

A module is loaded only once, regardless of the number of times it is imported. This prevents the module execution from happening over and over again if multiple imports occur.

7.3.1 *import* with renaming

We can import built-in or user-defined modules with an alias name. The following code shows how the built-in module math can be imported using an alias name.

Example Program

```
import math as m
print("The value of pi is", m.pi)
```

Output

```
The value of pi is 3.141592653589793
```

We have renamed the `math` module as `m`. This can save typing time in some cases. It is important to note that the name `math` is not recognized in our scope. Hence, `math.pi` is invalid, `m.pi` is the correct implementation.

7.3.2 *from...import* statement

We can import specific names from a module without importing the module as a whole. The module math contains a lot of built-in functions. But if we want to import only the `pi` function, the `from... import` statement can be used. The following example illustrates importing `pi` from `math` module.

Example Program

```
from math import pi
print("The value of pi is :", pi)
```

Output

```
The value of pi is : 3.14159265359
```

We have imported only the `pi` function from the `math` module. Hence no need to use the dot operator as given in example 7.3.1. We can also import multiple attributes from the module using `from...import` statement. The following example illustrates the import of `pi` as well as `sqrt()` from the `math` module using `from...import` statement.

Example Program

```
from math import pi,sqrt
print("The value of pi is :", pi)
print("The square root of 4 is:",sqrt(4))
```

Output

```
The value of pi is: 3.14159265359
The square root of 4 is: 2.0
```

7.3.3 *import* all names

We can import all names(definitions) from a module using the following construct. The following example shows how all the definitions from the `math` module can be imported. This makes all names except those beginning with an underscore, visible in our scope.

Example Program

```
from math import *
print("The value of pi is :", pi)
print("The square root of 4 is:",sqrt(4))
```

Output

```
The value of pi is: 3.14159265359
The square root of 4 is: 2.0
```

Here all functions in the module `math` are imported. But we have used only `pi` and `sqrt`. Importing everything with the asterisk (*) symbol is not a good programming practice. This can lead to duplicate definitions for an identifier. It also reduces the readability of our code.

7.4 Locating Modules

When we import a module, the Python interpreter searches for the module in the following sequence.

1. The current directory.
2. If the module isn't found, Python then searches each directory in the shell variable PYTHONPATH.
3. If the above two mentioned fails, Python checks the default path. On UNIX, this default path is normally /usr/local/lib/python/.

The module search path is stored in the system module `sys` as the `sys.path` variable. The `sys.path` variable contains the current directory, PYTHONPATH and the installation-dependent default.

7.4.1 PYTHONPATH variable

The PYTHONPATH is an environment variable, consisting of a list of directories. The syntax of PYTHONPATH is the same as that of the shell variable PATH. The following shows a typical PYTHONPATH from a Windows operating system.

```
set PYTHONPATH=c:\python34\lib
```

And here is a typical PYTHONPATH from a UNIX system.

```
set PYTHONPATH=/usr/local/lib/python
```

7.5 Namespaces and Scope

Variables are names (identifiers) that map to objects. A namespace is a dictionary of variable names (keys) and their corresponding objects (values). A Python statement can access variables in a local namespace and in the global namespace. If a local and a global variable have the same name, the local variable shadows the global variable.

Each function has its own local namespace. Python makes certain guesses on whether variables are local or global. It assumes that any variable assigned a value in a function is local. Therefore, in order to assign a value to a global variable within a function, you must first use the global statement. The statement `global variable_name` tells Python that `variable_name` is a global variable. Once a variable is declared global, Python stops searching the local namespace for that variable. Consider the following example.

Example Program

```
#Program to illustrate local and global namespace
a=10
def Add():
 a=a+1
 print(a)
Add()
print(a)
```

Output

```
Traceback (most recent call last):
  File "main.py", line 5, in <module>
    Add()
```

```
  File "main.py", line 3, in Add
    a=a+1
UnboundLocalError: local variable 'a' referenced before
assignment
```

When we run the above program, the output is listed above with errors. The reason is that we are trying to add 1 to a before a is assigned a value. This is because even though a is assigned a value 10, its scope is outside the function Add(). Further Python always searches for variables in the local namespace. Since a is not assigned a value inside the function, it resulted in an error. The below program is re-written using global variable concept.

Example Program

```
#Program to illustrate local and global namespace
a=10
print a
def Add():
  global a
  a=20
  a=a+1
  print(a)
Add()
print(a)
```

Output

```
10
21
21
```

In the above example, a is assigned a value 10 and it is printed. Inside the function, a is declared global and it is incremented by one. The result is 21. Even after, exiting the function, when we try to print the value of a, it is printing it as 21 since a is declared a global variable.

7.6 The *dir()* function

The dir() built-in function returns a sorted list of strings containing the names defined by a module. The list contains the names of all the modules, variables and functions that are defined in a module. The following example illustrates the use of dir() function for the built-in module called math.

Example Program

```
import math
c=dir(math)
print(c)
```

Output

```
['__doc__', '__file__', '__name__', '__package__', 'acos',
'acosh', 'asin', 'asinh', 'atan', 'atan2', 'atanh', 'ceil',
'copysign',, 'cos', 'cosh', 'degrees', 'e', 'erf', 'erfc',
'exp', 'expm1', 'fabs', 'factorial', 'floor', 'fmod', 'frexp',
'fsum', 'gamma', 'hypot', 'isinf', 'isnan', 'ldexp', 'lgamma',
'log', 'log10', 'log1p', 'modf', 'pi', 'pow', 'radians', 'sin',
'sinh', 'sqrt', 'tan', 'tanh', 'trunc']
```

In the above output, _doc_is present in every namespace. Initially it will be None, we can store documentation here.__file__ is the filename from which the module was loaded. __name__ is the name of the current module (minus the .py extension). In the top-level script or in conversational mode, this name is set to the string '__main__'. The module's __package__ attribute should be set. Its value must be a string, but it can be the same value as its __name__. If the attribute is set to None or is missing, the import system will fill it in with a more appropriate value. When the module is a package, its __package__ value should be set to its __name__. When the module is not a package, __package__ should be set to the empty string for top-level modules, or for submodules, to the parent package's name. The rest shows the built-in functions available in the math module.

Another example illustrates the use of dir() function along with user-defined modules.

Example Program

```
import test
c=dir(math)
print(c)
```

Output

```
['__builtins__', '__doc__', '__file__', '__name__', '__
package__', 'sum']
```

The output contains built-in strings and we have defined only one function called sum in that module. _builtins_ contain Python's built-in error handling functions which will be discussed in Chapter 10.

7.7 The *reload()* function

When the module is imported into a script, the code in the top-level portion of a module is executed only once. Therefore, if you want to reexecute the top-level code in a module, you can use the reload() function. The reload() function imports a previously imported module again. The syntax of the reload() function is as follows.

```
reload(module_name)
```

Here, module_name is the name of the module we want to reload and not the string containing the module name. For example, to reload `test` module, do the following

```
reload(test)
```

The following example illustrate the use of *reload()* function in Python.

7.8 Packages in Python

A package is a hierarchical file directory structure that defines a single Python application environment that consists of modules and subpackages and so on. As our application program grows larger in size with a lot of modules, we place similar modules in one package and different modules in different packages. This makes a project (program) easy to manage and conceptually clear. Similar, as a directory can contain sub-directories and files, a Python package can have sub-packages and modules. A directory must contain a file named `__init__.py` in order for Python to consider it as a package. This file can be left empty but we generally place the initialization code for that package in this file.

7.8.1 Importing modules from a Package

Consider a file `Asample.py` available in `pack` directory. This file has following line of source code.

```
def a:
 print("This is from A")
```

Similarly we have two more files `Bsample.py` and `Csample.py` available in `pack` directory with the following codes.

```
Bsample.py
 def b:
  print("This is from B")
 Csample.py
 def c:
  print("This is from C")
```

Now we have three files in the same directory `pack`. To make all of our functions available when we are importing `pack`, we need to put explicit import statements in __init__.py as follows.

```
from Asample import a
from Bsample import b
from Csample import c
```

After adding these lines to __init__.py, we have all of these functions available when we import the `pack` package. The following code shows how the package `pack` can be imported.

```
import pack
pack.a()
pack.b()
pack.c()
```

When the above code is executed, it gives the following result.

```
This is from A
This is from B
This is from C
```

In the above example, we have defined only one function in each module. It is also possible to have multiple definitions (more than one function) in each module and all these functions can be imported using the wildcard character `'*'`. Likewise if we have subfolders each subfolder can be separated by using dot operator while importing the package. For example, if the package `pack` resides in `/user/abc/level1`, we can give the `import` statement as follows.

```
import user.abc.level1.pack
```

7.9 Date and Time Modules

Conversion between various date and time formats is a common task to be done in almost all applications. Python provides various modules like time, calendar, datetime for parsing formatting and performing calculations on date and time.

7.9.1 The `time` Module

The time module contains a lot of functions to process time. Time intervals are represented as floating-point numbers in seconds. The time since January 1, 1970, 12:00 a.m is available and is termed as an epoch. The following example shows how many seconds have elapsed since the epoch.

Example Program

```
import time
seconds = time.time()
print("Number of seconds since 12:00am, January 1, 1970:",
seconds)
```

Output

```
Number of seconds since 12:00am, January 1, 1970:
1448080451.357909
```

The float representation is useful when storing or comparing dates, but not as useful for producing human readable representations. For printing the current time `ctime()` may be more useful. The following shows an example for `ctime()` method.

Example Program

```
import time
print("The time is:", time.ctime())
later = time.time() + 30
print("30 secs from now:", time.ctime(later))
```

Output

```
The time is: Sat Nov 21 10:10:08 2015
30 secs from now: Sat Nov 21 10:10:38 2015
```

7.9.1.1 struct_time Structure

Storing time as elapsed seconds is useful in some situations, but there are times when you need to have access to the individual fields of a date (year, month, etc.). The time module defines `struct_time` for holding date and time values with components broken out so they are easy to access. There are several functions that work with `struct_time` values instead of float. The `struct_time` has the following attributes listed in Table 7.2.

Table 7.2: Attributes of struct_time

Attribute	Values
tm_year	Current year
tm_mon	1 to 12
tm_mday	1 to 31
tm_hour	0 to 23
tm_min	0 to 59
tm_sec	0 to 61(60 and 61 are leap seconds)
tm_yday	0 to 6 (0 is Monday)
tm_wday	1 to 366 (Julian day)
tm_isdst	-1,0,1 -1 if library determines DST

Daylight saving time (DST) or summer time is the practice of advancing clocks during summer months by one hour so that in the evening, daylight is experienced an hour longer, while sacrificing normal sunrise times.

Example Program

```
import time
print("gmtime:", time.gmtime())
print("localtime:", time.localtime())
print("mktime:", time.mktime(time.localtime()))
t = time.localtime()
print("Current Year:",t.tm_year)
print("Current Month:",t.tm_mon)
print("Current Day:",t.tm_mday)
print("Day of month:", t.tm_mday)
print("Day of week:", t.tm_wday)
print("Day of year:", t.tm_yday)
print("DST:",t.tm_isdst)
```

Output

```
gmtime:time.struct_time(tm_year=2015, tm_mon=11, tm_mday=21,
tm_hour=5, tm_min=19, tm_sec=44, tm_wday=5, tm_yday=325, tm_
isdst=0)

localtime: time.struct_time(tm_year=2015, tm_mon=11, tm_mday=21,
tm_hour=10, tm_min=49, tm_sec=44, tm_wday=5, tm_yday=325, tm_
isdst=0)

mktime: 1448083184.0
Current Year: 2015
Current Month: 11
```

```
Current Day: 21
Day of month: 21
Day of week: 5
Day of year: 325
DST: 0
```

`gmtime()` returns the current time in Universal Time Clock. `localtime()` returns the current time with the current time zone applied. `mktime()` takes a `struct_time` and converts it to the floating point representation.

7.9.1.2 Parsing and Formatting Time

The two functions strptime() and strftime() convert between struct_time and string representations of time values. There is a long list of formatting instructions available to support input and output in different styles. The following example converts the current time from a string, to a struct_time instance, and back to a string.

Example Program

```
import time
now = time.ctime()
print(now)
parsed = time.strptime(now)
print(parsed)
print(time.strftime("%a %b %d %H:%M:%S %Y", parsed))
```

Output

```
Sat Nov 21 11:16:24 2015
time.struct_time(tm_year=2015, tm_mon=11, tm_mday=21, tm_
hour=11, tm_min=16, tm_sec=24, tm_wday=5, tm_yday=325, tm_
isdst=-1)
Sat Nov 21 11:16:24 2015
```

7.9.2 The `calendar` Module

The calendar module has many built-in functions for printing and formatting the output. By default, calendar takes Monday as the first day of the week and Sunday as the last one. To change this, call calendar.setfirstweekday() function. The following example shows a formatted text calendar.

Example Program

```
import calendar
c = calendar.TextCalendar(calendar.SUNDAY)
c.prmonth(2015,10)
```

Output

```
    October 2015
Su Mo Tu We Th Fr Sa
             1  2  3
 4  5  6  7  8  9 10
11 12 13 14 15 16 17
18 19 20 21 22 23 24
25 26 27 28 29 30 31
```

If we want to print the entire calendar for a year, the following code needs to be executed.

Example Program

```
import calendar
print(calendar.TextCalendar(calendar.SUNDAY).formatyear(2015))
```

Output

```
                                  2015

      January                   February                   March
Su Mo Tu We Th Fr Sa      Su Mo Tu We Th Fr Sa      Su Mo Tu We Th Fr Sa
             1  2  3       1  2  3  4  5  6  7       1  2  3  4  5  6  7
 4  5  6  7  8  9 10       8  9 10 11 12 13 14       8  9 10 11 12 13 14
11 12 13 14 15 16 17      15 16 17 18 19 20 21      15 16 17 18 19 20 21
18 19 20 21 22 23 24      22 23 24 25 26 27 28      22 23 24 25 26 27 28
25 26 27 28 29 30 31                                29 30 31

       April                      May                       June
Su Mo Tu We Th Fr Sa      Su Mo Tu We Th Fr Sa      Su Mo Tu We Th Fr Sa
          1  2  3  4                      1  2          1  2  3  4  5  6
 5  6  7  8  9 10 11       3  4  5  6  7  8  9       7  8  9 10 11 12 13
12 13 14 15 16 17 18      10 11 12 13 14 15 16      14 15 16 17 18 19 20
19 20 21 22 23 24 25      17 18 19 20 21 22 23      21 22 23 24 25 26 27
26 27 28 29 30            24 25 26 27 28 29 30      28 29 30
                          31

        July                     August                  September
Su Mo Tu We Th Fr Sa      Su Mo Tu We Th Fr Sa      Su Mo Tu We Th Fr Sa
          1  2  3  4                         1             1  2  3  4  5
 5  6  7  8  9 10 11       2  3  4  5  6  7  8       6  7  8  9 10 11 12
12 13 14 15 16 17 18       9 10 11 12 13 14 15      13 14 15 16 17 18 19
19 20 21 22 23 24 25      16 17 18 19 20 21 22      20 21 22 23 24 25 26
26 27 28 29 30 31         23 24 25 26 27 28 29      27 28 29 30
                          30 31
```

```
      October                      November                     December
Su Mo Tu We Th Fr Sa         Su Mo Tu We Th Fr Sa         Su Mo Tu We Th Fr Sa
             1  2  3          1  2  3  4  5  6  7                1  2  3  4  5
 4  5  6  7  8  9 10          8  9 10 11 12 13 14          6  7  8  9 10 11 12
11 12 13 14 15 16 17         15 16 17 18 19 20 21         13 14 15 16 17 18 19
18 19 20 21 22 23 24         22 23 24 25 26 27 28         20 21 22 23 24 25 26
25 26 27 28 29 30 31         29 30                        27 28 29 30 31
```

7.9.2.1 Built-in functions

1. calendar.firstweekday( ) - Returns the current setting for the weekday that starts each week. By default, when calendar is first imported, first week day is 0, i. e Monday.
2. calendar.setfirstweekday(weekday) - Sets the first day of each week to weekday with the parameter passed. Weekday codes are 0 (Monday) to 6 (Sunday).
3. calendar.isleap(year)- returns True if year is a leap year, False otherwise.
4. calendar.leapdays(y1,y2)- Returns the total number of leap days in the years within range(y1,y2).

   Example Program

```
import calendar
print("Default first weekday:",calendar.firstweekday())
calendar.setfirstweekday(calendar.SUNDAY)
print("New first weekday:",calendar.firstweekday())
print("Leap Year:",calendar.isleap(2014))
print("Leap days between 2010 and 2015:",calendar.
leapdays(2010,2015))
```

   Output

```
Default first weekday: 0
New first weekday: 6
Leap Year: False
Leap days between 2010 and 2015: 1
```

5. calendar.calendar(year,w=2,l=1,c=6) - Returns a multiline string with a calendar for year year formatted into three columns separated by c spaces. w is the width in characters of each date. l is the number of lines for each week. This is equivalent to the example given in Section 7.9.2

   Example Program

```
import calendar
print(calendar.calendar(2015,2,1,6))
```

Output

```
                                  2015

      January                   February                   March
Mo Tu We Th Fr Sa Su      Mo Tu We Th Fr Sa Su      Mo Tu We Th Fr Sa Su
          1  2  3  4                         1                         1
 5  6  7  8  9 10 11       2  3  4  5  6  7  8       2  3  4  5  6  7  8
12 13 14 15 16 17 18       9 10 11 12 13 14 15       9 10 11 12 13 14 15
19 20 21 22 23 24 25      16 17 18 19 20 21 22      16 17 18 19 20 21 22
26 27 28 29 30 31         23 24 25 26 27 28         23 24 25 26 27 28 29
                                                    30 31

       April                      May                       June
Mo Tu We Th Fr Sa Su      Mo Tu We Th Fr Sa Su      Mo Tu We Th Fr Sa Su
       1  2  3  4  5                   1  2  3       1  2  3  4  5  6  7
 6  7  8  9 10 11 12       4  5  6  7  8  9 10       8  9 10 11 12 13 14
13 14 15 16 17 18 19      11 12 13 14 15 16 17      15 16 17 18 19 20 21
20 21 22 23 24 25 26      18 19 20 21 22 23 24      22 23 24 25 26 27 28
27 28 29 30               25 26 27 28 29 30 31      29 30

        July                     August                  September
Mo Tu We Th Fr Sa Su      Mo Tu We Th Fr Sa Su      Mo Tu We Th Fr Sa Su
       1  2  3  4  5                      1  2          1  2  3  4  5  6
 6  7  8  9 10 11 12       3  4  5  6  7  8  9       7  8  9 10 11 12 13
13 14 15 16 17 18 19      10 11 12 13 14 15 16      14 15 16 17 18 19 20
20 21 22 23 24 25 26      17 18 19 20 21 22 23      21 22 23 24 25 26 27
27 28 29 30 31            24 25 26 27 28 29 30      28 29 30
                          31

      October                   November                  December
Mo Tu We Th Fr Sa Su      Mo Tu We Th Fr Sa Su      Mo Tu We Th Fr Sa Su
          1  2  3  4                         1          1  2  3  4  5  6
 5  6  7  8  9 10 11       2  3  4  5  6  7  8       7  8  9 10 11 12 13
12 13 14 15 16 17 18       9 10 11 12 13 14 15      14 15 16 17 18 19 20
19 20 21 22 23 24 25      16 17 18 19 20 21 22      21 22 23 24 25 26 27
26 27 28 29 30 31         23 24 25 26 27 28 29      28 29 30 31
                          30
```

6. calendar.month(year,month,w=2,l=1) -Returns a multiline string with a calendar for month, one line per week plus two header lines. w is the width in characters of each date l is the number of lines for each week.
7. calendar.prcal(year,w=2,l=1,c=6) – Same as that of calendar.calendar(year,w,l,c).
8. calendar.prmonth(year,month,w=2,l=1)–Same as that of calendar.month(year,month,w,l).

Example Program

```
import calendar
print(calendar.month(2015,11))
```

Output

```
   November 2015
Mo Tu We Th Fr Sa Su
                   1
 2  3  4  5  6  7  8
 9 10 11 12 13 14 15
16 17 18 19 20 21 22
23 24 25 26 27 28 29
30
```

7.9.3 The datetime Module

The datetime module includes functions and classes for doing date and time parsing, formatting, and arithmetic. It contains functions and classes for working with dates and times, separately and together.

7.9.3.1 The time Class

Time values are represented with the `time` class. Times have attributes for hour, minute, second, and microsecond. They can also include time zone information. A time instance only holds values of time, and not a date associated with the time.

Example Program

```
import datetime
t = datetime.time(1, 2, 3)
print(t)
print('hour  :', t.hour)
print('minute:', t.minute)
print('second:', t.second)
print('microsecond:', t.microsecond)
print('tzinfo:', t.tzinfo)
```

Output

```
01:02:03
hour  : 1
```

```
minute: 2
second: 3
microsecond: 0
tzinfo: None
```

7.9.3.2 The date Class

Calendar date values are represented with the date class. Instances have attributes for year, month, and day. It is easy to create a date representing today's date using the today() class method.

Example Program

```
import datetime
today = datetime.date.today()
print(today)
print('ctime:', today.ctime())
print('Year:', today.year)
print('Mon :', today.month)
print('Day :', today.day)
```

Output

```
2015-11-22
ctime: Sun Nov 22 00:00:00 2015
Year: 2015
Mon : 11
Day : 22
```

Another way to create new date instances uses the `replace()` method of an existing date. For example, we can change the year, leaving the day and month alone.

Example Program

```
import datetime
d1 = datetime.date(2015, 3, 12)
print('d1:', d1)
d2 = d1.replace(year=2016)
print('d2:', d2)
```

Output

```
d1: 2015-03-12
d2: 2016-03-12
```

7.9.3.3 timedeltas

Using `replace()` is not the only way to calculate future/past dates. You can use datetime to perform basic arithmetic on date values via the timedelta class. Subtracting dates produces a timedelta, and a timedelta can be added or subtracted from a date to produce another date. The internal values for a timedelta are stored in days, seconds, and microseconds. Intermediate level values passed to the constructor are converted into days, seconds, and microseconds.

Example Program

```
import datetime
print("microseconds:", datetime.timedelta(microseconds=1))
print("milliseconds:", datetime.timedelta(milliseconds=1))
print("seconds     :", datetime.timedelta(seconds=1))
print("minutes     :", datetime.timedelta(minutes=1))
print("hours       :", datetime.timedelta(hours=1))
print("days        :", datetime.timedelta(days=1))
print("weeks       :", datetime.timedelta(weeks=1))
```

Output

```
microseconds: 0:00:00.000001
milliseconds: 0:00:00.001000
seconds     : 0:00:01
minutes     : 0:01:00
hours       : 1:00:00
days        : 1 day, 0:00:00
weeks       : 7 days, 0:00:00
```

Date math uses the standard arithmetic operators. This example with date objects illustrates using timedelta objects to compute new dates, and subtracting date instances to produce timedeltas (including a negative delta value).

Example Program

```
import datetime
today = datetime.date.today()
print('Today    :', today)
one_day = datetime.timedelta(days=1)
print('One day  :', one_day)
yesterday = today - one_day
print('Yesterday:', yesterday)
tomorrow = today + one_day
print('Tomorrow :', tomorrow)
print('tomorrow - yesterday:', tomorrow - yesterday)
print('yesterday - tomorrow:', yesterday - tomorrow)
```

Output

```
Today    : 2015-11-22
One day  : 1 day, 0:00:00
Yesterday: 2015-11-21
```

```
Tomorrow : 2015-11-23
tomorrow - yesterday: 2 days, 0:00:00
yesterday - tomorrow: -2 days, 0:00:00
```

Both date and time values can be compared using the standard operators to determine which is earlier or later.

Example Program

```
import datetime
import time
print('Times:')
t1 = datetime.time(12, 55, 0)
print('\tt1:', t1)
t2 = datetime.time(13, 5, 0)
print('\tt2:', t2)
print('\tt1 < t2:', t1 < t2)
print('Dates:')
d1 = datetime.date.today()
print('\td1:', d1)
d2 = datetime.date.today() + datetime.timedelta(days=1)
print('\td2:', d2)
print('\td1 > d2:', d1 > d2)
```

Output

```
Times:
        t1: 12:55:00
        t2: 13:05:00
        t1 < t2: True
Dates:
        d1: 2015-11-23
        d2: 2015-11-24
        d1 > d2: False
```

In addition, we can use combine() a date instance and time instance to create a datetime instance.

Example Program

```
import datetime
t = datetime.time(1, 2, 3)
print('t :', t)
d = datetime.date.today()
print('d :', d)
```

```
dt = datetime.datetime.combine(d, t)
print('dt:', dt)
```

Output

```
t : 01:02:03
d : 2015-11-23
dt: 2015-11-23 01:02:03
```

The default string representation of a datetime object uses the ISO 8601 format (YYYY-MM-DDTHH:MM:SS.mmmmmm). Alternate formats can be generated using `strftime()`. Similarly, if your input data includes timestamp values parsable with `time.strptime()`, then `datetime.strptime()` is a convenient way to convert them to datetime instances.

Example Program

```
import datetime
format = "%a %b %d %H:%M:%S %Y"
today = datetime.datetime.today()
print('ISO     :', today)
s = today.strftime(format)
print('strftime:', s)
d = datetime.datetime.strptime(s, format)
print('strptime:', d.strftime(format))
```

Output

```
ISO     : 2015-11-23 09:52:29.427414
strftime: Mon Nov 23 09:52:29 2015
strptime: Mon Nov 23 09:52:29 2015
```

7.10 Solved Lab Exercises

1. Write a Python function to reverse a string. Import the module to reverse a string input by the user.

Program

```
StringReverse.py
def string_reverse(str1):
print("Reversed string:",str1[::-1])

#Main program importing the module
import StringReverse
str1=input("Enter a string:")
print("Original string:",str1)
StringReverse.string_reverse(str1)
```

Output

```
Enter a String:Python
Reversed String: nohtyP
```

2. **Write a Python function to check whether a number is in a given range. Import the module to input a number and check whether is in a given range.**

Program

```
NumberRange.py
  def test_range(a,b,n):
    if n in range(a,b):
        print( "%s is in the range"%str(n))
    else :
        print("The number is outside the given range.")

#Main Program importing the module
import NumberRange as num
a=int(input("Enter a lower limit:"))
b=int(input("Enter an Upper limit:"))
n=int(input("Enter a number:"))
num.test_range(a,b,n)
```

Output

```
Enter a lower limit:12
Enter an Upper limit:50
Enter a number:65
The number is outside the given range.
```

3. **Write a Python function to calculate the number of upper case letters and lower case letters in a string. Import the module to calculate the number of upper case letters and lower case letters from a string input by the user.**

Program

```
CountUpperLower.py
def string_test(s):
    d={"UPPER_CASE":0, "LOWER_CASE":0}
    for c in s:
      if c.isupper():
          d["UPPER_CASE"]+=1
      elif c.islower():
          d["LOWER_CASE"]+=1
```

```
    print("No:of Upper Case letters:",d["UPPER_CASE"])
    print("No:of Lower Case letters:",d["LOWER_CASE"])
#Main Program importing the module
import CountUpperLower as cul
s=input("Enter a String:")
cul.string_test(s)
```

Output

```
Enter a String:PYTHON Programming
No:of Upper Case letters: 6
No:of Lower Case letters: 11
```

4. **Write a Python function that takes a list and returns a new list with unique elements of the first list. Import the module and input a list to find the unique elements in a list.**

Program

UniqueList.py

```
def unique_list(l):
  x = []
  for a in l:
    if a not in x:
      x.append(a)
  return x

#Main Program importing the module
import UniqueList as ul
lis=input("Enter a list(space separated):")
lis1=list(lis.split())
print("Original List:",lis1)
print("Unique List:",ul.unique_list(lis1))
```

Output

```
Enter a list(space separated):1 2 3 1 4 2 6
Original List: ['1', '2', '3', '1', '4', '2', '6']
Unique List: ['1', '2', '3', '4', '6']
```

5. **Write a Python function that checks whether a passed string is palindrome or not. Import the module to find whether a string is palindrome.**

Program

```
PalindromeCheck.py
 def isPalindrome(string):
```

```
PalindromeCheck.py
 def isPalindrome(string):
    if string == string[::-1]:
        return True
    else:
        return False

#Main Program importing the module
from PalindromeCheck import isPalindrome
str1=input("Enter a String:")
f=isPalindrome(str1)
if f:
    print("The string ",str1," is a palindrome")
else:
    print("The string ",str1," is not a palindrome")
```

Output

```
Enter a String:malayalam
The string malayalam is a palindrome
```

6. **Write a Python function that that prints out the first n rows of the Pascal's triangle. Import the module and accept n from the user.**

Program

```
Pascal.py
def pascal_triangle(n):
   trow = [1]
   y = [0]
   for x in range(max(n,0)):
      print(trow)
      trow=[l+r for l,r in zip(trow+y, y+trow)]
   return n>=1

#Main Program importing the module
import Pascal as p
n=int(input("Enter a limit:"))
p.pascal_triangle(n)
```

Output

```
Enter a limit:7
[1]
```

```
[1, 1]
[1, 2, 1]
[1, 3, 3, 1]
[1, 4, 6, 4, 1]
[1, 5, 10, 10, 5, 1]
[1, 6, 15, 20, 15, 6, 1]
```

7. **Write a Python function to check whether a string is pangram or not. Pangrams are words or sentences containing every letter of the alphabet at least once. For example: "The quick brown fox jumps over the lazy dog". Import the package to see whether the input string is a pangram or not.**

Program

```
Pangram.py
import string, sys
def ispangram(str1, alphabet=string.ascii_lowercase):
    alphaset = set(alphabet)
    return alphaset <= set(str1.lower())

#Main Program importing the module
import Pack.Pangram as p
str1=input("Enter a String:")
print("The String",str1, "is a Pangram:",p.ispangram(str1))
```

Output

```
Enter a String:The quick brown fox jumps over the lazy dog
The String The quick brown fox jumps over the lazy dog is a
Pangram: True
```

8. **Write a Python function to create and print a list where the values are square of numbers between two limits (both included).Import the package to implement this.**

Program

```
SquaresOfNum.py
  def printValues(a,b):
     l = list()
     for i in range(a,b+1):
            l.append(i**2)
     print(l)

#Main Program importing the module
import Pack.SquaresOfNum as sqn
a=int(input("Enter the lower limit:"))
```

```
b=int(input("Enter the upper limit:"))
sqn.printValues(a,b)
```

Output

```
Enter the lower limit:1
Enter the upper limit:5
[1, 4, 9, 16, 25]
```

9. Write a function in file Armstrong.py to check whether a number is an Armstrong number. Import the module to generate Armstrong numbers between two limits.

```
Armstrong.py
#Function to Check Whether a Number is an Armstrong Number
def arm(n):
    num=0
    n1=n
    while n!=0:
        rem=n%10
        num+=rem*rem*rem
        n=n//10
    if num == n1: return True
    else : return False
```

Program

```
import Armstrong
l1=int(input("Enter lower limit: "))
l2= int(input("Enter upper limit:"))
print("Armstrong Numbers")
for i in range(l1, l2+1):
if Armstrong.arm(i): print(i)
```

Output

```
Enter lower limit: 1
Enter upper limit:500
Armstrong Numbers
1 153 370 371 407
```

10. Write a Python function to check whether a number is prime. Import the module to find the prime numbers between 2 limits.

```
PrimeNum.py
import math
#Function to check whether a number is prime
```

```
def prime(n):
  for j in range(2,int(math.sqrt(n))+1):
    if n%j==0:break
  else: return True
```

Program

```
import PrimeNum
m = int(input("Enter Lower Limit:"))
n = int(input("Enter Upper Limit:"))
print("Prime Numbers")
for i in range(m,n+1):
if PrimeNum.prime(i): print(i)
```

Output

```
Enter Lower Limit:5
Enter Upper Limit:19
Prime Numbers
5
7
11
13
17
19
```

11. The aliquot of a number is defined as: the sum of the proper of the number. For example, the aliquot(12) = 1 + 2 + 3 + 4 + 6 = 16. Write a function that returns the aliquot number of a given number. Import the module to find the aliquot of a number.

```
Aliquot.py
#Function to find the aliquot of a number
def aliquot(n):
  sum=0
  for i in range(1,n):
    if n%i==0: sum+=i
  return sum
```

Program

```
import Aliquot
num=int(input("Enter an integer:"))
print("Sum of all factors of",num,"is", Aliquot.aliquot(num))
```

Output

```
Enter an integer:12
Sum of all factors of 12 is 16
```

12. A pair of numbers (a, b) is said to be amicable if the aliquot number of a is b and the aliquot number of b is a. Example: 220, 284 Write a Program that prints all four digit amicable pairs between 1000 and 3000.

```
Amicable.py

#Program to find amicable pairs
import Aliquot as a
def amicable(m,n):
 if a.aliquot(m)==n and a.aliquot(n)==m:return True
 else: return False
```

Program

```
import Amicable as am
for i in range(1000,3000):
    for j in range(1000,i):
        if am.amicable(i,j):print(i,j)
```

Output

```
1210 1184
2924 2620
```

13. Write a Python script to display a) Current date and time, b) Current year, c) Month of year, d) Week number of the year, e) Weekday of the week, f) Day of year, g) Day of the month and h) Day of week.

Program

```
import time
import datetime
print("Current date and time: " , datetime.datetime.now())
print("Current year: ", datetime.date.today().strftime("%Y"))
print("Month of year: ", datetime.date.today().strftime("%B"))
print("Week number of the year: ", datetime.date.today().
strftime("%W"))
print("Weekday of the week: ", datetime.date.today().
strftime("%w"))
print("Day of year: ", datetime.date.today().strftime("%j"))
print("Day of the month : ", datetime.date.today().
strftime("%d"))
print("Day of week: ", datetime.date.today().strftime("%A"))
```

Output

```
Current date and time:  2015-11-23 10:25:53.149892
Current year:  2015
Month of year:  November
Week number of the year:  47
Weekday of the week:  1
Day of year:  327
Day of the month :  23
Day of week:  Monday
```

14. Write a Python program to determine whether a given year is a leap year.

Program

```
import calendar
def leap_year(y):
  if calendar.isleap(y):
      print(y,"is a leap year")
  else:
      print(y,"is not a leap year")
#Main program
y=int(input("Enter a year:"))
leap_year(y)
```

Output

```
Enter a Year:2004
2004 is a leap year: True
```

15. Write a Python program to convert a string to datetime.

Program

```
from datetime import datetime
str1=input("Enter a date and time:")
date_object = datetime.strptime(str1, '%b %d %Y %I:%M%p')
print(date_object)
```

Output

```
Enter a date and time:Nov 11 2015 12:00PM
2015-11-11 12:00:00
```

16. Write a Python program to get current time in Python.

Program

```
import datetime
print(datetime.datetime.now().time())
```

Output

```
10:41:38.283794
```

17. **Write a Python program to subtract five days from current date.**

Program

```
from datetime import date, timedelta
dt = date.today() - timedelta(5)
print('Current Date :',date.today())
print('5 days before Current Date :',dt)
```

Output

```
Current Date : 2015-11-23
5 days before Current Date : 2015-11-18
```

18. **Write a Python program to print yesterday, today, tomorrow.**

Program

```
import datetime
today = datetime.date.today()
yesterday = today - datetime.timedelta(days = 1)
tomorrow = today + datetime.timedelta(days = 1)
print('Yesterday : ',yesterday)
print('Today : ',today)
print('Tomorrow : ',tomorrow)
```

Output

```
Yesterday :  2015-11-22
Today :  2015-11-23
Tomorrow :  2015-11-24
```

19. **Write a Python program to print next 5 days starting from today.**

Program

```
import datetime
base = datetime.datetime.today()
for x in range(0, 5):
print(base + datetime.timedelta(days=x))
```

Output

```
2015-11-23 10:52:13.534924
2015-11-24 10:52:13.534924
2015-11-25 10:52:13.534924
2015-11-26 10:52:13.534924
2015-11-27 10:52:13.534924
```

20. **Write a Python program to add 5 seconds with current time.**

Program

```
import datetime
x= datetime.datetime.now()
y = x + datetime.timedelta(0,5)
print(x.time())
print(y.time())
```

Output

```
10:54:48.197057
10:54:53.197057
```

21. **Write a Python program to convert Year/Month/Day to Day of Year in Python.**

Program

```
import datetime
today = datetime.datetime.now()
day_of_year = (today - datetime.datetime(today.year, 1, 1)).days
+ 1
print(day_of_year)
```

Output

```
327
```

22. **Write a Python program to get current time in milliseconds in Python.**

Program

```
import time
milli_sec = int(round(time.time() * 1000))
print("Current time in milliseconds:",milli_sec)
```

Output

```
Current time in milliseconds: 1448256694588
```

23. **Write a Python program to get days between two dates.**

Program

```
from datetime import date
a = date(2014,2,28)
b = date(2015,2,28)
print(b-a)
```

Output

```
365 days, 0:00:00
```

7.11 Conclusion

This Chapter explains the concept of modules, built-in modules, how to import modules, various import statements for importing modules, how to locate modules, the importance of PYTHONPATH variable, namespaces and scope. The functions dir() and reload() is illustrated with examples. Another important concept called packages are covered with the import statements and examples. This Chapter also covers built-in modules like time, calendar, datetime with the built-in functions.

7.12 Review Questions

1. What is a module?
2. What are built-in modules? Give examples.
3. How will you create a user-defined module?
4. What is the purpose of import statement?
5. Explain various import statements in Python.
6. How a module is located in Python?
7. Explain the PYTHONPATH variable.
8. Explain the dir() function.
9. What is the purpose of reload() function?
10. Write short notes on namespace and scope of variables in Python.
11. Briefly explain the concept of packages with an example.
12. What is the importance of lib directory in Python?
13. What is the purpose of _init_.py in a Python package?
14. Write short notes on time module.
15. What is timedelta?
16. Write short notes on Calender module.
17. What are the functions available in datetime module?

08 File Handling

CONTENTS

File is a named location on disk to store related information. It is used to permanently store data in a non-volatile memory (e.g. hard disk). Since, random access memory (RAM) is volatile which loses its data when computer is turned off, we use files for future use of the data.

When we want to read from or write to a file we need to open it first. When we are done, it needs to be closed, so that resources that are tied with the file are freed. Hence, in Python, a file operation takes place in the following order.

a. Open a file
b. Read or write (perform operation)
c. Close the file

We have been reading and writing to the standard input and output. Now, we will see how to use actual data files. Python provides basic functions and methods necessary to manipulate files by default. We can do most of the file manipulation using a file object.

8.1 Opening a File

Before we can read or write a file, we have to open it using Python's built-in open() function. This function returns a file object, also called a handle, as it is used to read or modify the file accordingly.

We can specify the mode while opening a file. In mode, we specify whether we want to read 'r', write 'w' or append 'a' to the file. We also specify if we want to open the file in text mode or binary mode. The default is reading in text mode. In this mode, we get strings when reading from the file. On the other hand, binary mode returns bytes and this is the mode to be used when dealing with non-text files like image or exe files. The following shows the syntax for opening a file.

Syntax

```
file object = open(filename [, accessmode][, buffering])
```

The following gives the explanation of the parameters for opening a file.

`filename`: The `filename` argument is a string value that contains the name of the file that we want to access.

`accessmode`: The `accessmode` determines the mode in which the file has to be opened, i.e., read, write, append, etc. A complete list of possible values is given below in Section 8.1.1. This is optional parameter and the default file access mode is read (r).

`buffering`: If the buffering value is set to 0, no buffering takes place. If the buffering value is 1, line buffering is performed while accessing a file. If we specify the buffering value as an integer greater than 1, then buffering action is performed with the indicated buffer size. If negative, the buffer size is the system default. This is also an optional parameter.

Example

```
f = open("abc.txt",'r')      # open file in current directory
f = open("C:/Python34/sample.txt",'r')# specifying full path
```

In the above example, the file `abc.txt` is opened in the current working directory in read mode and `sample.txt` is opened in read mode inside `C:\Python34` folder.

8.1.1 Modes for Opening a File

1. `'r'` - Opens a file for reading only. The file pointer is placed at the beginning of the file. This is the default mode.
2. `'rb'` - Opens a file for reading only in binary format. The file pointer is placed at the beginning of the file.
3. `'r+'` - Opens a file for both reading and writing. The file pointer is placed at the beginning of the file.
4. `'rb+'` - Opens a file for both reading and writing in binary format. The file pointer is placed at the beginning of the file.
5. `'w'` - Opens a file for writing only. Overwrites the file if the file exists. If the file does not exist, creates a new file for writing.
6. `'wb'` - Opens a file for writing only in binary format. Overwrites the file if the file exists. If the file does not exist, creates a new file for writing.

7. `'w+'` - Opens a file for both writing and reading. Overwrites the existing file if the file exists. If the file does not exist, creates a new file for reading and writing.
8. `'wb+'` - Opens a file for both writing and reading in binary format. Overwrites the existing file if the file exists. If the file does not exist, creates a new file for reading and writing.
9. `'a'` - Opens a file for appending. The file pointer is at the end of the file if the file exists. That is, the file is in the append mode. If the file does not exist, it creates a new file for writing.
10. `'ab'` - Opens a file for appending in binary format. The file pointer is at the end of the file if the file exists. That is, the file is in the append mode. If the file does not exist, it creates a new file for writing.
11. `'a+'` - Opens a file for both appending and reading. The file pointer is at the end of the file if the file exists. The file opens in the append mode. If the file does not exist, it creates a new file for reading and writing.
12. `'ab+'` - Opens a file for both appending and reading in binary format. The file pointer is at the end of the file if the file exists. The file opens in the append mode. If the file does not exist, it creates a new file for reading and writing.
13. `'x'` - Open a file for exclusive creation. If the file already exists, the operation fails.

Since the version 3.x, Python has made a clear distinction between `str` (text) and `bytes` (8-bits). Unlike other languages, the character 'a' does not imply the number 97 until it is encoded using ASCII (or other equivalent encodings). Hence, when working with files in text mode, it is recommended to specify the encoding type. Files are stored in bytes in the disk, we need to decode them into `str` when we read into Python. Similarly, encoding is performed while writing texts to the file.

The default encoding is platform dependent. In Windows, it is `'cp1252'` but `'utf-8'` in Linux. Hence, we must not rely on the default encoding otherwise, our code will behave differently in different platforms. Thus, this is the preferred way to open a file for reading in text mode.

```
f = open("abc.txt", mode = 'r', encoding = 'utf-8')
```

8.1.2 Attributes of *file* object

Once a file is opened, we have one file object, we can get various information related to that file. The following shows various attributes for the file object.

1. file.closed - Returns True if file is closed, False otherwise.
2. file. mode - Returns access mode with which file was opened.
3. file.name - Returns name of the file.
4. file.softspace – Returns 0 if space is explicitly required with print, or 1 otherwise.

The following example shows the working of the above described attributes of file object.

Example Program

```
#Demo of file object attribute in Python
fo = open("abc.txt", "w")
print("Name of the file:", fo.name)
print("Closed or not:", fo.closed)
```

```
print("Opening mode:", fo.mode)
print("Softspace flag:", fo.softspace)
```

Output

```
Name of the file:  abc.txt
Closed or not: False
Opening mode: w
Softspace flag:0
```

8.2 Closing a File

When we have finished the operations to a file, we need to properly close it. Python has a garbage collector to clean up unreferenced objects. But we must not rely on it to close the file. Closing a file will free up the resources that were tied with the file and is done using the `close()` method. The following shows the syntax for closing a file.

Syntax

```
fileObject.close()
```

Example Program

```
# Open a file for writing in binary format
fo = open("bin.txt", "wb")
print("Name of the file: ", fo.name)
# Close opened file
fo.close()
print("File Closed")
```

Output

```
Name of the file:  bin.txt
File Closed
```

8.3 Writing to a File

In order to write into a file we need to open it in write 'w', append 'a' or exclusive creation 'x' mode. We need to be careful with the 'w' mode as it will overwrite into the file if it already exists. All previous data will be erased.

Writing a string or sequence of bytes (for binary files) is done using `write()` method. This method returns the number of characters written to the file. The `write()` method does not add a newline character ('\n') to the end of the string. The following shows the syntax of `write()` method.

Syntax

```
fileObject.write(string)
```

Here, passed parameter `string` is the content to be written into the opened file.

Example Program

```
# Open a file in writing mode
fo = open("test.txt", "w")
fo.write("Programming with Python is Fun.\nLet's try
Python!\n");
# Close opened file
fo.close()
print("File", fo.name, "closed.")
```

Output

```
File test.txt closed.
```

In the above program, we have opened a file `test.txt` in writing mode. The string to be written is passed to the `write()` method. This file is opened to see the contents in the example given in Section 8.4.

8.4 Reading from a File

To read the content of a file, we must open the file in reading mode. The `read()` method reads a string from an open file. It is important to note that Python strings can have binary data, apart from text data. The following gives the syntax for reading from a file.

Syntax

```
fileObject.read([size])
```

Here, the passed parameter size is the number of bytes to be read from the opened file. This method starts reading from the beginning of the file and if size is missing, then it tries to read as much as possible, maybe until the end of file. The following example shows how to read from the file test.txt which we have already created.

Example Program

```
# Open a file in read mode
fo = open("test.txt", "r")
str = fo.read(11)
print("String Read is : ", str)
# Close opened file
fo.close()
print("File", fo.name, "is closed.")
```

Output

```
String Read is: Programming
File test.txt is closed.
```

8.5 File Methods

1. file.close() – This method is already explained in Section 8.2.
2. file.fileno() - Returns an integer number (file descriptor) of the file.

   Example Program

```
# Example for fileno() in File Handling
fo=open("abc.txt","w")
str="Python Programming"
fo.write(str)
print("The file number is:",fo.fileno())
fo.close()
```

   Output

```
The file number is: 3
```

3. file.seek(offset,from=SEEK_SET)- Change the file position to offset bytes, in reference to from (start, current, end).
4. file.tell() – Returns the current file location.

   Example Program

```
#Demo Program for seek and tell
# Creating a file
str="Python Programming is fun"
fo=open("test.txt","w")
fo.write(str)
fo.close()
fo = open("test.txt", "r+")
s = fo.read(10);
print("Read String is : ", s)
# Check current position
pos = fo.tell();
print("Current file position : ", pos)
# Reposition pointer at the beginning once again
pos = fo.seek(0, 0);
s = fo.read(10);
print("Again read String is : ", s)
# Close opened file
fo.close()
```

5. file.write() – This method is already explained in Section 8.3.
6. file.read() – This method is already explained in Section 8.4.

7. file.readline()-The method readline() reads one entire line from the file. A trailing newline character is kept in the string. An empty string is returned only when EOF is encountered immediately.
8. file.truncate([size] - The method truncate() truncates the file's size. If the optional size argument is present, the file is truncated to (atmost) that size.

   Example Program

```
# Open a file
fo = open("test.txt", "r+")
line = fo.readline()
print("Read Line:",line)
# Now truncate remaining file.
fo.truncate()
# Try to read file now
line = fo.readline()
print("Read Line: ",line)
# Close opened file
fo.close()
```

   Output

```
Read Line: Python Programming is fun
Read Line:
```

9. file.readlines([sizeint]) - The method readlines() reads until EOF using readline() and returns a list containing the lines. sizeint is an optional argument and if it is present, instead of reading up to EOF, whole lines approximate to sizeint bytes are read. An empty string is returned only when EOF is encountered immediately.
10. file.writelines(sequence) - The method writelines() writes a sequence of strings to the file. The sequence can be any iterable object containing strings, typically a list of strings. There is no return value.

    Example Program

```
# Open a file in write mode
fo = open("Demo.txt", "w")
seq=["First Line\n", "Second Line\n", "Third Line\n", "Fourth
Line\n", "Fifth Line\n"]
fo.writelines(seq)
#close the file
fo.close()
#Open the file in read mode
fo = open("Demo.txt", "r")
line = fo.readlines()
```

```
print("readlines():", line)
line= fo.readlines(2)
print("readlines(2):",line)
# Close opened file
fo.close()
```

Output

```
readlines(): ['First Line\n', 'Second Line\n', 'Third Line\n',
'Fourth Line\n', 'Fifth Line\n']
readlines(2): []
```

8.6 Renaming a File

The os module Python provides methods that help to perform file-processing operations, such as renaming and deleting files. To use this os module, we need to import it first and then we can call any related functions. To rename an existing file, we can use the rename() method. This method takes two arguments, current filename and new filename. The following shows the syntax for rename() method.

Syntax

```
os.rename(current_file_name, new_file_name)
```

Example Program

```
import os
# Rename a file from test.txt to Newtest.txt
os.rename( "test.txt", "Newtest.txt" )
print("File renamed.")
```

Output

```
File renamed.
```

8.7 Deleting a File

We can delete a file by using the remove() method available in os module. This method receives one argument which is the filename to be deleted. The following gives the syntax for remove() method.

Syntax

```
os.remove(filename)
```

Example Program

```
import os
# Delete a file
os.remove("Newtest.txt")
print("File Deleted.")
```

Output

```
File Deleted.
```

8.8 Directories in Python

All files will be saved in various directories, and Python has efficient methods for handling directories and files. The os module has several methods that help to create, remove and change directories.

8.8.1 mkdir() method

The mkdir() method of the `os` module is used to create directories in the current directory. We need to supply an argument to this method which contains the name of the directory to be created. The following shows the syntax of `mkdir()` method.

Syntax

```
os.mkdir("dirname")
```

Example

```
import os
# Create a directory "Fruits"
os.mkdir("Fruits")
```

The above example creates a directory named `Fruits`.

8.8.2 chdir() method

To change the current directory, we can use the `chdir()` method. The `chdir()` method takes an argument, which is the name of the directory that we want to make the current directory. The following shows the syntax of `chdir()` method.

Syntax

```
os.chdir("dirname")
```

Example

```
import os
# Change a directory
os.chdir("/home/abc")
```

The above example goes to the directory `/home/abc`.

8.8.3 getcwd() method

The `getcwd()` method displays the current working directory. The following shows the syntax of `getcwd()` method.

Syntax

```
os.getcwd()
```

Example

```
import os
# Displays the location of current directory
os.getcwd()
```

8.8.4 rmdir() method

The rmdir() method deletes the directory, which is passed as an argument in the method.

Syntax

```
os.rmdir("dirname")
```

Example

```
import os
# Removes the directory
os.rmdir("Fruits")
```

It is intended to give the exact path of a directory. Otherwise it will search the current working directory.

8.9 Solved Lab Exercises

1. Write a program to copy a text file to another file.

Program

```
# Open the file to be copied in read mode
file1=input("Enter the source file to be copied:")
file2=input("Enter the destination file name:")
fr=open(file1, "r")
# Open a file to be copied in write mode
fw=open(file2, "w")
for line in fr.readlines():
    fw.write(line)
#close the files
fr.close()

fw.close()
print("1 File Copied")
```

Output

```
1 File Copied
```

2. Program to count the number of lines in a file.

Program

```
fr=open("Demo.txt", "r")
countlines=0
for line in fr.readlines():
    countlines=countlines+1
print("Number of Lines:",countlines)
#close the file
fr.close()
```

Output

```
Number of Lines: 2
```

3. **Write a program to count the frequencies of each word from a file.**

Program

```
# Open the file to be read in read mode
fr=open("Demo.txt","r")
wordcount={}
for word in fr.read().split():
    if word not in wordcount:
        wordcount[word] = 1
    else:
        wordcount[word] += 1
for k,v in wordcount.items():
    print(k, v)
#close the file
fr.close()
```

Output

```
Handling 1
easy 1
Python 2
is 2
Programming 1
File 1
fun 1
```

4. **Write a program to append a file with the contents of another file.**

Program

```
file1=input("Enter the file to be opened for appending:")
file2=input("Enter the file name to be appended:")
```

```
# Open the file to in append mode
fa=open(file1, "a")
# Open a file in read mode
fr=open(file2, "r")
for line in fr.readlines():
    fa.write(line)
#close the files
fr.close()
fa.close()
print("1 File Appended")
```

Output

```
Enter the file to be opened for appending:TruncateDemoCopy.py
Enter the file name to be appended:TruncateDemo.py
1 File Appended
```

5. **Write a program, that counts the number of times the first three letters of the alphabet (A, a, B, b, C, c) occur in a file. Do not distinguish between the lowercase and uppercase letters.**

Program

```
file1=input("Enter the file to be opened :")
# Open the file in read mode
fr=open(file1, "r")
counta,countb,countc=0,0,0
for ch in fr.readlines():
 counta=counta+(ch.count('A',0,len(ch))or
ch.count('a',0,len(ch)))
 countb=countb+(ch.count('B',0,len(ch)) or
ch.count('b',0,len(ch)))
 countc=countc+(ch.count('C',0,len(ch)) or
ch.count('c',0,len(ch)))
#close the file
fr.close()
print("Number of occurences of 'A' or 'a'=",counta)
print("Number of occurencesof 'B' or 'b'=",countb)
print("Number of occurences of 'C' or 'c'=",countc)
```

Output

```
Enter the file to be opened :test.txt
Number of occurences of 'A' or 'a'= 3
Number of occurencesof 'B' or 'b'= 2
Number of occurences of 'C' or 'c'= 3
```

6. **Write a program to compare two files.**

Program

```
import filecmp
file1=input("Enter the first file to be compared:")
file2=input("Enter the second file to be compared:")
b=filecmp.cmp(file1,file2)
if b: print("Files are equal")
else: print("Files are not equal")
```

Output

```
Enter the first file to be compared:test.txt
Enter the second file to be compared:test1.txt
Files are equal
```

7. **Write a program to delete a sentence from the specified position in a file.**

Program

```
#Program to delete a sentence from a specified position from a
file
def filedel(n):
  with open(str,'r') as file :
   lis = file.readlines()
   file.close()
   print(lis)
   del lis[n]
   print(lis)
  with open(str,'w') as file:
   file.writelines(lis)
   file.close()
#main Program
str=input("Enter the filename:")
n=int(input("Enter the position of the word to be deleted:"))
filedel(n)
print("Sentence Deletion Successful")
```

Output

```
Enter the filename:abc.txt
Enter the position of the word to be deleted:1
['Python Programming is Fun\n', 'Learning Python is Fun\n',
'Welcome to python\n', 'Guido van Rossum\n', 'Open Source']
```

```
['Python Programming is Fun\n', 'Welcome to python\n', 'Guido
van Rossum\n', 'Open Source']
File Deletion Successful
```

8. Write a program to delete the sentences from a file, if the file contains a specific word.

Program

```
#Program for deleting the line if the line contains a particular
word
import os
def fileDEL(str,word):
   file = open(str,"r")
   newfile = open("new.txt","w")
   while True:
      line = file.readline()
      if not line :
       break
      elif word in line :
       pass
      else :
       print(line)
       newfile.write(line)
   file.close()
   newfile.close()
   os.remove(str)
   os.rename("new.txt",str)
#main Program
str=input("Enter the name of the file:")
word=input("Enter the word:")
fileDEL(str,word)
```

Output

```
Enter the name of the file:abc.txt
Enter the word:fun
Learn Python
```

9. Write a program to delete comment lines (lines beginning with a #) from a file.

Program

```
#Program for deleting comment lines or lines beginning with a #
import os
def fileDEL(str):
```

```
    file = open(str,"r")
    newfile = open("new.txt","w")
    while True:
        line = file.readline()
        if not line :
         break
        elif line.startswith('#',0,len(line)):
         pass
        else :
         newfile.write(line)
    file.close()
    newfile.close()
    os.remove(str)
    os.rename("new.txt",str)
#Main Program
str=input("Enter the name of the file:")
fileDEL(str)
print("Lines beginning with # deleted")
```

Output

```
Enter the name of the file:abc.txt
Lines beginning with # deleted
```

10. Write a Python function to capitalize each word in a file.

Program

```
#Program for deleting the line if the line contains a particular
word
import os
def fileCapitalize(str):
    file = open(str,"r")
    newfile = open("new.txt","w")
    while True:
        line = file.readline()
        if not line :
         break
        else :
         newfile.write(line.title())
    file.close()
    newfile.close()
```

```
    os.remove(str)
    os.rename("new.txt",str)
#main Program
str=input("Enter the name of the file:")
fileCapitalize(str)
print("File Capitalized")
```

Output

```
Enter the name of the file:abc.txt
File Capitalized
```

11. **Write a Python program to search a word and replace with another word for all the occurrences.**

Program

```
#Program for deleting the line if the line contains a particular
word
import os
def fileSearchandReplace(str,oldword,newword):
    file = open(str,"r")
    newfile = open("new.txt","w")
    while True:
        line = file.readline()
        if not line :
         break
        else :
         newfile.write(line.replace(oldword,newword))
    file.close()
    newfile.close()
    os.remove(str)
    os.rename("new.txt",str)
#main Program
str=input("Enter the name of the file:")
oldword=input("Enter the word to be replaced:")
newword=input("Enter the new word:")
fileSearchandReplace(str,oldword,newword)
print("Replacements Successful")
```

Output

```
Enter the name of the file:abc.txt
Enter the word to be replaced:Is
```

```
Enter the new word:was
Replacements Successful
```

12. **Write a Python program to insert a sentence into a specified position in a file.**

Program

```
#Program to insert a sentence in a specified position in a file
def fileinsert(str,n,line):
    with open(str,'r') as file :
     lis = file.readlines()
     lis.insert(n,line)
     lis.insert(n+1,'\n')
     file.close()
     print(lis)

    with open(str,'w') as file:
     file.writelines(lis)
     print(lis)
     file.close()
#main Program
str=input("Enter the filename:")
n=int(input("Enter the position of the sentence to be
inserted:"))
line=input("Enter the Sentence to be inserted:")
fileinsert(str,n,line)
print("Sentence Insertion Successful")
```

Output

```
Enter the filename:abc.txt
Enter the position of the sentence to be inserted:1
Enter the Sentence to be inserted:Python Program
['Why Python\n', 'Python Program', '\n', 'Python is fun\n',
'Guido van Rossum']
['Why Python\n', 'Python Program', '\n', 'Python is fun\n',
'Guido van Rossum']
Sentence Insertion Successful
```

13. **Write a program to read a file in reverse order. The last sentence should be read first and continue till the first sentence is read.**

Program

```
#Program to read a file and display contents backwards
```

```
def filebackward(str):
  with open(str,'r') as file :
    lis = file.readlines()
    lis.reverse()
    file.close()
    print(lis)
    for line in lis:
     print(line)
#main Program
str=input("Enter the filename:")
filebackward(str)
```

Output

```
Enter the filename:abc.txt
['Guido van Rossum', 'Python is fun\n', 'Python Program\n', 'Why
Python\n']
Guido van Rossum
Python is fun
Python Program
Why Python
```

8.10 Conclusion

This Chapter covers the concepts of file handling which covers how to open a file, different modes of opening a file, how to close a file, how to read and write data to files, various built-in methods available in file handling, how to rename and delete a file. This Chapter also covers various directory methods like mkdir(), chdir(), getcwd and rmdir() methods available in Python.

8.11 Review Questions

1. Briefly explain various modes for opening a file.
2. What are the various attributes for a file object?
3. Explain the built-in methods available in Python for file handling.
4. How will you rename a file in Python?
5. How will you delete a file in Python?
6. Briefly explain the various methods available in Python for processing directories.
7. Explain the seek() and tell() method in Python.
8. What is the purpose of truncate() method in Python?
9. Explain readline(), readlines() and writelines() method in Python.
10. Explain the methods fileno() and filename() with examples.

09 Object Oriented Programming

CONTENTS

Object Oriented Programming is a powerful method for creating programs. So far we have discussed the procedural concepts in programming. Before going into Object Oriented Programming (OOPs), we need to understand the basic terminologies used in Object Oriented Programming. While procedure oriented programming gives importance to functions, Object Oriented Programming focuses on objects. A class is the base of Object Oriented Programming.

A class contains a collection of data (variables) and methods (functions) that act on those data. Class is considered as a blueprint for an object. For example consider the design of a house with details of windows, doors, roofs and floors. We can build the house based on the descriptions. This can be considered as a class while the object is the house itself. An object is said to be an instance of a class and the process of creating a class is called instantiation. The basic concepts related to OOP are as follows:

1. Classes
2. Objects
3. Encapsulation
4. Data Hiding
5. Inheritance
6. Polymorphism

Advantages of Object Oriented Programming

Object Oriented Programming has following advantages:

- **Simplicity:** The objects in case of OOP are close to the real world objects, so the complexity of the program is reduced making the program structure very clear and simple. For example by looking at the class Student, we can simply identify with the properties and behavior of a student. This makes the class Student very simple and easy to understand.
- **Modifiability:** It is easy to make minor changes in the data representation or the procedures in an OOP. Changes inside a class do not affect any other part of a program, since the only public interface that the external world has to a class is through the use of methods.
- **Extensibility and Maintainability:** It is quite easy to add new features and extend the program in case of Object Oriented Programming. It can be simply done by introducing a few new objects and modifying some existing ones. The original base class need not be modified at all. Even objects can be maintained separately, there by making locating and fixing problems easier. For example if a new attribute of the class Student needs to be added, a new derived class of the class Student may be created and no other class in the class hierarchy need to be modified.
- **Re-usability:** Objects can be reused in different programs. The class definitions can be reused in various applications. Inheritance makes it possible to define subclasses of data objects that share some or all of the main class characteristics. It forces a more thorough data analysis, reduces development time and ensures more accurate coding.
- **Security:** Since a class defines only the data it needs to be concerned with, when an instance of that class (an object) is run, the code will not be able to accidentally access other program data. This characteristic of data hiding provides greater system security and avoids unintended data corruption.

9.1 Class Definition

The class definition in Python begins with the keyword class. The first statement after class definition will be the docstring which gives a brief description about the class. The following shows the syntax for defining a class.

Syntax

```
class ClassName:
    'Optional class documentation string'
    class_suite
```

A class creates a new local namespace where all its attributes are defined. Attributes may be data or functions. There are also special attributes in it that begins with double underscores (__). For example, __doc__ gives us the docstring of that class. As soon as we define a class, a new class object is created with the same name. This class object allows us to access the different attributes as well as to instantiate new objects of that class.

Example Program

```
class Student:
 "Common base class for all students"
 studentcount = 0
 def __init__(self, rollno,name,course):
     self.rollno=rollno
     self.name = name
     self.course = course
     Student.studentcount += 1
 def displayCount(self):
     print("Total Students=", Student.studentcount)
 def displayStudent(self):
     print("Roll Number:", self.rollno)
     print("Name: ", self.name)
     print("Course: ", self.course)
```

In the above program, we have created a class called Student. The variable `studentcount` is a class variable whose value is shared among all instances of this class. This can be accessed from inside the class or outside the class by giving `Student.studentcount`.

The first method __init__() is a special method, which is called class constructor or initialization method that Python calls when we create a new instance of this class.

Class methods have only one specific difference from ordinary functions - they must have an extra argument in the beginning of the parameter list. This particular argument is `self` which is used for referring to the instance. But we need not give any value for this parameter when we call the method. Python provides it automatically. `self` is not a reserved word in Python but just a strong naming convention and it is always convenient to use conventional names as it makes the program more readable. So while defining our class methods, we must explicitly list `self` as the first argument for each method, including __init__.

It also implies that if we have a method which takes no arguments, then we still have to define the method to have a `self` argument. `Self` is an instance identifier and is required so that the statements within the methods can have automatic access to the current instance attributes.

9.2 Creating Objects

An object is created by calling the class name with the arguments defined in the _init_ method. We can access a method by using the dot operator along with the object. Similarly a class name can be accessed by specifying the method name with the dot operator with the class.

Example Program

```
# First student object is created
stud1=Student(10, "Jack", "MS")
# Second student object is created.
stud2=Student(20, "Jill", "BE")
# Displays the details of First Student
stud1.displayStudent()
# Displays the details of Second Student.
stud2.displayStudent()
print("Total Number of Students:", Student.studentcount)
```

When the above code is executed, it produces the following result.

```
Roll Number: 10
Name:  Jack
Course:  MS
Roll Number: 20
Name:  Jill
Course:  BE
Total Number of Students: 2
```

9.3 Built-in Attribute Methods

There are built-in functions to access the attributes. We can access the attribute value, check whether an attribute exists or not, modify an attribute value or delete an attribute. The following gives the built-in attribute methods.

1. getattr(obj, name[, default]) : This method is used to access the attribute of object.
2. hasattr(obj,name) : This attribute is used to check if an attribute exists or not.
3. setattr(obj,name,value) : This method is used to set an attribute. If attribute does not exist, then it would be created.
4. delattr(obj, name) : This method is used to delete an attribute.

Example Program

```
  class Student:
  "Common base class for all students"
 def __init__(self, rollno,name,course):
      self.rollno=rollno
      self.name = name
      self.course = course
 def displayStudent(self):
     print("Roll Number:", self.rollno)
```

```
        print("Name: ", self.name)
        print("Course: ", self.course)
stud1=Student(10, "Jack", "MS")
stud1.displayStudent()
at=getattr(stud1,'name')
print("getattr(stud1,'name'):",at)
print("hasattr(stud1,age):" , hasattr(stud1,'age'))
#New attribute inserted
print("setattr(stud1,age,21):",setattr(stud1, 'age', 21))
stud1.displayStudent()
print("Age:", stud1.age)
# Attribute age deleted
print("delattr(stud1,age):", delattr(stud1, 'age'))
stud1.displayStudent()
```

Output

```
Roll Number: 10
Name:  Jack
Course:  MS
getattr(stud1,'name'): Jack
hasattr(stud1,age): False
setattr(stud1,age,21): None
Roll Number: 10
Name:  Jack
Course:  MS
Age: 21
delattr(stud1,age): None
Roll Number: 10
Name:  Jack
Course:  MS
```

9.4 Built-in Class Attributes

Python contains several built-in class attributes. These attributes are accessed using the dot operator. The following gives the list of built-in class attributes.

1. __dict__: This attribute contains the dictionary containing the class's namespace.
2. __doc__: It describes the class or it contains the class documentation string. If undefined, it contains None.
3. __name__: This attribute contains the class name.

4. __module__: This contains the module name in which the class is defined. This attribute is "__main__" in interactive mode.
5. __bases__: This contains an empty tuple containing the base classes, in the order of their occurrence in the base class list.

The following program shows the usage of built-in class attributes.

Example Program

```
class Student:
 "Common base class for all students"
 def __init__(self, rollno,name,course):
       self.rollno=rollno
       self.name = name
       self.course = course
 def displayStudent(self):
      print("Roll Number:", self.rollno)
      print("Name: ", self.name)
      print("Course: ", self.course)
stud1=Student(10, "Jack", "MS")
stud1.displayStudent()
print("Student.__doc__:", Student.__doc__)
print("Student.__name__:", Student.__name__)
print("Student.__module__:", Student.__module__)
print("Student.__bases__:", Student.__bases__)
print("Student.__dict__:", Student.__dict__)
```

Output

```
Roll Number: 10
Name:  Jack
Course:  MS
Student.__doc__: Common base class for all students
Student.__name__: Student
Student.__module__: __main__
Student.__bases__: ()
Student.__dict__: {'displayStudent': <function displayStudent at
0x7efdcc047758>, '__module__': '__main__', '__doc__': 'Common ba
se class for all students', '__init__': <function __init__ at
0x7efdcc0476e0>}
```

9.5 Destructors in Python

Python automatically deletes an object that is no longer in use. This automatic destroying of objects is known as garbage collection. Python periodically performs the garbage collection to free the blocks off memory that are no longer in use. But a class can implement the special method __del__(), called a destructor, that is invoked when the instance is about to be destroyed. This method might be used to clean up any non memory resources used by an instance. The following program shows the destructors in Python.

Example Program

```
class Student:
  "Common base class for all students"
  def __init__(self, rollno,name,course):
      self.rollno=rollno
      self.name = name
      self.course = course
  def displayStudent(self):
      print("Roll Number:", self.rollno)
      print("Name: ", self.name)
      print("Course: ", self.course)
  def __del__(self):
      class_name = self.__class__.__name__
      print(class_name, "destroyed")
stud1=Student(10, "Jack", "MS")
stud1.displayStudent()
del stud1
```

Output

```
Roll Number: 10
Name:  Jack
Course:  MS
Student destroyed
```

9.6 Encapsulation

Encapsulation is the most basic concept of OOP. It is the combining of data and the functions associated with that data in a single unit. In most of the languages including Python, this unit is called a class. In simple terms we can say that encapsulation is implemented through classes. In fact the data members of a class can be accessed through its member functions only. It keeps the data safe from any external interference and misuse. The only way to access the data is through the functions of the class. In the example of the class Student, the class encapsulates the data (rollno, name, course) and the associated functions into a single independent unit.

9.7 Data Hiding

We can hide data in Python. For this we need to prefix double underscore for an attribute. Data hiding can be defined as the mechanism of hiding the data of a class from the outside world or to be precise, from other classes. This is done to protect the data from any accidental or intentional access. In most of the Object Oriented Programming languages, encapsulation is implemented through classes. In a class, data may be made private or public. Private data or function of a class cannot be accessed from outside the class while public data or functions can be accessed from anywhere. So data hiding is achieved by making the members of the class private. Access to private members is restricted and is only available to the member functions of the same class. However the public part of the object is accessible outside the class. Once the attributes are prefixed with the double underscore, it will not be visible outside the class. The following program shows an example for data hiding in Python.

Example Program

```
class HidingDemo:
 "Program for Hiding Data"
 __num=0
 def numbercount(self):
     self.__num+=1
     print("Number Count=", self.__num)
number=HidingDemo()
number.numbercount()
print(number.__num)
```

Output

```
Number Count= 1
Traceback (most recent call last):
  File "main.py", line 9, in <module>
    print number.__num
AttributeError: HidingDemo instance has no attribute '__num'
```

The output shows that numbercount is displayed once. When it is attempted to call the variable number.__num from outside the function, it resulted in an error.

9.8 Inheritance

The mechanism of deriving a new class from an old class is known as inheritance. The old class is known as base class or super class or parent class. The new one is called the subclass or derived class or child class. Inheritance allows subclasses to inherit all the variables and methods to their parent class. The advantage of inheritance is the reusability of code. Fig. 9.1 illustrates the single inheritance. The attributes and methods of parent class will be available in child class after inheritance.

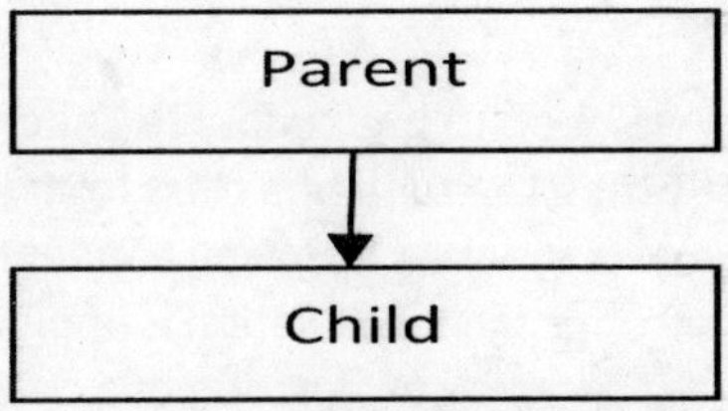

Fig. 9.1: Single Inheritance

9.8.1 Deriving a Child Class

The following shows the syntax for deriving a child class in Python.

Syntax

```
class SubClassName (ParentClass1[, ParentClass2, ...]):
    'Optional class documentation string'
class_suite
```

The following program shows an example for single inheritance.

Example Program

```
class Student:
 "Common base class for all students"
 def getData(self,rollno,name,course):
       self.rollno=rollno
       self.name = name
        self.course = course
 def displayStudent(self):
      print("Roll Number:", self.rollno)
      print("Name:", self.name)
      print("Course:", self.course)
 #Inheritance
class Test(Student):
 def getMarks(self, marks):
    self.marks=marks
 def displayMarks(self):
    print("Total Marks:", self.marks)
r = int(input("Enter Roll Number:"))
n = input("Enter Name:")
c = input("Enter Course Name:")
m = int(input("Enter Marks:"))
```

```
#creating the object
print("Result")
stud1=Test()#instance of child
stud1.getData(r,n,c)
stud1.getMarks(m)
stud1.displayStudent()
stud1.displayMarks()
```

Output

```
Enter Roll Number:20
Enter Name:Smith
Enter Course Name:MS
Enter Marks:200
Result
Roll Number: 20
Name: Smith
Course: MS
Total Marks: 200
```

9.8.2 Multilevel Inheritance

We have already discussed the mechanism of deriving a new class from one parent class. We can further inherit the derived class to form a new child class. Inheritance which involves more than one parent class but at different levels is called multilevel inheritance. Figure 9.2 illustrates multilevel inheritance.

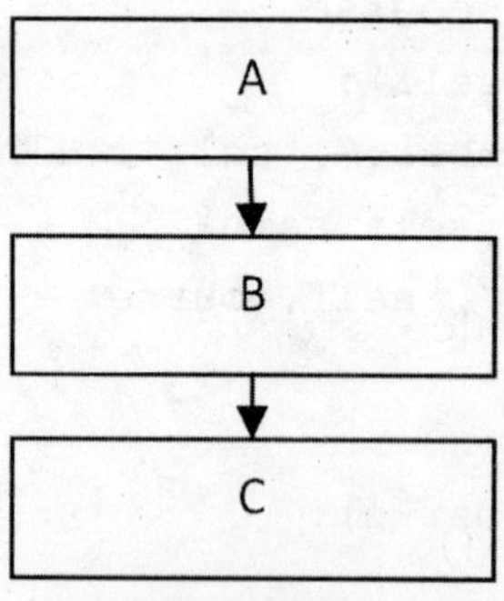

Fig. 9.2: Multilevel Inheritance

Here B is derived from A. Hence all attributes and methods that are available in A is now available in B also. C is derived from B. Hence all methods and attributes of B and A is now available in C. The following program shows an example for multilevel inheritance.

Example Program

```
def displayStudent(self):
    print("Roll Number:", self.rollno)
    print("Name:", self.name)
    print("Course:", self.course)
 #Inheritance
class Test(Student):
 def getMarks(self, marks):
   self.marks=marks
 def displayMarks(self):
   print("Total Marks:", self.marks)
#Multilevel Inheritance
class Result(Test):
 def calculateGrade(self):
   if self.marks>480: self.grade="Distinction"
   elif self.marks>360: self.grade="First Class"
   elif self.marks>240: self.grade="Second Class"
   else: self.grade="Failed"
   print("Result:", self.grade)
#Main Program
r = int(input("Enter Roll Number:"))
n = input("Enter Name:")
c = input("Enter Course Name:")
m = int(input("Enter Marks:"))
#creating the object
print("Result")
stud1=Result()#instance of child
stud1.getData(r,n,c)
stud1.getMarks(m)
stud1.displayStudent()
stud1.displayMarks()
stud1.calculateGrade()
```

Output

```
Enter Roll Number:12
Enter Name:Jones
Enter Course Name:MS
```

```
Enter Marks:400
Result
Roll Number: 12
Name: Jones
Course: MS
Total Marks: 400
Result: First Class
```

9.8.3 Multiple Inheritance

It is possible to inherit from more than one parent class. Such type of inheritance is called multiple inheritance. In this case all the attributes and methods of both the parent class will be available in the child class after inheritance. Fig 9.3 illustrates multiple inheritance.

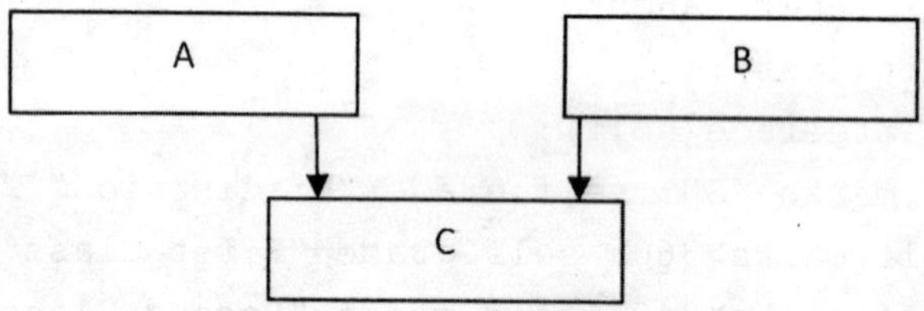

Fig. 9.3: Multiple Inheritance

Here A and B are the parent classes and C is the child class. The attributes and methods of both classes A and B are now available in C after inheritance.

Example Program

```
class Student:
 "Common base class for all students"
 def getData(self,rollno,name,course):
      self.rollno=rollno
      self.name = name
      self.course = course
 def displayStudent(self):
     print("Roll Number:", self.rollno)
     print("Name:", self.name)
     print("Course:", self.course)
 #Inheritance
class Test(Student):
 def getMarks(self, marks):
   self.marks=marks
 def displayMarks(self):
```

```
    print("Total Marks:", self.marks)
class Sports:
  def getSportsMarks(self, spmarks):
    self.spmarks=spmarks
  def displaySportsMarks(self):
    print("Sports Marks:", self.spmarks)

#Multiple Inheritance
class Result(Test,Sports):
  def calculateGrade(self):
    m=self.marks+self.spmarks
    if m>480: self.grade="Distinction"
    elif m>360: self.grade="First Class"
    elif m>240: self.grade="Second Class"
    else: self.grade="Failed"
    print("Result:", self.grade)
#Main Program
r = int(input("Enter Roll Number:"))
n = input("Enter Name:")
c = input("Enter Course Name:")
m = int(input("Enter Marks:"))
s = int(input("Enter Sports marks:"))
#creating the object
print("Result")
stud1=Result()#instance of child
stud1.getData(r,n,c)
stud1.getMarks(m)
stud1.getSportsMarks(s)
stud1.displayStudent()
stud1.displayMarks()
stud1.displaySportsMarks()
stud1.calculateGrade()
```

Output

```
Enter Roll Number:10
Enter Name:Bob
Enter Course Name:MS
Enter Marks:190
```

```
Enter Sports marks:200
Result
Roll Number: 10
Name: Bob
Course: MS
Total Marks: 190
Sports Marks: 200
Result: First Class
```

9.8.4 Invoking the Base Class Constructor

In the above examples of inheritance, we have used member functions. Instead we can use constructors to pass value to the objects. In Python the constructor of the base class can be invoked by extending __init__ ().

The class Student and class Teacher both have __init__ () method. The __init__ () method is defined in class Student and Teacher is extended in class School. In Python, name of the base class can also be used to access the method of the base class which has been extended in derived class.

Example Program

```
class Student(object):
 def __init__(self,Id,name):
  self.Id=Id
  self.name=name
 def showStudent(self):
  print("Id number of the Student:",self.Id)
  print("Name of the Student:",self.name)
class Teacher(object):
 def __init__(self,tec_Id,tec_name, subject):
  self.tec_Id=tec_Id
  self.tec_name=tec_name
  self.subject=subject
 def showTeacher(self):
  print("Id of the Teacher:",self. tec_Id)
  print("Name of the Teacher:",self.tec_name)
  print("Subject:",self.subject)
class School(Student,Teacher):
  def __init__(self, ID, name, tec_Id, tec_name, subject, sch_
Id):
   Student.__init__ (self,ID,name)
   Teacher. __init__(self,tec_Id,tec_name, subject)
```

```
    self.sch_Id= sch_Id
   def showSchool(self):
    print("Id of the School:",self.sch_Id)
#main Program
sc=School(10,"Jones",100,"Jack","Math",80)
sc.showStudent()
sc.showTeacher()
sc.showSchool()
```

Output

```
Id number of the Student: 10
Name of the Student: Jones
Id of the Teacher: 100
Name of the Teacher: Jack
Subject: Math
Id of the School: 80
```

9.9 Method Overriding

Polymorphism is an important characteristic of Object Oriented Programming language. In Object-Oriented Programming, polymorphism refers to a programming language's ability to process objects differently depending on their data type or class. More specifically, it is the ability to redefine methods for derived classes. We can override methods in the parent class.

Method overriding is required when we want to define our own functionality in the child class. This is possible by defining a method in the child class that has the same name, same arguments and same return type as a method in the parent class. When this method is called, the method defined in the child class is invoked and executed instead of the one in the parent class. The following shows an example program for method overriding.

Example Program

```
class Parent:
 "Base class"
 def __init__(self,name):
       self.name = name
 def displayName(self):
      print("Name: ", self.name)
 def __del__(self):
      class_name = self.__class__.__name__
      print(class_name, "destroyed")
class Child(Parent):
 def __init__(self,name,address):
```

```
            self.name = name
            self.address= address
      def displayName(self):
            print("Name: ", self.name)
            print("Address:",self.address)
      def __del__(self):
            class_name = self.__class__.__name__
            print(class_name, "destroyed")
#Main Program
n=input("Enter Name:")
a=input("Enter Address:")
obj=Child(n,a)#instance of child
obj.displayName() #Calling child's method
del obj
```

Output

```
Enter Name:Jill
Enter Address:Klos
Name:  Jill
Address: Klos
Child destroyed
```

In the above program, even though there are two methods with the same name displayName() is available in child class, the method in the child class will be invoked. The method in the child class has overridden the method in the parent class.

The following shows some generic functionality that can be overriden.

```
1__init__ ( self [,args...] )
Constructor (with any optional arguments)
Sample Call : obj = className(args)
2__del__( self )
Destructor, deletes an object
Sample Call : del obj
3__repr__( self )
Evaluatable string representation
Sample Call : repr(obj)
4__str__( self )
Printable string representation
Sample Call : str(obj)
5__cmp__ ( self, x )
```

```
Object comparison
Sample Call : cmp(obj, x)
```

9.10 Polymorphism

The word polymorphism is formed from two words - poly and morph where poly means many and morph means forms. So polymorphism is the ability to use an operator or function in various forms. That is a single function or an operator behaves differently depending upon the data provided to them. Polymorphism can be achieved in two ways: operator overloading and function overloading. Unlike in C++ and Java, Python does not support function or method overloading.

9.10.1 Operator Overloading

Operator overloading is one of the important features of Object Oriented Programming. C++ and Python supports operator overloading, while Java does not support operator overloading. The mechanism of giving special meanings to an operator is known as operator overloading. For example the operator '+' is used for adding two numbers. In Python this operator can also be used for concatenating two strings. This '+' operator can be used for adding member variables of two different class. The following example shows how '+' operator can be overloaded.

Example Program

```
class Abc:
    def __init__(self, a, b):
        self.a = a
        self.b = b
    def __str__(self):
        return "Abc (%d, %d)" % (self.a, self.b)
    def __add__(self,other):
        return Abc(self.a + other.a, self.b + other.b)
a1 = Abc(2,4)
a2 = Abc(5,-2)
print(a1 + a2)
```

Output

```
Abc (7, 2)
```

9.11 Solved Lab Exercises

1. Write a Python class to convert an integer to a roman numeral.

   Program

```
class py_solution:
def int_to_Roman(self, num):
    val = [
```

```
                1000, 900, 500, 400,
                100, 90, 50, 40,
                10, 9, 5, 4,
                1
                ]
            syb = [
                "M", "CM", "D", "CD",
                "C", "XC", "L", "XL",
                "X", "IX", "V", "IV",
                "I"
                ]
            roman_num = ''
            num1=num
            i = 0
            while  num > 0:
                for _ in range(num // val[i]):
                    roman_num += syb[i]
                    num -= val[i]
                i += 1
            print("Roman Numeral of",num1,"is", roman_num)
#Main Program
n=int(input("Enter an integer:"))
obj=py_solution()
obj.int_to_Roman(n)
```

Output

```
Enter an integer:10
Roman Numeral of 10 is X
```

2. **Write a Python class to convert a roman numeral to an integer.**

Program

```
class pyth_solution:
def roman_to_int(self, s):
rom_val = {'I': 1, 'V': 5, 'X': 10, 'L': 50, 'C': 100, 'D': 500,
'M': 1000}
            int_val = 0
            for i in range(len(s)):
                if i > 0 and rom_val[s[i]] > rom_val[s[i - 1]]:
                    int_val += rom_val[s[i]] - 2 * rom_val[s[i - 1]]
```

```
            else:
                int_val += rom_val[s[i]]
        return int_val
#Main Program for object creation
r=input("Enter a roman numeral:")
obj=pyth_solution()
print("The decimal number equivalent of",r,"is",obj.roman_to_
int(r))
```

Output

```
Enter a roman numeral:XV
The decimal number equivalent of XV is 15
```

3. **Write a program to find the area and perimeter of a rectangle using classes and objects.**

Program

```
class Rectangle:
 def getData(self,length,breadth):
     self.length=length
     self.breadth=breadth
 def area(self):
     a=self.length*self.breadth
     print("Area of rectangle with length",self.length,"and
breadth",self.breadth, "is",a)
 def perimeter(self):
     p=2*(self.length+self.breadth)
     print("Perimeter of rectangle with length",self.length,"and
breadth",self.breadth, "is",p)
#main Program
ch=0
l=int(input("Enter Length of a Rectangle:"))
b=int(input("Enter Breadth of a Rectangle:"))
obj=Rectangle()
obj.getData(l,b)
while  ch!=3:
    print("1.Area")
    print("2.Perimeter")
    print("3.Exit")
    ch=int(input("Enter your choice:"))
    if ch==1:obj.area()
```

```
        if ch==2:obj.perimeter()
    else: print("End of the Program")
```

Output

```
Enter Length of a Rectangle:12
Enter Breadth of a Rectangle:3
1.Area
2.Perimeter
3.Exit
Enter your choice:1
Area of rectangle with length 12 and breadth 3 is 36
1.Area
2.Perimeter
3.Exit
Enter your choice:2
Perimeter of rectangle with length 12 and breadth 3 is 30
1.Area
2.Perimeter
3.Exit
Enter your choice:3
End of the Program
```

4. **Define a class to represent a bank account. Include the following details like name of the depositor, account number, type of account, balance amount in the account. Write methods to assign initial values, to deposit an amount, withdraw an amount after checking the balance, to display name, account number, account type and balance.**

Program

```
class Customer:
  "Common base class for all Customers"
  def getData(self,name,accno,acctype,balance):
        self.name=name
        self.accno=accno
        self.acctype=acctype
        self.balance=balance
  def displayCustomer(self):
        print("Customer Name:", self.name)
        print("Account Number:", self.accno)
        print("Account Type:", self.acctype)
        print("Balance amount:", self.balance)
```

```
    def deposit(self,amount):
        self.balance=self.balance+amount
    def withdrawal(self,amount):
        if self.balance-amount<0: print("Insufficient Funds")
        else: self.balance=self.balance-amount
#Main Program
ch=0
while  ch!=5:
    print("1.New Customer")
    print("2.Deposit")
    print("3.Withdrawal")
    print("4.Display")
    print("5.Exit")
    ch=int(input("Enter your choice:"))
    if ch==1:
        obj=Customer()
        n=input("Enter Name:")
        no=int(input("Enter Account Number:"))
        t=input("Enter Account Type(SB/C):")
        b=int(input("Enter the Amount:"))
        obj.getData(n,no,t,b)
    if ch==2:
        b=int(input("Enter the amount to be deposited:"))
        obj.deposit(b)
    if ch==3:
        b=int(input("Enter the amount to be withdrawn:"))
        obj.withdrawal(b)
    if ch==4:
        obj.displayCustomer()
else:print("Program Terminated")
```

Output

```
1.New Customer
2.Deposit
3.Withdrawal
4.Display
5.Exit
Enter your choice:1
```

```
Enter Name:Jith
Enter Account Number:123
Enter Account Type(SB/C):SB
Enter the Amount:100
1.New Customer
2.Deposit
3.Withdrawal
4.Display
5.Exit
Enter your choice:2
Enter the amount to be deposited:100
1.New Customer
2.Deposit
3.Withdrawal
4.Display
5.Exit
Enter your choice:3
Enter the amount to be withdrawn:250
Insufficient Funds
1.New Customer
2.Deposit
3.Withdrawal
4.Display
5.Exit
Enter your choice:4
Customer Name: Jith
Account Number: 123
Account Type: SB
Balance amount: 200
1.New Customer
2.Deposit
3.Withdrawal
4.Display
5.Exit
Enter your choice:5
Program Terminated
```

5. Write a program to implement the following. Create a base class called Person consisting of name and code. Create 2 child classes a) Account with member_ pay and b) Admin with experience and

inherit the base class. Create a class Employee with name, code, experience and pay by inheriting the above classes.

Program

```
class Person:
    def getPerson(self,name,code):
        self.name=name
        self.code=code
    def displayPerson(self):
        print("Name:",self.name)
        print("Code:",self.code)
class Account(Person):
    def getAccount(self,pay):
        self.pay=pay
    def displayAccount(self):
        print("Payment:",self.pay)
class Admin(Person):
    def getAdmin(self,exp):
        self.exp=exp
    def displayAdmin(self):
        print("Experience:",self.exp)
class Employee(Account,Admin):
    print("New Final Class")
n=input("Enter Name:")
c=input("Enter Code:")
p=int(input("Enter payment:"))
e=input("Enter experience:")
obj=Employee()
obj.getPerson(n,c)
obj.getAccount(p)
obj.getAdmin(e)
obj.displayPerson()
obj.displayAccount()
obj.displayAdmin()
```

Output

```
New Final Class
Enter Name:jons
Enter Code:101
```

```
Enter payment:100000
Enter experience:3
Name:jons
Code:101
Payment:10000
Experience:3
```

6. **Create a class called Staff with code and name. Create classes Teacher(subject, publication),Typist(speed),Officer(grade). Using the typist class as base class, create 2 classes Regular(salary) and Casual(daily wages). Implement a menu driven program for the same.**

Program

```
class Staff:
    def getStaff(self,code,name):
        self.code=code
        self.name=name
    def displayStaff(self):
        print("Code:",self.code)
        print("Name:",self.name)
class Teacher(Staff):
    def getTeacher(self,subject,pub):
        self.subject=subject
        self.pub=pub
    def displayTeacher(self):
        print("Subject:",self.subject)
        print("Publication:",self.pub)
class Typist(Staff):
    def getTypist(self,speed):
        self.speed=speed
    def displayTypist(self):
        print("Speed of Typing:",self.speed)
class Officer(Staff):
    def getOfficer(self,grade):
        self.grade=grade
    def displayOfficer(self):
        print("Grade of Officer:",self.grade)
class Regular(Typist):
    def getRegular(self,salary):
        self.salary=salary
```

```
    def displayRegular(self):
        print("Salary of Regular Typist:",self.salary)
class Casual(Typist):
    def getCasual(self,wages):
        self.wages=wages
    def displayCasual(self):
        print("Wages of Casual Typist:",self.wages)
#Main Program
ch=0
while  ch!=5:
    print("1.Teacher")
    print("2.Officer")
    print("3.Regular Typist")
    print("4.Casual Typist")
    print("5.Exit")
    ch=int(input("Enter your choice:"))
    if ch==1:
        obj=Teacher()
        c=input("Enter the code:")
        n=input("Enter Name:")
        s=input("Enter Subject:")
        p=input("Enter Publication:")
        obj.getStaff(c,n)
        obj.getTeacher(s,p)
        obj.displayStaff()
        obj.displayTeacher()
    if ch==2:
        obj=Officer()
        c=input("Enter the code:")
        n=input("Enter Name:")
        g=input("Enter the Grade:")
        obj.getStaff(c,n)
        obj.getOfficer(g)
        obj.displayStaff()
        obj.displayOfficer()
    if ch==3:
        obj=Regular()
```

```
            c=input("Enter the code:")
            n=input("Enter Name:")
            sp=input("Enter the speed:")
            sal=input("Enter the salary:")
            obj.getStaff(c,n)
            obj.getTypist(sp)
            obj.getRegular(sal)
            obj.displayStaff()
            obj.displayTypist()
            obj.displayRegular()
        if ch==4:
            obj=Casual()
            c=input("Enter the code:")
            n=input("Enter Name:")
            sp=input("Enter the speed:")
            w=input("Enter the daily wages:")
            obj.getStaff(c,n)
            obj.getTypist(sp)
            obj.getCasual(w)
            obj.displayStaff()
            obj.displayTypist()
            obj.displayCasual()
    else:print("Program Terminated")
```

Output

```
1.Teacher
2.Officer
3.Regular Typist
4.Casual Typist
5.Exit
Enter your choice:1
Enter the code:100
Enter Name:Smith
Enter Subject:Science
Enter Publication:Wiley
Code: 100
Name: Smith
Subject: Science
```

```
Publication: Wiley
1.Teacher
2.Officer
3.Regular Typist
4.Casual Typist
5.Exit
Enter your choice:2
Enter the code:156
Enter Name:John
Enter the Grade:First
Code: 156
Name: John
Grade of Officer: First
1.Teacher
2.Officer
3.Regular Typist
4.Casual Typist
5.Exit
Enter your choice:3
Enter the code:210
Enter Name:Jack
Enter the speed:200
Enter the salary:2000
Code: 210
Name: Jack
Speed of Typing: 200
Salary of Regular Typist: 2000
1.Teacher
2.Officer
3.Regular Typist
4.Casual Typist
5.Exit
Enter your choice:4
Enter the code:406
Enter Name:Jill
Enter the speed:180
Enter the daily wages:180
```

```
Code: 406
Name: Jill
Speed of Typing: 180
Wages of Casual Typist: 180
1.Teacher
2.Officer
3.Regular Typist
4.Casual Typist
5.Exit
Enter your choice:5
Program Terminated
```

9.12 Conclusion

This Chapter covers the Object Oriented Programming concepts, creation of classes, instantiation of objects, constructors, methods, destructors and characteristics of OOPs like data hiding, method overriding, operator overloading and inheritance.

9.13 Review Questions

1. Explain the concept of class and objects in Python.
2. Explain constructors with an example.
3. What are destructors in Python?
4. What is data hiding?
5. Explain method overriding with an example.
6. What is operator overloading?
7. Explain single inheritance with an example.
8. Explain multiple inheritance with an example.
9. Write short notes on built-in attribute methods.
10. Explain built-in class attributes.
11. What are the advantages of Object Oriented Programming?

10 Exception Handling

CONTENTS

An exception is an abnormal condition that is caused by a runtime error in the program. It disturbs the normal flow of the program. An example for an exception is division by 0. When a Python script encounters a situation that it cannot deal with, it raises an exception. An exception is a Python object that represents an error.

If the exception object is not caught and handled properly, the interpreter will display an error message. If we want the program to continue with the execution of the remaining code, then we should try to catch the exception object thrown by the error condition and then display appropriate messages for taking corrective actions. This task is known as exception handling.

10.1 Built-in Exceptions

Python has a collection of built-in exception classes. If the runtime error belongs to any of the pre-defined built-in exception, it will throw the object of the appropriate exception. The following Table 10.1 gives a detailed explanation of built-in exceptions and the situation in which they are invoked.

Table 10.1: Built-in Exceptions

Exception Name	When it is raised
AssertionError	Raised in case of failure of the Assert statement.
AttributeError	Raised in case of failure of attribute reference or assignment.

Exception Name	When it is raised
EnvironmentError	Base class for all exceptions that occur outside the Python environment.
EOFError	Raised when there is no input from either the raw_input() or input() function and the end of file is reached.
Exception	Base class for all exceptions
ImportError	Raised when an import statement fails.
IndentationError	Raised when indentation is not specified properly.
IndexError	Raised when an index is not found in a sequence.
IOError	Raised when an input/ output operation fails, such as the print statement or the open() function when trying to open a file that does not exist.
KeyboardInterrupt	Raised when the user interrupts Program execution, usually by pressing Ctrl+c.
KeyError	Raised when the specified key is not found in the dictionary.
LookupError	Base class for all lookup errors.
NameError	Raised when an identifier is not found in the local or global namespace.
NotImplementedError	Raised when an abstract method that needs to be implemented in an inherited class is not actually implemented.
OSError	Raised for operating system-related errors.
RuntimeError	Raised when a generated error does not fall into any category.
SyntaxError	Raised when there is an error in Python syntax.
SystemError	Raised when the interpreter finds an internal problem, but when this error is encountered the Python interpreter does not exit.
SystemExit	Raised when Python interpreter is quit by using the sys.exit() function. If not handled in the code, causes the interpreter to exit.
TypeError	Raised when an operation or function is attempted that is invalid for the specified data type.
UnboundLocalError	Raised when trying to access a local variable in a function or method but no value has been assigned to it.
ValueError	Raised when the built-in function for a data type has the valid type of arguments, but the arguments have invalid values specified.
ArithmeticError	Base class for all errors that occur for numeric calculation.
AssertionError	Raised in case of failure of the Assert statement
AttributeError	Raised in case of failure of attribute reference or assignment.
Exception	Base class for all exceptions
EOFError	Raised when there is no input from either the raw_input() or input() function and the end of file is reached.
EnvironmentError	Base class for all exceptions that occur outside the Python environment.
FloatingPointError	Raised when a floating point calculation fails.

Exception Name	When it is raised
IndentationError	Raised when indentation is not specified properly.
ImportError	Raised when an import statement fails.
IndexError	Raised when an index is not found in a sequence.
IOError	Raised when an input/ output operation fails, such as the print statement or the open() function when trying to open a file that does not exist.
KeyboardInterrupt	Raised when the user interrupts Program execution, usually by pressing Ctrl+c.
NameError	Raised when an identifier is not found in the local or global namespace.
NotImplementedError	Raised when an abstract method that needs to be implemented in an inherited class is not actually implemented.
OverflowError	Raised when a calculation exceeds maximum limit for a numeric type.
OSError	Raised for operating system-related errors.
RuntimeError	Raised when a generated error does not fall into any category.
StopIteration	Raised when the next() method of an iterator does not point to any object.
SystemExit	Raised by the sys.exit() function.
StandardError	Base class for all built-in exceptions except StopIteration and SystemExit.
SyntaxError	Raised when there is an error in Python syntax.
SystemError	Raised when the interpreter finds an internal problem, but when this error is encountered the Python interpreter does not exit.
SystemExit	Raised when Python interpreter is quit by using the sys.exit() function. If not handled in the code, causes the interpreter to exit.
TypeError	Raised when an operation or function is attempted that is invalid for the specified data type.
UnboundLocalError	Raised when trying to access a local variable in a function or method but no value has been assigned to it.
ValueError	Raised when the built-in function for a data type has the valid type of arguments, but the arguments have invalid values specified.
ZeroDivisonError	Raised when division or modulo by zero takes place for all numeric types.

10.2 Handling Exceptions

Python uses a keyword `try` to prepare a block of code that is likely to cause an error and throw an exception. An `except` block is defined which catches the exception thrown by the `try` block and handles it. The `try` block can have one or more statements that could generate an exception. If anyone statement generates an exception, then the remaining statements in the block are skipped and execution jumps to the `except` block that is placed next to the `try` block.

The `except` block can have more than one statement and if the except parameter matches with the type of the exception object, then the exception is caught and statements in the `except` block will be executed. Every `try` block should be followed by atleast one `except` statement.

10.2.1 try.... except

The following gives the syntax of try....except statement.

Syntax

```
try:
   suite

except Exception1:
   Exception1_suite#Executes when Exception1 occurs.

except Exception2:
   Exception2_suite#Executes when Exception2 occurs.


else:
   else_suite #Executes if there is no exception in the try
block.
```

When an exception occurs inside a try block, it will go to the corresponding except block. If no exception is raised inside a try block then after the try block, the statements in the else block is executed. The else block can also be considered a place to put the code that does not raise any exception.

Example Program 1

```
#Exception Handling
try:
    a=int(input("First Number:"))
    b=int(input("Second Number:"))
    result=a/b
    print("Result=",result)
except ZeroDivisionError:
    print("Division by Zero")
else:
    print("Successful Division")
```

Output

```
First Number:10
Second Number:0
Division by Zero
```

In the above example, the second number is 0. Since division by zero is not possible, an exception is thrown and the execution goes to the except block. All the rest of the statements is bypassed in the try block. Hence the output is displayed as Division by Zero.

Example Program 2

```
#Exception Handling
try:
    a=int(input("First Number:"))
    b=int(input("Second Number:"))
    result=a/b
    print("Result=",result)
except ZeroDivisionError:
    print("Division by Zero")
else:
    print("Successful Division")
```

Output

```
First Number:20
Second Number:10
Result= 2
Successful Division
```

In the above example exception is not thrown and hence all the statements in the `try` block is executed. After executing the `try` block, the control passes on to the `else` block. Hence the print statement in the `else` block is executed.

10.2.2 except clause with no Exception

We can use except statement with no exceptions. This kind of try-except statement catches all the exceptions. Since it catches all the exceptions, it will not help the programmer to exactly identify what is the cause for the error occurred. Hence it is not considered as a good programming practice. The following shows the syntax for except clause with no exception.

Syntax

```
try:
    suite

except:
    Exception_suite #Executes when whatever Exception occurs.

else:
    else_suite #Executes if there is no exception in the try
block.
```

Example Program

```
#Exception Handling
try:
    a=int(input("First Number:"))
    b=int(input("Second Number:"))
    result=a/b
    print("Result=",result)
except:
    print("Error Occured")
else:
    print("Successful Division")
```

Output

```
First Number: 2
Second Number: 0
Error Occurred
```

10.2.3 except clause with multiple Exceptions

This is used when we want to give multiple exceptions in one `except` statement. The following shows the syntax of the `except` clause with multiple exceptions.

Syntax

```
try:
   suite

except(Exception1[, Exception2[,...ExceptionN]]]):

   Exception_suite #Executes when whatever Exception specified
occurs.

else:
   else_suite #Executes if there is no exception in the try
block.
```

Example Program

```
#Exception Handling
try:
    a=int(input("First Number:"))
    b=int(input("Second Number:"))
    result=a/b
    print("Result=",result)
except(ZeroDivisionError,TypeError):
    print("Error Occured")
```

```
else:
    print("Successful Division")
```

Output

```
First Number:10
Second Number:0
Error Occurred
```

10.2.4 try...finally

A finally block can be used with a `try` block. The code placed in the `finally` block is executed no matter exception is caused or caught. We cannot use `except` clause and `finally` clause together with a `try` block. It is also not possible to use `else` clause and `finally` together with a `try` block. The following gives the syntax for a `try...finally` block.

Syntax

```
try:
    suite

finally:
    finally_suite #Executed always after the try block.
```

Example Program 1

```
#Exception Handling
try:
    a=int(input("First Number:"))
    b=int(input("Second Number:"))
    result=a/b
    print("Result=",result)
finally:
    print("Executed Always")
```

Output

```
First Number:20
Second Number:0
Executed Always
Traceback (most recent call last):
  File "main.py", line 5, in <module>
    result=a/b
ZeroDivisionError: integer division or modulo by zero
```

In the above example, an error occurred in the try block. It is caught by the Python's error handling mechanism. But the statement in the finally block is executed even though an error has occurred.

Example Program 2

```
#Exception Handling
try:
    a=int(input("First Number:"))
    b=int(input("Second Number:"))
    result=a/b
    print("Result=",result)
finally:
    print("Executed Always")
```

Output

```
First Number:10
Second Number:5
Result= 2
Executed Always
```

In the above example there was no exception thrown. Hence after the try block, the finally block is executed.

10.3 Exception with Arguments

It is possible to have exception with arguments. An argument is a value that gives additional information about the problem. This variable receives the value of the exception mostly containing the cause of the exception. The variable can receive a single value or multiple values in the form of a tuple. This tuple usually contains the error string, the error number and an error location. The syntax of exception with arguments is as follows.

Syntax

```
try:
   suite

except ExceptionType, argument:
   except_suite #Executed when exception occurs.
```

Example Program

```
def display(a):
  try:
          return int(a)
  except ValueError,argument1:
print("Argument does not contain numbers", argument1)
#Function Call
display("a")
```

Output

```
Argument does not contain numbers invalid literal for int() with
base 10: 'a'
```

In the above example, the function `display` is called with string arguments. But the actual function is defined with integer parameter. Hence an exception is thrown and it is caught by the `except` clause.

10.4 Raising an Exception

We have discussed about raising built-in exceptions. It is also possible to define a new exception and raise it if needed. This is done using the `raise` statement. The following shows the syntax of `raise` statement. An exception can be a string, a class or an object. Most of the exceptions that the Python raises are classes, with an argument that is an instance of the class. This is equivalent to `throw` clause in Java.

Syntax

```
raise [Exception [, argument [, traceback]]]
```

Here, Exception is the type of exception (for example, IOError) and `argument` is a value for the exception argument. This argument is optional. The exception argument is `None` if we does not supply any argument. The argument, `traceback`, is also optional. If this is used, then the `traceback` object is used for the exception. This is rarely used in programming.

In order to catch the exception defined using the `raise` statement, we need to use the `except` clause which is already discussed. The following code shows how an exception defined using the `raise` statement can be used.

Example Program

```
# Raising an Exception
a=int(input("Enter the parameter value:"))
try:
  if a<=0:
    raise  ValueError("Not a Positive Integer")
except ValueError as err:
    print(err)
else:print("Positive Integer=",a)
```

Output

```
Enter the parameter value:-9
Not a Positive Integer
```

10.5 User-defined Exception

Python also allows us to create our own exceptions by deriving classes from the standard built-in exceptions. In the try block, the user-defined exception is raised and caught in the except block. This is useful when we need to provide more specific information when an exception is caught. The following shows an example for user-defined exception.

Example Program

```
# define Python user-defined exceptions
class Error(Exception):
   """Base class for other exceptions"""
   pass
class ValueTooSmallError(Error):
   """Raised when the input value is too small"""
   pass
class ValueTooLargeError(Error):
   """Raised when the input value is too large"""
   pass
# Main Program
number = 10
while True:
   try:
      i_num = int(input("Enter a number: "))
      if i_num < number:
         raise ValueTooSmallError
      elif i_num > number:
         raise ValueTooLargeError
      break
   except ValueTooSmallError:
      print("This value is too small, try again!")
   except ValueTooLargeError:
      print("This value is too large, try again!")
print("Congratulations! You guessed it correctly.")
```

Output

```
Enter a number: 13
This value is too large, try again!
Enter a number: 9
This value is too small, try again!
Enter a number: 10
Congratulations! You guessed it correctly.
```

Here, we have defined a base class called Error. The other two exceptions (ValueTooSmallError and ValueTooLargeError) that are actually raised by our program are derived from this class. This is the standard way to define user-defined exceptions in Python programming, but you are not limited to this way only.

10.6 Assertions in Python

An assertion is a checking in Python that can be turned on or off while testing a program. In assertion, an expression is tested and if the result is false, an exception is raised. Assertions are done using the assert statement. The application of assertion is to check for a valid input or for a valid output. The following shows the syntax for assert statement.

When Python interpreter encounters an assertion statement, it evaluates the accompanying expression. If the expression is evaluated to `False`, Python raises an AssertionError exception. AssertionError exceptions can be caught and handled like any other exception using the `try-except` statement, but if not handled, they will terminate the program and produce a traceback.

Example Program

```
#Python Assertions
def sum(a,b):
 sum=a+b
 assert(sum>0), "Too low value"
 return(sum)
a=int(input("First Number:"))
b=int(input("Second Number:"))
print(sum(a,b))
```

Output

```
First Number:-8
Second Number:-2
Traceback (most recent call last):
  File "main.py", line 8, in <module>
    print sum(a,b)
  File "main.py", line 4, in sum
    assert(sum>0), "Too low value"
AssertionError: Too low value
```

10.7 Conclusion

This Chapter covers exception handling mechanisms, built-in exceptions, how to handle exceptions using try....except, except clause with no exception, except clause with multiple exceptions and try... finally statements. It also covers exception with arguments, how to raise an exception, user-defined exception and assertions in Python.

10.8 Review Questions

1. Briefly explain exception handling in Python.
2. What are built-in exceptions?
3. Explain try....except statement in Python.

4. Explain except clause with no exception.
5. Explain except clause with multiple exceptions.
6. What is try...finally in Python?
7. Explain exception with arguments.
8. How to raise an exception in Python using the raise statement?
9. Write short notes on user-defined exceptions.
10. What are assertions in Python?

11 Regular Expressions

CONTENTS

Regular expressions (called REs, or regexes, or regex patterns) are essentially a tiny, highly specialized programming language embedded inside Python and made available through the `re` module. A regular expression helps to match or find other strings or sets of strings, using a specialized syntax held in a pattern. They are widely used in UNIX world.

The `re` module raises the exception `re.error` if an error occurs while compiling or using a regular expression. There are various characters, which have special meaning when they are used in regular expression. While dealing with regular expressions, we use raw strings as r'expression'.

11.1 The *match()* function

The purpose of *match()* function is to match regular expression pattern to string with optional flags. For using this function, the `re` module needs to be imported. The following shows the syntax of *match()* function.

Syntax

```
re.match(pattern, string, flags=0)
```

where pattern is the regular expression to be matched, string is searched to match the pattern at the beginning of string, flags are modifiers specified using bitwise OR(|). The modifiers will be explained in Section 11.4. The re.match() function returns a match object if the matching was success and returns None, if matching was a failure.

Two functions group(n) and groups() of match object are used to get matched expression. The group(n) method returns entire match (or specific subgroup n) and groups() method returns all matching subgroups in a tuple or empty if there weren't any matches.

Example Program

```
#Example Program for match() function
import re
line = "Python Programming is fun";
matchObj = re.match( r'fun', line, re.M|re.I)
if matchObj:
   print("match --> matchObj.group() : ", matchObj.group())
else:
   print("No match!!")
```

Output

```
No match!!
```

The match() function always checks the beginning of the string. Even though the keyword "fun" is there in the string it is not considered as a match since it does not appear at the beginning of the string. Consider the below example.

Example Program

```
#Example Program for match() function
import re
line = "Python Programming is fun";
matchObj = re.match( r'python', line, re.M|re.I)
if matchObj:
   print("match --> matchObj.group() : ", matchObj.group())
else:
   print("No match!!")
```

Output

```
match --> matchObj.group() :  Python
```

In the above example the word "python" is found as a match since it appears at the beginning of the string.

11.2 The *search()* function

The *search()* function searches for first occurrence of regular expression pattern within a string with optional flags. The following shows the syntax for *search()* function.

Syntax

```
re.search(pattern, string, flags=0)
```

where `pattern,string` and `flags` have the same meaning as that of `match()` function. The re.search() function returns a match object if the matching was success and returns None, if matching was a failure.

The difference between `match()` and `search()` is that `match()` checks for a match only at the beginning of the string, while `search()` checks for a match anywhere in the string. The following shows an example between `match()` and `search()` functions.

Example Program

```
#Example Program for difference between match() & search()
function
import re
line = "Python Programming is fun";
matchObj = re.match( r'fun', line, re.M|re.I)
if matchObj:
   print("match --> matchObj.group() : ", matchObj.group())
else:
   print("No match!!")
searchObj = re.search( r'fun', line, re.M|re.I)
if searchObj:
   print("search --> searchObj.group() : ", searchObj.group())
else:
   print("Nothing found!!")
```

Output

```
No match!!
search --> searchObj.group() :  fun
```

In the above example, match() function returns nothing while search() function searches the entire string to find a match.

11.3 Search and Replace

Search and replace is done in Python with the help of `sub` method in `re` module. The following shows the syntax of `sub` method.

Syntax

```
re.sub(pattern, repl, string, max=0)
```

This method replaces all occurrences of the regular expression pattern in string with `repl`, substituting all occurrences. If value for `max` is provided, it will replace only the number of occurrences specified in `max`. This method returns modified string. The following example shows the application of `sub` method.

Example Program

```
import re
zipcode = "2004-959-559 # This is zipcode"
# Remove anything other than digits
num = re.sub(r'\D', "", zipcode)
print("Zip Code: ", num)
```

Output

```
Zip Code:  2004959559
```

11.4 Regular Expression Modifiers: Option Flags

Regular expression literals may include an optional modifier to control various aspects of matching. The modifiers are specified as an optional flag. We can provide multiple modifiers using exclusive OR (|), as shown in the previous examples. The following Table 11.1 shows various modifiers and their description available in the `re` module.

Table 11.1: Modifiers and Descriptions in re Module

Modifier	Description
re.I	Performs case-insensitive matching.
re.L	Interprets words according to the current locale. This interpretation affects the alphabetic group (\w and \W), as well as word boundary behavior (\b and \B).
re.M	Makes $ match the end of a line (not just the end of the string) and makes ^ match the start of any line (not just the start of the string).
re.S	Makes a period (dot) match any character, including a newline.
re.U	Interprets letters according to the Unicode character set. This flag affects the behavior of \w, \W, \b, \B.
re.X	Permits "cuter" regular expression syntax. It ignores whitespace (except inside a set [] or when escaped by a backslash) and treats unescaped # as a comment marker.

11.5 Regular Expression Patterns

All characters match themselves except for control characters, (+ ? . * ^ $ ( ) [ ] { } | \). We can escape a control character by preceding it with a backslash. Table 11.2 shows the regular expression patterns and their descriptions.

Table 11.2: Regular Expression Patterns and Descriptions

Pattern	Description
^	Matches beginning of line.
$	Matches end of line.
.	Matches any single character except newline. Using m option allows it to match newline as well.
[...]	Matches any single character in brackets.
[^...]	Matches any single character not in brackets
re*	Matches 0 or more occurrences of preceding expression.
re+	Matches 1 or more occurrence of preceding expression.
re?	Matches 0 or 1 occurrence of preceding expression.
re{ n}	Matches exactly n number of occurrences of preceding expression.
re{ n,}	Matches n or more occurrences of preceding expression.
re{ n, m}	Matches at least n and at most m occurrences of preceding expression.
a| b	Matches either a or b.
(re)	Groups regular expressions and remembers matched text.
(?imx)	Temporarily toggles on i, m, or x options within a regular expression. If in parentheses, only that area is affected.
(?-imx)	Temporarily toggles off i, m, or x options within a regular expression. If in parentheses, only that area is affected.
(?: re)	Groups regular expressions without remembering matched text.
(?imx: re)	Temporarily toggles on i, m, or x options within parentheses.
(?-imx: re)	Temporarily toggles off i, m, or x options within parentheses.
(?#...)	Comment
(?= re)	Specifies position using a pattern. Doesn't have a range.
(?! re)	Specifies position using pattern negation. Doesn't have a range.
(?> re)	Matches independent pattern without backtracking.
\w	Matches word characters.
\W	Matches nonword characters.
\s	Matches whitespace. Equivalent to [\t\n\r\f].
\S	Matches nonwhitespace.
\d	Matches digits. Equivalent to [0-9].
\D	Matches nondigits.
\A	Matches beginning of string.
\Z	Matches end of string. If a newline exists, it matches just before newline.
\z	Matches end of string.
\G	Matches point where last match finished.

\b	Matches word boundaries when outside brackets. Matches backspace (0x08) when inside brackets.
\B	Matches nonword boundaries.
\n, \t, etc.	Matches newlines, carriage returns, tabs, etc.
\1...\9	Matches nth grouped subexpression.
\10	Matches nth grouped subexpression if it matched already. Otherwise refers to the octal representation of a character code.

11.6 Character Classes

The Table 11.3 shows example of various character classes and their description used in regular expression of Python.

Table 11.3: Example of Character Classes

Example	Description
[Pp]ython	Match "Python" or "python"
rub[ye]	Match "ruby" or "rube"
[aeiou]	Match any one lowercase vowel
[0-9]	Match any digit; same as [0123456789]
[a-z]	Match any lowercase ASCII letter
[A-Z]	Match any uppercase ASCII letter
[a-zA-Z0-9]	Match any of the above
[^aeiou]	Match anything other than a lowercase vowel
[^0-9]	Match anything other than a digit

11.7 Special Character Classes

Table 11.4 shows example of various special character classes and their description used in regular expression of Python.

Table 11.4: Example of Special Character Classes

Example	Description
.	Match any character except newline
\d	Match a digit: [0-9]
\D	Match a nondigit: [^0-9]
\s	Match a whitespace character: [\t\r\n\f]
\S	Match nonwhitespace: [^ \t\r\n\f]
\w	Match a single word character: [A-Za-z0-9_]
\W	Match a nonword character: [^A-Za-z0-9_]

11.8 Repetition Cases

Table 11.5 shows example of various repetition cases and their description used in regular expression of Python.

Table 11.5: Repetition cases with examples

Example	Description
ruby?	Match "rub" or "ruby": the y is optional
ruby*	Match "rub" plus 0 or more ys
ruby+	Match "rub" plus 1 or more ys
\d{3}	Match exactly 3 digits
\d{3,}	Match 3 or more digits
\d{3,5}	Match 3, 4, or 5 digits

11.9 findall() method

The findall() method searches all patterns and returns a list. The following shows an example for findall() method.

Example Program

```
import re
a = "hello 234789 world 63678 ok 1 ok 1115 alpha 88 beta 999g"
print(re.findall("\d+", a))
```

Output

```
['234789', '63678', '1', '1115', '88', '999']
```

In the above example, \d is any numeric characters ie 0,1,2,3,4,5,6,7,8,9, "+" represents one or more previous character. Hence the regular expression searches for only numeric characters.

11.10 compile() method

The compile method compiles a regular expression pattern into a regular expression object, which can be used for matching using its match() and search() methods. The syntax of compile is as follows.

```
re.compile(pattern, flags=0)
```

The expression's behaviour can be modified by specifying a flags value. Values can be any of the following variables, combined using bitwise OR (the | operator). The sequence

```
prog = re.compile(pattern)
result = prog.match(string)
```

is equivalent to `result = re.match(pattern, string)`

Similarly the sequence

```
prog = re.compile(pattern)
```

```
result = prog.search(string)
```

is equivalent to `result = re.search(pattern, string)`

Using re.compile() and saving the resulting regular expression object for reuse is more efficient when the expression will be used several times in a single program.

Example Program

```
import re
file = open("Abc.txt","r")
text = file.readlines()
file.close()
# compiling the regular expression:
keyword = re.compile(r'a ')
# searching the file content line by line:
for line in text:
    if keyword.search (line):
        print(line)
```

Output

```
#Only lines containing a is displayed
Ram is a boy
Geeta is a girl
```

11.11 Solved Lab Exercises

1. Given a string like, "1, 3-7, 12, 15, 18-21", produce the list [1,3,4,5,6,7,12,15,18,19,20,21]

Program

```
import re
listString = []
string = "1,4,6-9,12-19"
def matches(l):
    start, end = l.groups()
    return ','.join(str(i) for i in range(int(start),
int(end)+1))
listString = (re.sub('(\d+)-(\d+)', matches, string)).split(',')
print(listString)
```

Output

```
['1', '4', '6', '7', '8', '9', '12', '13', '14', '15', '16',
'17', '18', '19']
```

2. **Write a Python program to check the validity of password input by users. Validation(At least 1 letter between [a-z] and 1 letter between [A-Z]. At least 1 number between [0-9]. At least 1 character from [$#@]. Minimum length 6 characters. Maximum length 16 characters.**

   Program

```
import re
p= input("Input your password:")
while True:
    if (len(p)<6 or len(p)>16):
        print("Invalid Password")
        break
    elif not re.search("[a-z]",p):
        print("Invalid Password")
        break
    elif not re.search("[0-9]",p):
        print("Invalid Password")
        break
    elif not re.search("[A-Z]",p):
        print("Invalid Password")
        break
    elif not re.search("[$#@]",p):
        print("Invalid Password")
        break
    else:
        print("Valid password")
        break
```

   Output

```
Input your password:ASD232@sdfl
Valid password
```

3. **Create a file Test.txt. Retrieve all lines that contain "the ".**

   Program

```
import re
file = open("Test.txt","r")
text = file.readlines()
file.close()
# compiling the regular expression:
keyword = re.compile(r'the ')
```

```
    # searching the file content line by line:
    for line in text:
        if keyword.search(line):
            print(line)
```

Output

```
    # Only lines containing "the" is displayed
    Green computing is the environmentally responsible use of
    computers and related resources.

    Such practices include the implementation of energy-efficient
    central processing units (CPUs).
    One of the earliest initiatives toward green computing in the
    United States was the voluntary labeling Program known as Energy
    Star.
```

4. **Retrieve all lines that contain "the" with lower or upper case letters.**

Program

```
    import re
    # open a file
    file = open("Test.txt","r")
    text = file.readlines()
    file.close()
    # searching the file content line by line:
    keyword = re.compile(r"the ", re.I)
    for line in text:
        result = keyword.search(line)
        if result:
            print(result.group(), ":",line)
```

Output

```
    the: Green computing is the environmentally responsible use of
    computers and related resources.
    the: Such practices include the implementation of energy-
    efficient central processing units (CPUs).
    the: One of the earliest initiatives toward green computing in
    the United States was the voluntary labeling Program known as
    Energy Star.
    The: The use of notebook computers rather than desktop computers
    whenever possible.
```

5. **Retrieve lines that have two consecutive o's.**

Program

```
import re
# open a file
file = open("Test.txt","r")
text = file.readlines()
file.close()
# searching the file content line by line:
keyword = re.compile(r"oo")
for line in text:
    result = keyword.search(line)
    if result:
        print(result.group(),":",line)
```

Output

```
oo : The use of notebook computers rather than desktop computers
whenever possible.
```

6. **Retrieve lines that contain a three letter string consisting of "s", then any character, then "e", such as "she".**

Program

```
import re
# open a file
file = open("Test.txt","r")
text = file.readlines()
file.close()
# searching the file content line by line:
keyword = re.compile(r"s.e")
for line in text:
    result = keyword.search(line)
    if result:
        print(result.group(),":",line)
```

Output

```
ste :  Minimize the use of paper and properly recycle waste paper.
ste : Dispose of e-waste according to federal, state and local
regulations.
```

7. **Retrieve lines with a three letter word that starts with s and ends with e.**

Program

```
import re
# open a file
```

```
file = open("Test.txt","r")
text = file.readlines()
file.close()
# searching the file content line by line:
keyword = re.compile(r"\bs\we\b")
for line in text:
    result = keyword.search(line)
    if result:
        print(result.group(),":",line)
```

Output

```
she : she advocates green computing
```

8. **Retrieve lines that contain a word of any length that starts with s and ends with e.**

Program

```
import re
# open a file
file = open("Test.txt","r")
text = file.readlines()
file.close()
# searching the file content line by line:
keyword = re.compile(r"\bs\w*e\b")
for line in text:
    result = keyword.search(line)
    if result:
        print(result.group(),":",line)
```

Output

```
state :Dispose of e-waste according to federal, state and local
regulations.
she : she advocates green computing
```

9. **Retrieve lines that contain a word of any length that starts with s and ends with e and the word has at least four characters.**

Program

```
import re
# open a file
file = open("Test.txt","r")
text = file.readlines()
file.close()
```

```
# searching the file content line by line:
keyword = re.compile(r"\bs\w\w+e\b")
for line in text:
    result = keyword.search(line)
    if result:
       print(result.group(),":",line)
```

Output

```
state :   Dispose of e-waste according to federal, state and
local regulations.
```

10. Retrieve lines that start with a.

Program

```
import re
# open a file
file = open("Test.txt","r")
text = file.readlines()
file.close()
# searching the file content line by line:
keyword = re.compile(r"^a")
for line in text:
    result = keyword.search(line)
    if result:
       print(result.group(),":",line)
```

Output

```
a : any energy sources for computing workstation
```

11. Retreive lines that start with a and ends with n.

Program

```
import re
# open a file
file = open("Test.txt","r")
text = file.readlines()
file.close()
# searching the file content line by line:
keyword = re.compile(r"^a.*n$")
for line in text:
    result = keyword.search(line)
    if result:
       print(line)
```

Output

```
any energy sources for computing workstation
```

12. **Retrieve lines that do not contain the blank space character.**

Program

```
import re
# open a file
file = open("Test.txt","r")
text = file.readlines()
file.close()
# searching the file content line by line:
keyword = re.compile(r" ")
for line in text:
    if not keyword.search(line):
        print(line)
```

Output

```
power-upandpower-downenergy-intensiveperipherals
```

13. **Retreive an odd digit followed by an even digit.**

Program

```
import re
# open a file
file = open("Test.txt","r")
text = file.readlines()
file.close()
# searching the file content line by line:
keyword = re.compile(r"[13579][02468]")
for line in text:
    result = keyword.search(line)
    if result:
        print(line)
```

Output

```
any energy sources for computing workstation 54
33 45 23 54 31 23 44 66 55
```

14. **Retrieve all lines with a letter followed by a non-letter followed by a number.**

Program

```
import re
# open a file
```

```
file = open("Test.txt","r")
text = file.readlines()
file.close()
# searching the file content line by line:
keyword = re.compile(r"[A-Za-z][^A-Za-z]\d")
for line in text:
    result = keyword.search(line)
    if result:
        print(line)
```

Output

```
any energy sources for computing workstation54
```

15. Retrieve all lines in which a word that starts with an upper case letter.

Program

```
import re
# open a file
file = open("Test.txt","r")
text = file.readlines()
file.close()
# searching the file content line by line:
keyword = re.compile(r"\b[A-Z]\w*\b")
for line in text:
    result = keyword.search(line)
    if result:
        print(line)
```

Output

```
Green computing is the environmentally responsible use of
computers and related resources.

Such practices include the implementation of energy-efficient
central processing units (CPUs).
```

16. Retrieve lines with one or more times the word "the".

Program

```
import re
# open a file
file = open("Test.txt","r")
text = file.readlines()
file.close()
```

```
# searching the file content line by line:
keyword = re.compile(r"(the )+")
for line in text:
    result = keyword.search(line)
    if result:
        print(line)
```

Output

```
Green computing is the environmentally responsible use of
computers and related resources.

Such practices include the implementation of energy-efficient
central processing units (CPUs).

One of the earliest initiatives toward green computing in the
United States was the voluntary labeling Program known as Energy
Star.
```

17. **Retrieve all lines with a date in the form of one or two digits, a dot, one or two digits, a dot, two digits.**

    Program

```
import re
# open a file
file = open("Test.txt","r")
text = file.readlines()
file.close()
# searching the file content line by line:
keyword = re.compile(r"\d\d?\.\d\d?\.\d\d")
for line in text:
    result = keyword.search(line)
    if result:
        print(line)
```

Output

```
12.05.15


12.5.2014
```

18. **You are given date strings of the form "29, Jul 2009", or "4 January 2008". In other words a number a string and another number, with a comma sometimes separating the items. Write a function that takes such a string and returns a tuple (yyyy, mm, dd) where all three elements are ints.**

Program

```
import re
def myDate(date):
    tmp_date=re.findall(r"[\w']+", date)
    mdic=dict(jan=1, feb=2, mar=3, apr=4, may=5, jun=6, jul=7,
aug=8, sep=9, oct=10, nov=11, dec=12)
    for key, value in mdic.items():
        x=re.search(key, date, re.IGNORECASE)
        if x:
            month=value
    return int(tmp_date[-1]), int(month), int(tmp_date[0])
date=input("Date form "29, Jul 2009", or "4 January 2008": ")
y, m, d = myDate(date)
print("Became: (%.4d, %.2d, %.2d)" %(y, m, d))
```

Output

```
Date form "29, Jul 2009", or "4 January 2008": 8, April,2015
Became: (2015, 04, 08)
```

19. Given a dictionary of the names of students and their marks, identify how many duplicate marks are there and what are these?

Program

```
dic=dict(Adam=45, Pick=33, Tom=48, Aaron=27, Smith=25, Bob=25,
Lubber=33, Horatio=33, Jack=45, Jill=50)
print(dic)
new_dic = {}
for k, v in dic.items():
    new_dic.setdefault(v, []).append(k)
for k, v in new_dic.items():
    if(len(new_dic[k]))>1:
        print("%s have the same mark=%d" %(new_dic[k],k))
```

Output

```
{'Lubber': 33, 'Smith': 25, 'Adam': 45, 'Jill': 50, 'Tom': 48,
'Bob': 25, 'Jack': 45, 'Pick': 33, 'Horatio': 33, 'Aaron': 27}
['Lubber', 'Pick', 'Horatio'] have the same mark=33
['Smith', 'Bob'] have the same mark=25
['Adam', 'Jack'] have the same mark=45
```

20. Given a string of the form "4-7, 9, 12, 15" find the numbers missing in this list for a given range.

Program

```
import re
def from_ex20(str):
    list=[]
    tmp=str.replace(" ", "").split(",") # to remove whitespace
and make tmp_list
    for i in tmp:
        if re.search(r".+-.+", i, flags=0): # if it found "x-y"
sign => make range(x,y+1)
            x=i.split("-")
            for j in range(int(x[0]), int(x[1])+1):
                list.append(int(j))
        else:
            list.append(int(i))
    return list

str=input("Give a range of value, e.g: 3-7, 12, 15: ")
print("You've input: '%s'" %str, end="")
l=from_ex20(str)
print("\nSo it will become:", l)

print("Elements not in range: ", end="")
for i in range(min(l), max(l)):
    if i not in l:
        print(i, end=",  ")
```

Output

```
Give a range of value, e.g: 3-7, 12, 15: 4-7,9,18
You've input: '4-7,9,18'
So it will become: [4, 5, 6, 7, 9, 18]
Elements not in range: 8,  10,  11,  12,  13,  14,  15,  16,
17,
```

11.12 Conclusion

This Chapter covers the regular expressions, the use of match() function, the use of search() function, the application of search and replace, various regular expression modifiers, regular expression patterns, character classes, special character classes, repetition cases and use of findall() method.

11.13 Review Questions

1. What is the purpose of match() function in a regular expression?
2. What is the purpose of search() function in a regular expression?
3. Explain the importance of re module in regular expressions.
4. Explain findall() method with an example.
5. Explain search() and replace() in regular expression.
6. Explain compile() method with an example.

12 Database Programming

CONTENTS

Python allows us to connect to various databases though database interfaces. Python's database interface is DB-API (Data Base – Application Programming Interface). We can choose the database which we want to connect to Python. Python DB-API supports a large number of databases like Oracle, MS-SQL server 2000, MySQL, mSQL, Sybase etc. For using each database we need to download separate DB-API modules.

The API includes the following steps which include importing the API module, acquiring a connection with the database, issuing SQL statements and stored procedures and closing the connection. This Chapter explains all the concepts and examples using MySQL. MySQL is an open source database. For connecting to MySQL database, we need pymysql, which is an interface connecting MySQL and Python. Before establishing a connection between Python and MySQL, we should make sure that pymysql is installed in our machine.

12.1 Connecting to a Database

Before connecting to a database, following things should be done to assure the right connectivity.

1. Create a database called SAMPLE in MySQL.
2. The user id and password used to access SAMPLE database is "user" and "pass" respectively.
3. Create a table STUDENT in SAMPLE.
4. The table STUDENT has fields ROLLNO, NAME, AGE, COURSE, GRADE.

The following code shows how to connect MySQL database with Python.

Example Program

```
import pymysql

# Open database connection
db = pymysql.connect("localhost","user","pass","SAMPLE" )

# prepare a cursor object using cursor() method
cursor = db.cursor()

# execute SQL query using execute() method.
cursor.execute("SELECT VERSION()")

# Fetch a single row using fetchone() method.
data = cursor.fetchone()

print("Database version:",data)

# disconnect from server
db.close()
```

While running this script, it is producing the following output in Windows machine.

Output

```
Database version: 5.6.36-log
```

In the above example, a connection is established with the data source and a connection object is returned. In our example, the connection object is saved to db. If connection is not properly established, db will store the value None. The database object db is used to create a cursor object cursor and this cursor is used for executing SQL queries. At the end, database connection is closed and resources are released.

12.2 Creating Tables

Once a connection is successfully established, we can create the tables. Creation of tables, insertion, updation and deletion operations are performed in Python with the help of `execute()` statement. The following example shows how to create a table in MySQL from Python.

Example Program

```
import pymysql

# Open database connection
db = pymysql.connect("localhost","user","pass","SAMPLE" )

# prepare a cursor object using cursor() method
cursor = db.cursor()
# Create table as per requirement
sql = """CREATE TABLE DEPT (
         DEPTNO INT,
         DEPT_NAME CHAR(20),
         LOCATION CHAR(25))"""
cursor.execute(sql)

# disconnect from server
db.close()
```

The program creates a table called DEPT with fields DEPTNO, DEPT_NAME and LOCATION. The SQL statement for creating the table is stored in sql and the sql is passed to `execute()` method for creating the table.

12.3 INSERT Operation

Once a table is created, we need to insert values to the table. The values can be inserted using the INSERT statement of SQL. The following example shows an example for insert operation.

Example Program

```
import pymysql

# Open database connection
db = pymysql.connect("localhost","user","pass","SAMPLE" )

# prepare a cursor object using cursor() method
cursor = db.cursor()
# Prepare SQL query to INSERT a record into the database.
sql = """INSERT INTO DEPT(DEPTNO,DEPT_NAME,LOCATION)
         VALUES (10,'Sales', 'Chennai')"""
cursor.execute(sql)
db.commit()
```

```
# disconnect from server
db.close()
```

A record with specified values will be inserted into the DEPT table.

12.4 UPDATE Operation

UPDATE operation is done to modify existing values available in the table. We can update one or more records at the same time. The following example shows how to update records in a table from Python.

Example Program

```
import pymysql

# Open database connection
db = pymysql.connect("localhost","user","pass","SAMPLE" )

# prepare a cursor object using cursor() method
cursor = db.cursor()
# Prepare SQL query to UPDATE records into a table.
sql = "UPDATE DEPT SET LOCATION = 'Delhi'
       WHERE DEPT_NAME = 'SALES'"
cursor.execute(sql)
db.commit()
# disconnect from server
db.close()
```

The above example updates the location of sales department from Chennai to Delhi. If there is more than one record with the satisfied condition, then all those records will be updated.

12.5 DELETE Operation

DELETE operation is required when we want to delete some undesired or unwanted records from a table. We can specify DELETE operation with or without conditions. The following example shows how to delete records from a table.

Example Program

```
import pymysql

# Open database connection
db = pymysql.connect("localhost","user","pass","SAMPLE" )

# prepare a cursor object using cursor() method
cursor = db.cursor()
```

```
# Prepare SQL query to DELETE records from a table.
sql = "DELETE FROM DEPT WHERE LOCATION = 'Delhi'"
cursor.execute(sql)
db.commit()
# disconnect from server
db.close()
```

The above example will delete all the records with location Delhi.

12.6 READ Operation

READ operation is used to fetch desired records from a database. There are several methods for fetching records from a database. Once a connection is established, we can make queries to a database. The following methods are used in READ operation.

1. **fetchone():** It fetches the next row of a query result set. A result set is an object that is returned when a cursor object is used to query a table.

   Example Program

```
import pymysql

# Open database connection
db = pymysql.connect("localhost","user","pass","SAMPLE" )

# prepare a cursor object using cursor() method
cursor = db.cursor()
# Prepare SQL query
sql = "SELECT LOCATION FROM DEPT"
cursor.execute(sql)
# Fetches the next Record. In this case first Record
row = cursor.fetchone()
if row:
   print("Location:", row[0])
# disconnect from server
db.close()
```

   Output

```
Location:Delhi
```

2. **fetchall():** It fetches all the rows in a result set. If some rows have already been extracted from the result set, then it retrieves the remaining rows from the result set.

   Example Program

```
import pymysql
```

```
# Open database connection
db = pymysql.connect("localhost","user","pass","SAMPLE" )

# prepare a cursor object using cursor() method
cursor = db.cursor()
# Prepare SQL query
sql = "SELECT LOCATION FROM DEPT"
cursor.execute(sql)
# Fetches all the records.
rows = cursor.fetchall()
for row in rows:
    print("Location:", row[0])
# disconnect from server
db.close()
```

Output

```
Location:Delhi
Location:Chennai
Location:Mumbai
```

3. **rowcount:** This is a read-only attribute and returns the number of rows that were affected by an execute() method.

Example Program

```
import pymysql

# Open database connection
db = pymysql.connect("localhost","user","pass","SAMPLE" )

# prepare a cursor object using cursor() method
cursor = db.cursor()
# Prepare SQL query
sql = "SELECT LOCATION FROM DEPT"
numrows = cursor.execute(sql)
# Displays number of records.
numrows = cursor.rowcount
print("Number of Records:", numrows)
# disconnect from server
db.close()
```

Output

```
Number of Records:3
```

12.7 Transaction Control

A transaction is a logical unit of work that contains one or more SQL statements. A transaction is an atomic unit. The effects of all the SQL statements in a transaction can be either all committed (applied to the database) or all rolled back (undone from the database). Transaction is a mechanism to ensure data consistency. Transaction ensures 4 properties generally referred to as ACID properties.

- **Atomicity:** ensures that all operations within the work unit are completed successfully; otherwise, the transaction is aborted at the point of failure, and previous operations are rolled back to their former state.
- **Consistency:** ensures that the database properly change states upon a successfully committed transaction.
- **Isolation:** enable transactions to operate independently and transparent to each other.
- **Durability:** ensures that the result or effect of a committed transaction persists in case of a system failure.

12.7.1 COMMIT Operation

The COMMIT command is the transactional command used to save changes invoked by a transaction to the database. The COMMIT command saves all transactions to the database since the last COMMIT or ROLLBACK command. The syntax for a commit statement is `db.commit()`.

12.7.2 ROLLBACK Operation

The ROLLBACK command is the transactional command used to undo transactions that have not already been saved to the database. The ROLLBACK command can only be used to undo transactions since the last COMMIT or ROLLBACK command was issued. The syntax for rollback is `db.rollback()`.

Example Program for COMMIT and ROLLBACK

```
import pymysql

# Open database connection
db = pymysql.connect("localhost","user","pass","SAMPLE" )

# prepare a cursor object using cursor() method
cursor = db.cursor()
# Prepare SQL query to INSERT a record into the database.
sql = """INSERT INTO DEPT(DEPTNO,DEPT_NAME,LOCATION)
         VALUES (10,'Sales', 'Chennai')"""
cursor.execute(sql)
# Commit changes in the database
```

```
    db.commit()
    except:
        # Rollback in case there is any error
        db.rollback()

    # disconnect from server
    db.close()
```

In the above example, `commit()` statement makes changes to the database permanently. If there is any error, `rollback()` is called to undo the changes.

12.8 Disconnecting from a Database

A `close()` method is called to disconnect from the database. The syntax for closing is `db.close()`. If the connection to a database is closed by the user with the `close()` method, any outstanding transactions are rolled back by the database. However, instead of depending on any of database lower level implementation details, our application would be better to call commit or rollback explicitly.

12.9 Exception Handling in Databases

There are many sources of errors in databases. A few examples are a syntax error in an executed SQL statement, a connection failure, or calling the fetch method for an already canceled or finished statement handle. The database API defines a number of errors that must exist in each database module. The following Table 12.1 list the exceptions and their descriptions related to databases.

Table 12.1: Exceptions related to databases

Exception	Description
DatabaseError	Used for errors in the database. Must subclass Error.
DataError	Subclass of DatabaseError that refers to errors in the data.
Error	Base class for errors. Must subclass StandardError.
IntegrityError	Subclass of DatabaseError for situations that would damage the relational integrity, such as uniqueness constraints or foreign keys.
InterfaceError	Used for errors in the database module, not the database itself. Must subclass Error.
InternalError	Subclass of DatabaseError that refers to errors internal to the database module, such as a cursor no longer being active.
NotSupportedError	Subclass of DatabaseError that refers to trying to call unsupported functionality.
OperationalError	Subclass of DatabaseError that refers to errors such as the loss of a connection to the database. These errors are generally outside the control of the Python scripter.
ProgrammingError	Subclass of DatabaseError that refers to errors such as a bad table name
Warning	Used for non-fatal issues. Must subclass StandardError.

12.10 Solved Lab Exercises

1. Create a table sailor with fields sid: integer, sname: char, age:int, rating:int with sid as the primary key.

   Program

```
import pymysql
# Open database connection
db = pymysql.connect("localhost","user","pass","SAMPLE" )

# prepare a cursor object using cursor() method
cursor = db.cursor()
# Create table as per requirement
sql = """CREATE TABLE SAILOR (
         SID INT,
         SNAME CHAR(20),
         AGE INT,
         RATING INT PRIMARY KEY(SID))"""
cursor.execute(sql)
db.commit()
# disconnect from server
db.close()
```

2. Insert values into sailor.

   Program

```
import pymysql

# Open database connection
db = pymysql.connect("localhost","user","pass","SAMPLE" )

# prepare a cursor object using cursor() method
cursor = db.cursor()
# Prepare SQL query to INSERT a record into the database.
sql = """INSERT INTO SAILOR(SID,SNAME,AGE,RATING)
         VALUES (10,'Smith',25,3)"""
cursor.execute(sql)
db.commit()
# disconnect from server
db.close()
```

3. **Update sailors with rating incremented by one.**

```
import pymysql

# Open database connection
db = pymysql.connect("localhost","user","pass","SAMPLE" )

# prepare a cursor object using cursor() method
cursor = db.cursor()
# Prepare SQL query to UPDATE records into a table.
sql = "UPDATE SAILORS SET RATING = RATING +1"
cursor.execute(sql)
db.commit()
# disconnect from server
db.close()
```

4. **Delete sailors whose age>40.**

```
import pymysql

# Open database connection
db = pymysql.connect("localhost","user","pass","SAMPLE" )

# prepare a cursor object using cursor() method
cursor = db.cursor()
# Prepare SQL query to DELETE records from a table.
sql = "DELETE FROM SAILORS WHERE AGE > 40"
cursor.execute(sql)
db.commit()
# disconnect from server
db.close()
```

5. **Find the result of the following SQL queries.**

a. **Find the details of sailors.**

Program

```
import pymysql

# Open database connection
db = pymysql.connect("localhost","user","pass","SAMPLE" )
```

```
# prepare a cursor object using cursor() method
cursor = db.cursor()
# Prepare SQL query
sql = "SELECT * FROM SAILORS"
cursor.execute(sql)
# Fetches all the records.
result = cursor.fetchall()
for row in result:
    id=row[0]
    name=row[1]
    age=row[2]
    rating=row[3]
    print("Sailor ID:", id)
    print("Name:", name)
    print("Age:", age)
    print("Rating:", rating)
# disconnect from server
db.close()
```

b. **Find the sailor names with age>20 and age<40.**

Program

```
import pymysql

# Open database connection
db = pymysql.connect("localhost","user","pass","SAMPLE" )

# prepare a cursor object using cursor() method
cursor = db.cursor()
# Prepare SQL query
sql = "SELECT SNAME FROM SAILORS WHERE AGE BETWEEN 20 AND 40"
cursor.execute(sql)
# Fetches all the records.
result = cursor.fetchall()
for row in result:
    print ("Name:", row[0])
# disconnect from server
db.close()
```

c. Find the name and rating of the sailors with age>40.

Program

```
import pymysql

# Open database connection
db = pymysql.connect("localhost","user","pass","SAMPLE" )

# prepare a cursor object using cursor() method
cursor = db.cursor()
# Prepare SQL query
sql = "SELECT SNAME,RATING FROM SAILORS WHERE AGE > 40"
cursor.execute(sql)
# Fetches all the records.
result = cursor.fetchall()
for row in result:
   print("Name:", row[0])
   print("Rating:", row[1])
# disconnect from server
db.close()
```

12.11 Conclusion

This Chapter explains how databases can be connected from Python. All operations including creation of tables, insert, delete, update and SQL statements are explained in detail. The read operation which includes methods like fetchone(), fetchall() and rowcount are illustrated with examples. Further, the transactions in a database which involves commit() and rollback() are explained. The last section discusses the exceptions related to databases.

12.12 Review Questions

1. How will you connect to MySQL from Python?
2. How will you create tables in MySQL from Python?
3. Explain the INSERT operation in MySQL from Python.
4. Describe the UPDATE command in MySQL from Python.
5. Write short notes on COMMIT and ROLLBACK.
6. Briefly explain fetchone(), fetchall() and rowcount.
7. How DELETE operations can be done in MySQL from Python?
8. Give an account of exceptions related to databases.